D1649004

ADVANCE PRAISE FOR QUEST FOR JUSTICE

"*Quest for Justice* is both a gripping legal thriller and a chilling indictment of the death penalty. The inside story of how Richard Jaffe saved the lives of three innocent men who were already on Death Row illustrates why he is one of the most remarkable criminal defense attorneys in America."

Maryanne Vollers, author, *Ghosts of Mississippi* and
Lone Wolf: Eric Rudolph and the Legacy of American Terror

"This riveting book takes you inside the intricate human drama of real death penalty cases—defendants who are guilty and those who are innocent—in a way you will not forget. Some of these stories will shock and challenge even the strongest proponents of capital punishment. '*Quest for Justice: Defending the Damned*' is a must read for those who care about justice in America."

Barry Scheck, Prof. of Law, Benjamin N. Cardozo
School of Law, Co-Director of the Innocence Project

"*Quest for Justice* is a rare look inside the mind of an attorney who has devoted his life to fighting for justice and freeing the innocent. His courage, persistence and intelligence are a gift to all of us who care about true justice and liberty. Richard's gripping story should be required reading for anyone interested in criminal justice in America."

Jessica Blank and Erik Jensen, authors of *The Exonerated* and *Living Justice*

"This book tells the stories of people once convicted and sentenced to death and later acquitted of the same charges. It tells how it happened, shows the criminal courts are fallible and that poor people facing the death penalty may live or die depending on the competence and dedication of the lawyers appointed to defend them."

Charles J. Ogletree, Jr., Harvard Law Professor

"The criminal justice system has been the least impacted by change in matters related to race in our nation. This writing by Richard Jaffe is a 'rock in a weary land' on the subject. We owe him a great deal for this important, yea, critical work."

Reverend Joseph Lowery, Recipient of the
Presidential Medal of Freedom, delivered the closing
prayer at the inauguration of President Barack Obama

"An excellent account of what passes for justice in Alabama—innocent people sentenced to death and saved from execution only by the good fortune of getting Richard Jaffe to take their case, eccentric pistol-packing judges, and pervasive racism. It is also about the humanity of the guilty and well as the innocent. We meet them up close, get to know them and realize that they are much more than the worst thing they did in their lives."

Stephen Bright, President and Senior Counsel
of the Southern Center for Human Rights

"This poignant and insightful book tells the story of America's experience with capital punishment as only a person on the front lines can tell it. Richard Jaffe is the person to tell this story. With each new chapter, you meet the people who the state has sought to kill and begin to understand why Jaffe has devoted his life to saving them. *Quest for Justice* will change the way you feel about capital punishment and the men and women on America's death row."

Professor Penny White, Elvin E. Overton Distinguished Professor
of Law and Director, Center for Advocacy and Dispute
Resolution, University of Tennessee College of Law

"The sad truth is that the justice system is imperfect at best and a death sentence, once served, is flat and final. Richard Jaffe has for years stood in the way of that rush to justice, and here, with real drama, tells his story. He takes us inside a world where a rusty gun in the weeds, not fired in recent memory, can somehow become a murder weapon that can send a man to death row, a world where flawed and even fictional testimony can put a needle in a man's arm."

Rick Bragg, Professor of writing at the University of Alabama,
author of *All Over but the Shoutin'* and winner of the Pulitzer Prize

QUEST FOR JUSTICE

QUEST FOR JUSTICE

Defending the Damned

By
Richard S. Jaffe

New Horizon Press
Far Hills, New Jersey

DEDICATION

To my parents Herman and Raye, my wife Linda and daughter Lana,
for their unconditional love and support.

Jaffe, Richard S.
Quest for Justice: Defending the Damned
Cover design: Robert Aulicino
Interior design: Susan Sanderson

Library of Congress Control Number: 2011928840

ISBN 13: 978-0-88282-374-4
New Horizon Press

Manufactured in the U. S. A.

16   15   14   13   12   1   2   3   4   5

AUTHOR'S NOTE

This book is based on the experiences of Richard S. Jaffe and reflects his perceptions of the past, present and future. The personalities, events, actions and conversations portrayed within the story have been taken from his memories, court documents, interviews, testimony, research, letters, personal papers, press accounts and the memories of some participants.

In an effort to safeguard the privacy of certain people, names and a few identifying characteristics have, in some cases, been changed. Events involving the characters happened as described. Only minor details have been altered.

CONTENTS

PROLOGUE

One bleak November night, a lone man pointed a gun at a young female cashier and demanded money at a grocery store in Homewood, Alabama, a suburb that stands on the edge of both Birmingham and the affluent town of Mountain Brook. After the cashier doled out a few hundred dollars in rolled cash and coins, the robber left. Shaken, the cashier called 911, reporting the armed robbery.

The 911 operator alerted the police departments of Homewood, Mountain Brook and Birmingham. Officers from all three jurisdictions quickly responded, but before they could apprehend the robber, violence erupted.

The twenty-three-year-old store manager followed the robber out of the grocery store. The unarmed manager and the robber played a dangerous game of "cat and mouse" for two or three minutes. As the robber started to cross the street, the store manager came closer to him. The robber turned and pointed his gun at the store manager, who retreated toward the store entrance. Then the store manager retraced his pursuit. The robber again turned and pointed his gun. The young manager again retreated. Finally, they both disappeared deep in a dark trailer park across the street. They were out of sight of both the cashier and a customer who had witnessed the alarming scene through the store's plate glass windows.

Within five minutes of the cashier's call to 911, two Homewood plainclothes police officers arrived on the scene. After speaking to the cashier, they approached and entered the trailer park. Three confused students walked out on the front porch of their trailer after hearing "Halt! Police!" and two gunshots. The officers ordered them to go back inside, close the door and remain there until further notice. Several other residents later reported they also heard the sounds of two rapidly fired gunshots. For some unknown reason, the plainclothes police officers raced from the trailer park after the shots were fired.

Additional police officers who had arrived at the grocery store converged on the darkened trailer park. No more than thirty minutes after the trailer residents heard the gunshots, a group of three officers searching for the robber found Bo Cochran hiding in thick brush just outside the trailer park, approximately one-quarter mile from the scene of the shooting. The police located a .38 revolver in the bushes about ten feet from Bo. Officers noticed that the worn weapon appeared rusty and brown, with a scratched four-inch barrel. When an officer examined the weapon, he discovered that the cylinder contained four rounds and turned clockwise. He further noted and later put in his report that from the position of the cylinder, the weapon's most recent turn would not have discharged a bullet, because it was empty. *The last time someone pulled the trigger, the gun did not fire.* Trailer residents had reported gunshots, but when the officers came upon Bo Cochran and his gun, they discovered the weapon was cold and without the scent of burned gun powder. The officers did not conduct a Paraffin test, then a standard technique, to determine the probability of whether a person had recently handled or fired the gun. One of the three officers conducting the search put a gun to Bo's head and said, "I ought to put a bullet right through your head."

With his heart pounding, Bo was curled up in a fetal position among the dark weeds and grassy woods. The officers immediately cuffed and thoroughly searched him, finding nothing of interest and no money of any kind. Before placing him in a nearby squad car, two other officers searched Bo, again finding nothing.

It wasn't until forty-five minutes after the reported gunshots that, after an intense search, numerous officers discovered the store manager's lifeless corpse under the trailer shared by the three students. The body was still warm. About an hour after the students heard the shots, officers went inside their trailer and took their statements.

When the coroner arrived at the scene, he examined the dead store manager's body. He discovered that one penetrating gunshot to the manager's left arm travelled through his side, perforated his heart and caused his death. The bullet then lodged in his right arm. This was extremely significant, because the bullet had not passed *through* his right arm; there was no exit wound. The coroner never found the bullet, nor did a search party of police officers who searched both that night and over the next several days using a metal detector. However, the coroner did find a rather large scraping mark at the site of the entrance wound in the manager's right arm, as if someone had used a pocket knife to remove the bullet.

Crime scene photos revealed no signs of blood on the grass or grass marks on the store manager's clothes. It seemed that at least two people must have lifted the young man's body and placed it underneath the trailer.

At the police station, the booking officers searched Bo for a third time. This time, they claimed to find a wad of money in a jacket pocket that already had been searched twice. The money matched that found in a grocery sack in the trailer park by another group of officers who had been conducting a search for shell casings, bullets and any other potential evidence.

When the officers "discovered" the rolled money in Bo's jacket, Bo yelled out, "You planted that money on me! You planted it! You already searched me twice. You planted it!"

The officers responded by booking Bo for capital murder.

1

A LIFE AT STAKE

It felt no different from any other day in the life of a court-appointed lawyer. My trial practice was thriving. I rushed from courtroom to courtroom like a madman, representing a string of indigent defendants. I defended a drug case before Judge Robert Gwin, represented another client in a probation hearing with Judge James Hard and went before Judge Jasper, who entered a guilty plea for a third client on the charges of buying, receiving and concealing stolen property. Judge Cole sought me out, discussing for a few minutes the appeal for James Willie "Bo" Cochran, whom he had just sentenced to die in the electric chair.

Later I received a phone message that I knew, from the intensity with which my secretary tracked me, demanded my attention. The pink message slip was from Judge William Cole. It read "Bo Cochran" and the case designation "appeal." Instead of being addressed to Richard, it said "To Lucky." How lucky was I?

Although I was still a novice, I had already secured a string of not guilty verdicts in Judge Cole's courtroom. Previously, a jury had acquitted Julia Mitchell of the more serious charge of murder and instead found her guilty of second-degree manslaughter for stabbing her drunken boyfriend while he beat her face with his fists. Prior to that, another jury had acquitted a young man of stealing hubcaps, since the police failed to produce the fingerprints they took from the victim's car at the scene. Several other felony cases that I defended had ended in acquittals or lesser sentences, even though courtroom observers had predicted guilty verdicts beforehand. Although Judge Cole never commented about my successes directly to me, he'd begun to refer to me as "Lucky Jaffe." I preferred to view my handling of these defendants as effective lawyering that revealed discrepancies and mistakes in the prosecutions' cases, resulting in more appropriate verdicts for my clients.

While I appreciated the notice and compliment, I held neither any intention nor desire to handle an appeal of a capital murder case. For one thing, simple cost-of-living economics were not in my favor. During the time I spent handling appeals as an assistant attorney general for the State of Alabama immediately after graduating law school, I experienced firsthand the considerable time required to research the law and prepare an appellate brief. To handle a capital murder appeal competently, I knew I would spend hundreds of hours or more of legal work on the case before the appeal was heard and resolved. I also knew the case would drag on for years in the court system.

In exchange for my tireless and thankless efforts, the State would pay me one thousand dollars. I would be working for two or three dollars an hour while shouldering the enormous emotional pressure of someone's life as it hung in the balance.

Thanks but no thanks, I thought about Judge Cole's appointment.

There were other factors. If I accepted the responsibility, I was to perform the legal work from a desk situated within the humble halls of the local law school library. If I had preferred the monastic corridors of the law library to the combat and drama of the courtroom, I would never have left the attorney general's office in the first place. As a young, hard-charging attorney, I wanted to defend high-profile cases.

I tried to find Judge Cole. I planned to explain my situation calmly. Surely he would hear me out, conclude I could not sink my heart and mind into this appeal and appoint another attorney.

A short while later, though, Judge Cole caught me off guard as I passed him in the hallway heading to my next case. "Lucky, I called your office and left a message," he said in his gravelly, staccato voice. "I've appointed you to represent Bo Cochran. I sentenced him to death yesterday. I didn't have any choice. I like ol' Bo, but there was nothing else I could do. He needs a good lawyer for his appeal, a fighter. That's you, my boy."

The shock that registered across my face must have looked like that of a nighttime burglar caught by the police as he left a vacant house with the loot in his arms. *Damn!* I thought. Only thirty-one and in private practice for just three years, I already carried a caseload better suited for two or three lawyers; it was filled mostly with appointed cases, all of which seemed fated for trial.

"But, Judge," I protested, "I don't do appeals. I'm a trial lawyer and I've never handled a capital murder case. There are plenty of experienced lawyers..."

Judge Cole lacked familiarity with the concept of refusal, unless he was the one who did the refusing. Still robust and intensely energetic in his mid-sixties, the former FBI agent had once partnered in one of the most prestigious civil law firms in the state. Brazen, crusty and full of stature, he barked orders that he expected others to obey.

"Listen, Lucky." Judge Cole's eyes narrowed and his voice turned into an impatient, low-scale bark. "You are Bo's lawyer and that's the end of it. He needs a good lawyer and I've decided it's you."

The judge turned away, abruptly terminating the discussion. I felt helplessly screwed.

As my ears rang from his latest bark, I considered one more maneuver. I went to the chambers of Judge James Hard, the presiding judge of the Criminal Division, and asked him to talk to Judge Cole on my behalf. I had known Jim Hard for most of my life. He and I grew up within a mile of each other in Birmingham. I attended elementary, junior high and high school with his brother, who was a gifted athlete before his untimely death due to complications from a debilitating spinal injury.

Five years my senior, Jim Hard possessed even more athletic ability than his brother. I spent many childhood days watching in awe as he ran track, high jumped, broad jumped and hit home runs on the elementary school baseball field where the neighborhood children routinely gathered after school and on weekends. Only a few years after Governor Fob James had appointed him as a state circuit judge for the criminal division of Jefferson County, Jim rose to become the presiding criminal court judge.

Judge Hard replied to my request with a friendly promise to handle things. "Piece of cake, Richard," he reassured me. The confidence in his voice was pretty clear; I'd be returning to my normal criminal law practice in no time. "Wait here. I'll go right now and talk to Cole. If he knows you feel that strongly about it, he won't make you do it."

Five minutes later, Judge Hard returned to his chambers. "You're on the case, Richard. There's nothing you can do about it," he said, his voice as sheepish as the look in his eyes. "Cole wouldn't listen to me. You'll never win against him. It's not worth it. You're the attorney. It'll be more trouble to fight Cole over this than to go ahead and handle the case."

On that humbling note, I embarked as Bo Cochran's attorney. I had never read the capital statutes carefully, let alone defended a capital murder case. After all, I had been in private practice for just over three years; I was still a virtual neophyte.

Questions rattled like hailstones in my head: *Where would I find the time? The expertise? What if my inexperience contributed to Bo Cochran's execution?*

A deep gnaw settled in the pit of my stomach as my fears and apprehensions caught up with the uncertain burdens I faced. A heaviness enveloped me almost like a fog as I slowly made my way out of Judge Hard's chambers.

Despite my frustration and the overwhelming feelings, duty called. I rushed to the county jail to meet Bo before he was shipped back to the Alabama State Penitentiary.

The old facility which I made my way into afforded lawyers face-to-face contact with the inmates. That can be both good and bad. Talking through telephones while looking at each other through a glass panel compromises communication, especially when a lawyer has never met his client. For one thing, while you are literally sitting a pane of glass apart, the connection often sounds like you're talking to someone in another world; in some ways, I suppose you are. However, in a face-to-face meeting, when the deputies clang that solid iron door shut, it locks securely. In the five-by-seven cubicle, no distance remains between you and your client, which can cause you some discomfort when sitting across from a man sentenced to die by electrocution after being convicted of capital murder.

James Willie "Bo" Cochran was already seated at the metal table in the attorney conference room when I arrived and introduced myself. As was customary, deputies had escorted my leg-chained client into the room. When I walked into the tiny space and sat directly opposite him, I could feel his distrust and anger. Bo's glaring eyes, which sunk deeply into his clenched face, reflected palpable tension in the air. Not a particularly large man, Bo had a strong, compact and solid five-foot-seven, 175-pound build. His physique grew more imposing due to his intensity, which bordered on menacing. I reached out my hand to grip his firm handshake and introduced myself.

"Bo," I began, "I am Richard Jaffe. Judge Cole just appointed me to represent you on appeal. I wanted to meet you as soon as I could, so we can get started."

Bo sat silently for at least fifteen seconds, clearly studying me. He had never before heard my name; it had only been a day since Judge Cole had sentenced him to death. I must have looked as inexperienced as I was to the convicted man. Now, only a series of appeals stood between him and a new trial or an execution date, when a guard would pull a lever that would send two thousand volts of electricity surging through his body while he was strapped into "Yellow Mama," Alabama's infamous electric chair.

Obviously despondent and still somewhat in a daze, Bo politely pretended to be glad to meet me. "What did you say your name was?"

"Richard Jaffe." I looked squarely into his fiercely glaring eyes. "I handled many appeals while I worked for the attorney general's office a few years ago. I want you to know I will do anything I can to help you."

"That's what the court-appointed lawyers said for five years and look where I am now: heading back to death row." His every word was filled with bitterness as he told me the story of what happened on the night a murder occurred and he was arrested.

I listened carefully as Bo explained how he'd come to be arrested. He went over the November night five years before: a robbery at a grocery store in Homewood had turned deadly when the young store manager followed the robber out of the store and they both entered a dark trailer park. Later, after hearing gunshots, officers raced to the scene and the store manager's body was discovered under a trailer. No blood was on the grass; no grass marks were on the manager's body. Officers found Bo cowering in the bushes. After one put a gun to his head, threatening him, they took Bo to the station and soon booked him for capital murder.

Following Bo's arrest, Judge Cole appointed lawyers from the Southern Poverty Law Center to represent him. The State of Alabama tried Bo, but after a few days Judge Cole declared a mistrial, because the young cashier who had tentatively identified Bo in a lineup had undergone psychological counseling. However, the prosecution failed to disclose this important information until the middle of the trial. Bo remained incarcerated while he waited for his second trial to begin.

The next year, Bo arrived in the courtroom for his second trial with newly appointed counsel. His lawyers put up practically no defense. They lacked the critical resources and funds to adequately investigate Bo's adamant denials that he shot the store manager. They did not speak to any of the trailer residents or call them as witnesses. They had no money to hire experts to challenge any of the prosecution's evidence. Instead, Bo's lawyers relied on a theory of defense that suggested a lack of proof beyond a reasonable doubt. This time, the jury convicted him in less than an hour.

After finding Bo guilty, the jury recommended a death sentence. Bo's lawyers didn't have the resources to explore his background and childhood or to hire mental health experts. Bo's lawyers offered the jury no evidence of Bo's life history, which contained critical information the jury needed to properly determine whether Bo should live or die.

Because the United States Supreme Court later found Alabama's capital sentencing statute unconstitutional, Bo received yet another new trial. As before, in spite of many requests, the court denied Bo's lawyers the crucial financial resources and experts necessary for them to conduct an adequate inquiry and challenge the prosecution's evidence. For the second time, a jury convicted Bo and sentenced him to death.

Now I sat across from the man convicted of this heinous crime, knowing that I had never before handled a death penalty case and my efforts could make the difference in whether Bo lived or died. I felt overwhelmed, inadequate and scared. There would be literally thousands of pages of court transcripts to review, law to research and briefs to file.

Bo Cochran's anger began to melt into tears. They slowly welled up and then began to roll down his cheeks. Bo had already experienced the horror of death row and now he would occupy it again, perhaps until his execution, unless the courts granted him another new trial. That could take years.

"Mr. Jaffe, no one believes me, but I did not shoot that man," he said as tears continued to pool in his eyes. "God knows I didn't. The gun I had was so old and rickety that it wouldn't have fired anyway. I did the robbery, but I did not shoot him. I swear before God that I didn't. Do you believe me?"

"I believe you, Bo. I believe you."

The look of desperation never left his lonely eyes. I left the jail after failing to either assure or comfort Bo. I walked away knowing my words rang hollow.

Bo stayed on Alabama's death row for nearly fifteen more years. By then my initially reluctant foray into the death penalty arena had become, for better or worse, the centerpiece of my legal career: I defended the right to live within a system and a locale that had no qualms about throwing the switch—even if the condemned man was innocent.

At the time of Judge Cole's decision to give me the Bo Cochran case, I could not grasp his prescience. He saw characteristics that it took me years to recognize within myself: a tenacious fighter with a friendly, persuasive personality; an ability to research and dig for a detail or the hidden truth; a tendency to look for the best in others; a knack for putting people at ease in a courtroom. *How* he saw so much in a young lawyer who did not yet know the extent of his own capabilities became, for me, the kind of riddle I tend to ponder retrospectively.

Especially when I peer back to view my past and the journey to the time and place my life changed forever.

PLANTING THE SEEDS
OF A TRIAL LAWYER

Birmingham is the largest city in Alabama, but it is still a rather small town. Although nearly a million people live in the metropolitan area, fewer than 250,000 reside in the city itself. Nashville, Memphis, Charlotte and Atlanta offer vibrant night life, but downtown Birmingham is desolate—and dangerous—after the sun goes down. That is most unfortunate, since the city is quite lovely, with rolling hills and deep valleys. There is a real divide between the luscious suburbs over the mountain and the empty, shadowlike downtown that never seems to get revived.

Still, today's Birmingham is a much different place than in 1950, the year I was born. For example, I didn't know as a boy that Birmingham was nicknamed "Bombingham."[1] Like many who lived sheltered lives "over the mountain," I understood very little about the Civil Rights Movement. Although I was thirteen when the 16th Street bombing killed four innocent African-American children, it was as if it happened thousands of miles away, rather than just a few miles from my home.

Not a single African-American lived in the suburb of Mountain Brook where most everyone I knew grew up. There was a huge disconnect in the segregated world of my youth. When I played high school basketball for Mountain Brook Junior High and Senior High, the black kids I knew went to all-black high schools or were the sons

9

and daughters of the customers of Jaffe Auto Supply, the business my father opened when I was about four years old. At City Hall and other public places, blacks and whites drank water from separate fountains, used separate bathroom facilities and ate at different restaurants.

Still, I could not help but notice that blacks worked for whites and that countless blacks could not afford automobiles. Instead, they took the bus to the nearest stop and then walked to their respective homes to perform their domestic chores. That made the dividing line clear but did not alter my perception of a societal disconnect nor my questions as to why blacks were treated differently when the only difference I saw was the color of their skin.

While growing up, I knew nothing of the cruelties and lynchings that occurred so nonchalantly, especially in the Deep South. I suppose that the decisions of my parents and most others to shelter their children offered us naïve and ignorant bliss, although it could not help but contribute to the deeply embedded culture that perpetuated this casual racism.

Blacks were easy targets because of the color of their skin. Even today, blacks are still far from reaching totally equal status as citizens, especially from an economic perspective, in spite of the fact that we currently have an African-American president and many cities, such as Birmingham, have black majority city councils and black mayors.

My family faced our own form of discrimination as Jews. Our collective soul was ripped apart from the six million fellow Jews annihilated in Hitler's genocide. Every Jewish person I knew had multiple family members who were victims of the gas chambers. Even within the small population of Jews in Birmingham, more than a few who had managed to escape and survive still wore evidence stamped on their flesh: their assigned numbers from the Nazi concentration camps where they were slated for death.

When I played varsity basketball at Mountain Brook High School, I was the only Jew on the team. Each Sunday, the team visited a different church in the area. A church, sometimes more than one, sits on practically every corner in many southern cities, especially in smaller towns. When several of my teammates implored our coach to take the team to Temple on one occasion, the coach punished not only those who asked but me as well.

Understandably, no one made that request again.

So it was not a surprise that, during the civil rights movement, Jews aligned with blacks and supported their quest. Although I was sheltered from the politics, my personal experiences and exposure left me confused. The vitriolic rhetoric of our governor, George Wallace, and the treatment of Jews and blacks not only made no sense to me, but also seemed cruel, humiliating and wrong. It shaped attitudes I would carry against authority for my entire life. Although we were a middle-class family growing up in a mixed neighborhood of Christians and Jews in an affluent suburb, I was a rebel and a renegade. I resisted authority and did not appreciate the value of education. I did not study at all in high school and only went to college because my mother informed me that my only other option would be to move out and get a job working for my father at Jaffe Auto Supply. College became an easy choice.

During my first semester, I skipped classes constantly, gambled incessantly on practically any sport and embraced the student counter-culture. My report card grades reflected my irresponsibility: three Fs and two Ds. I had to drop three courses.

Then things changed. I became roommates with Mark Mandell, a fraternity brother from Providence, Rhode Island. He was brilliant, kind, empathetic, inspiring and a true leader. Mark possessed a real moral compass. He singularly changed my life. A voracious reader and an astute student of national politics, Mark exposed me to books on various social and political topics. This took place around the time of the Chicago Eight trial, the Charles Manson slayings and Woodstock. My formerly poor grades turned high enough for me to make the dean's list. I had also entered a new frontier: politics.

Mark was already a leader in the student government association and a straight-A student. I endeavored to follow in his footsteps. It didn't matter to me that I was in a fraternity that was part of the "Greek political machine." I ran as an independent so that no one would control my vote. With the help of another fraternity brother, I circumvented the fifty-dollar-per-candidate spending limit by collecting six car hoods for free from local junkyards. We painted "Jaffe for Off-Campus Representative" on each one and placed them at strategic places around campus. The next year, I handily won a coveted Student Senate seat. We were now legislators. We enacted laws related to student affairs.

During my junior year, Mark Mandell was elected vice president and I was appointed to the Honor Court, comprised of students and faculty, to judge other students who allegedly violated the Student Honor Code.

Everywhere, the Vietnam controversy pervaded the air and sound waves. We decided that the time had come to protest. Mark's core group met one day at a spot near the Student Center and distributed materials to create black armbands. The demonstrations would occur only on campus at designated places. Those participating would remain peaceful and some would carry signs. The protests were to begin in the afternoon and continue for as long as the students wanted to protest.

As the day progressed and the number of students wearing black armbands continued to increase, the atmosphere on campus thickened. Slowly but surely, the presence of local and state law enforcement increased. With that came greater tension. Officials at the University of Alabama were not happy, nor were the local police. It had been less than a decade since Governor George C. Wallace, backed by state troopers, had stood in the way of the first black student who tried to enroll at the university. On this occasion, in response to the protests, Governor Albert Brewer called in armed National Guard soldiers and state troopers.

Soon there seemed to be as many National Guardsmen and police officers as protesting students. However, they had quite an advantage; they were armed with batons and weapons along with their physical appearances: grim, determined faces and tightened jaws. We felt more than intimidated; we were scared, yet too young and naïve to be deterred. The demonstrations stretched into the evening with only scattered arrests. We appeared to be making our point but we had no intention of shutting down. Then we began to hear of more arrests, including students being beaten. Some were rushed to the hospital.

Around 11:30 P.M. the protest was still going strong. The violence perpetrated upon the students escalated as well. Mark and I ended up outside the local diner, ever mindful of the now swarming uniformed law enforcement officers stepping out of patrol cars and wielding batons. The streets of the university had been transformed into a police state. Martial order was instituted. They took over. Instead of restoring order, they created chaos, with more injuries and arrests.

As we edged our way inside the diner, we observed a plethora of patrol cars circling the area. Suddenly, students began to run in all directions, pursued by officers clubbing any student within their reach. Our black armbands prominent, our hearts beating faster, we sank into a booth occupied by a young student with waist-length hair but no black armband. He moved to the inside of the booth and I sat on his right. Across from him sat a young female student who slid over to make room for Mark. We all watched in horror through the windows as officers chased and beat any student they could catch. I saw one girl knocked to the ground and then dragged off, along with many others struck and beaten by cops swinging batons.

Suddenly, the officers and National Guardsmen stormed into the diner itself. We froze, shocked with fear. The troopers burst through the entrance and circulated throughout the diner. All four of us remained still, as if in a trance.

Then one of the troopers stopped at our booth, glanced quickly at me and then at the long-haired boy to my left. It happened too quickly for me to grasp as the officer reached over my shoulder and I felt a thin swoosh of wind from the vacancy left as the trooper lifted up the boy next to me by his hair. The officer carried the helpless student outside. Through the glass window, we watched the officer beat him senseless and toss him, like a sack of potatoes, into a paddy wagon.

The better part of discretion convinced Mark and me to remain seated in our booth. Quickly, the students dispersed and the officers disappeared. Frightened but undeterred, Mark and I continued to walk the campus in protest before I returned to our apartment to watch news reports. The demonstrations had been quelled. Law enforcement's efforts prevailed. As we watched the news on television, we tried to make sense of the violence and the school's overreaction to a *planned* and *peaceful* First Amendment expression of political differences. These experiences only reinforced my distrust for authority and the sheer brutish nature of it.

One evening, I flipped through the television channels and saw Alabama's new attorney general give an interview. I was mesmerized by the difference between his determined quest for justice and that of former Governor George C. Wallace, who preached the necessity of segregation "now, today and forever." At that very moment I decided that if I were fortunate enough I would one day work for Attorney General Baxley. The next day, I sent him a handwritten letter praising him for his vision and courage, simply hoping that he would write back to me. And he did!

The next year, the University of Alabama accepted me for law school. I returned to Tuscaloosa with an attitude of seriousness and focus. There would be no more wasting my parent's resources and my life. I learned about the incredible number of influential legal cases that had sprung from courageous lawyers and their clients who stood up for civil rights and the freedoms that are guaranteed to all of us by the United States Constitution and the Bill of Rights.

During the summer of my last year of law school, I moved back to Birmingham to clerk for a highly successful, quickly expanding, small law firm. The law firm was so busy that it retained eight clerks working feverishly on criminal, civil and divorce cases. I worked for $150 a month, which amounted to less than a dollar per hour. Yet the experience I gained proved invaluable, in learning to conduct both legal research and investigations.

As investigators, we always purposely made some minor typographical but immaterial mistake in a witness's sworn statement so that we could persuade the potential witness to correct it in his or her own hand and then initial the correction. In this way, the potential witness could not later claim he or she did not read it. The investigatory experiences I honed as a law clerk would serve me well as a prosecutor and, ultimately, as a criminal defense lawyer.

Throughout my three years in law school, I continued to write Attorney General Baxley and he always wrote me back. During the first semester of my senior year, I wrote him one more time, asking that he hire me as an assistant attorney general.

After one face-to-face interview, that's what he did.

3

PROSECUTING VIOLENT CRIMES

As an assistant attorney general in Montgomery, Alabama, I worked alongside and supervised employees from the same law enforcement agencies that forcibly quashed the protests I helped lead at the University of Alabama just five years earlier. Mainly, though, I served in the Criminal Appellate Department, handling appeals of criminal trials prosecuted by deputy district attorneys and defended by criminal defense lawyers. When it came to seniority, I lingered far back in the line of attorneys, hired by Attorney General Baxley and Chief Assistant Attorney General George Beck, who longed to live and die in the courtroom, not the library. Although I relished my position and immensely enjoyed the people with whom I worked and the contacts I made, impatience for the battlefield beat in my heart like distant drums.

One true highlight during the time I worked for Baxley was my miniscule involvement in the Whitehurst civil rights case.[1] Attorney General Baxley initiated this action against Montgomery police officers, who allegedly shot and killed a criminal suspect and then allegedly planted a murder weapon on him. Unfortunately for the officers involved, it was proven that the murder weapon had been obtained from the police department property room. Baxley tried this case with Montgomery District Attorney Jimmy Evans.

The presiding federal judge was the brilliant, courageous and famous United States District Judge, the Honorable Frank Johnson, a champion of civil rights and at one time the archenemy of Governor George C. Wallace. While governor, Wallace ranted and raved against those "liberal activist" federal judges. He considered them the sworn enemies of "states' rights"—thinly veiled code for segregation. At the head of the line was Judge Johnson.

I watched in awe as Baxley controlled the courtroom as much as anyone could in Judge Johnson's presence. Judge Johnson was austere and stern, intimidating to the most experienced and skillful warriors and utterly frightening to a greenhorn like me. I observed the trial with several other assistants and my immediate boss and supervisor, Assistant Attorney General Sally Greenhaw. Judge Johnson enjoyed a reputation for ordering a brief submission on a point of law to be delivered to his chambers by 7:30 A.M. the following morning. He usually issued the order at the end of a long day. The thought of sleep that night never occurred to my colleagues and me. After rubbing our eyes and our stomachs from no sleep and too much coffee, we hand-delivered the trial brief by the 7:30 A.M. deadline.

Meanwhile, a Tuscaloosa insurance defense lawyer named Wayne Williams had just defeated longtime Tuscaloosa District Attorney Lou Lackey. Upon winning the election, Wayne fired every deputy district attorney in the office except for Tommy Smith and Jerry Hudson. (The district attorney is an elected position and can hire and fire at will.) Although an experienced and seasoned civil defense lawyer, Wayne had neither prosecuted nor defended a criminal case. Wisely, Wayne kept Smith to coordinate the grand jury and Hudson as a trial lawyer.

A mutual friend suggested that Wayne interview me for one of the now-open positions. Less than three weeks later, I drove from Montgomery to Tuscaloosa, feeling scared but brash.

I sat before the newly-elected Williams, a young and boyish-looking former high school football coach, and got right to the point: "If you decide to hire me," I brazenly asked, "and I choose to leave my current position as an assistant attorney general, would you consider making me your chief deputy district attorney?"

Like any talented trial lawyer or good poker player, Wayne did not wince. "I can't in good conscience appoint you as my chief assistant. Jerry and Tommy have been in the office even before I was elected. But I can promise you this: if you are as good as I think you could be and you prove it, I will give you the biggest and most challenging cases."

A month later, I went to work for Wayne Williams in Tuscaloosa. Within days of starting, he asked me to assist him as second chair in a drug prosecution. The following Monday, I learned I would serve as a lead lawyer in a first-degree murder prosecution and Deputy District Attorney Tommy Smith would assist me.

Rarely have I felt more scared than the day my first murder trial commenced in the courtroom of the Honorable Claude Harris. The only morsel of sanity I retained lay hidden in my knowledge that Tommy would support me when an unfamiliar rule of evidence stymied me. Low-key and understated but bright and wily, Tommy would make sure I did not mishandle my first murder trial.

On the day the trial commenced, the insides of my legs felt paralyzed as I trudged slowly to take my seat at counsel table, just a few feet from where twelve unknown strangers would soon decide the guilt or innocence of Willie Brown, the accused killer, who fearfully faced the front of the courtroom. Behind counsel table, directly behind me, sat Mike Bishop, the lead detective in the case.

Unlike many in his position today, Mike had no interest in obtaining a conviction for conviction's sake. He investigated his cases correctly and carefully and left the outcome to the jury. He believed in letting the system run its course. Quiet and thoughtful, Mike conducted solid investigations.

Lawyers, on the other hand, knew their principal role to be that of producer and director of the most persuasive and convincing story they could present to the jurors they hoped to convince. Mike had arrested

Brown after he stabbed and killed his friend at a neighborhood barbecue. Both he and the victim were inebriated. Unfortunately, the victim was much smaller and was unarmed. The claim of self-defense appeared rather weak.

As I seated myself uneasily in my chair, I saw the defendant for the first time. All I knew previously about him consisted of what eyewitnesses had stated to Mike: how the suspect inflicted a fatal blow in the chest of the deceased with a pocket knife. However, the Willie Brown who slumped in his chair next to his lawyer wore a look of dejection and sadness across his face. He did not look like a cold-blooded killer, just a poor, uneducated manual laborer who seemed to regret allowing the effects of too much bad whiskey arouse his passions at a routine family gathering on a hot Sunday.

For the moment I could relax, because Tommy Smith had agreed to take the responsibility of questioning the prospective jurors who had filed into the solemn mahogany and marble courtroom. In less than half an hour, I would deliver the opening statement in this first-degree murder case and all eyes would focus upon me.

Finally the time had come. After Judge Harris swore in the jury, he looked over to the prosecutor's table and, in a matter-of-fact tone, asked: "Who will be making the opening statement for the State?"

"Mr. Jaffe will, on behalf of the State, Your Honor."

Fear gripped me. My heart raced into overdrive. I knew that I had to stand up, but I didn't know if I could speak. I slowly walked to within eight feet of the jury rail, my eyes glazed over with fear. I tried to speak…nothing came out. Finally, I managed to deliver the opening statement in a painstakingly quivering voice, as if my mouth was full of gravel.

The trial lasted only two days. By the time that I made the final closing statement, the nervousness and fear that plagued me during my opening statement had dissipated. Sensing victory, I was on fire, hardly able to contain my excitement. With the righteous indignation of a true prosecutor, I actually yelled some of my closing. In those days, the jury not only decided innocence or guilt, but also meted out the punishment with its verdict.

It did not take much time for the normally conservative law-and-order rural Tuscaloosa jury to find Brown guilty of murder and sentence him to thirty years in the state penitentiary.

After the verdict, I commented to Mike, "I think I may have been a little more aggressive than I needed to be."

Mike paused for a few seconds. "Yeah," he quietly agreed, "you probably didn't need to be so loud. You could have toned it down some and still got the conviction."

With Tommy's support, the trial had proceeded smoothly. Yet when Mike confirmed what I sensed was my unnecessarily over-the-top performance, I felt a little hollow. I vowed to be more controlled at my next trial, which was a week or two away. I recognized just how powerful the position of a prosecutor can be and became sensitized to the fact that the men and women who sit in the defendant's chair are people, too.

Trials involving violent crimes carry not only a tremendous burden but also raw emotion. If convicted, the accused faces decades in prison or even death. In every case, the victims suffer permanent, unimaginable losses that will forever define their futures. The families of the victims will never be the same, nor experience the world as safely or securely as they did before being victimized. As a prosecutor, I made sure to get to know the victims and family members.

So it was with Josh Varlett. While drunk at an outdoor neighborhood gathering, defendant Bobby Day shot Josh's left arm off just above the elbow. Every time this case was continued for one reason or another, Josh and his wife retreated back into their discombobulated lives, waiting eagerly but patiently for the trial to be held and, they hoped, for justice to be served.

Finally, Josh got his day in court. The jury convicted his assailant and sentenced him to fifteen years in prison for attempted murder.[2] The perpetrator would serve approximately one-third of that sentence, but Josh would never get back his fingers, his forearm or his elbow. For every minute of every day, the now unemployable carpenter would know the trauma and helpless sense of loss, yet never be able to understand this heinous act.

Though what I had learned would be with me always, after Josh's case I had no choice but to move on to the next one, leaving Josh, his wife and their two small children to navigate their shattered lives.

I tried more than thirty major felony cases while I was at the Tuscaloosa District Attorney's Office. While I rarely gloated when a jury convicted someone I had prosecuted and the court sent him or her to prison, I liked winning trials and felt part of the law enforcement community.

4

THE DIXIE MAFIA

While at the District Attorney's office, I began to familiarize myself with a country club robbery case, in which the "Dixie Mafia" robbed a group of well-heeled professionals in the middle of their weekly poker game, where they played for high stakes and plenty of cash flowed.

It was no wonder that no other prosecutor had volunteered to take this to trial. No eyewitness could identify any of the four robbers, each of whom wore a ski mask. The prospect of a successful prosecution did not seem particularly promising. Those who were robbed were seen as pillars of the community and would not be pleased with an acquittal; no prosecutor relished causing such disappointment. The local law enforcement agencies called in the Alabama Bureau of Investigation (ABI) for similar reasons. ABI Agent Larry Smelley served as the lead investigator.

The sparse contents of the District Attorney's case file did not offer me much hope, other than the fact that one of the four robbers, Nick Jameson, had cooperated with the ABI and would receive immunity in exchange. The other three defendants were represented by Don Holt, a very skillful and extremely aggressive defense attorney from Florence, Alabama. The Dixie Mafia made its presence most known in northern Alabama and Don had built a longstanding reputation by successfully defending many of its members—so much so that he was nearly a legend in the mountainous rural areas where bootleggers and drug dealers thrived. Although Don represented each of the three codefendants, the Tuscaloosa Circuit Court set each trial separately.

First was defendant Neal Rogers. I read over the prosecution file in our office, which included police reports, the ABI reports and statements from the poker players. In addition, I reviewed transcripts of the recorded conversations between Jameson, who wore a wire, and each of the three codefendants. Apparently, Nick Jameson possessed a knack for gaining the trust of his cohorts, as each made damning admissions when Nick pretended to be upset over the division of the poker pot heisted in the smoothly-engineered armed robbery.

As I reviewed the file, I noticed that something important was missing. The file contained no motion for discovery. I could not believe it. At the time, statements made to non-law enforcement officers were not to be turned over to the defense without a written or oral motion for discovery. More than likely, with Don's demanding trial schedule, he delegated the filing of motions in the case. I checked the official court file in the clerk's office; no motion for discovery, motion to suppress or request for a pre-trial hearing had been filed.

Meanwhile, Jameson was in the witness protection program and under constant guard by investigators. I didn't even have access to my witness. From the public's perspective, it appeared that Jameson had simply disappeared to avoid being prosecuted. Since the State had charged him with the same robbery offenses, there was no obvious reason for Don to assume he was cooperating with police. At that time, no one had ever cooperated against members of the "Dixie Mafia" and certainly not one of their own. Don knew the ski masks ensured no eyewitness testimony and anticipated a rapid victory against a young, rookie deputy district attorney such as myself.

I had never met ABI Investigator Larry Smelley or coopera- tor Nick Jameson. On the weekend before the trial, I was scheduled to meet both. Smelley had given me specific instructions: go to the lobby of a particular hotel in Tuscaloosa at precisely 1:55 P.M. on the Saturday afternoon before the Monday trial. Once there, I was to call a number and ask for a fictitious person, then await further instructions. I was to wear street clothes.

Proceeding as instructed, I arrived at the hotel precisely on time, dressed in blue jeans, tennis shoes and a sweatshirt. I brought along a blank yellow legal pad. I made the call from a phone in the hotel lobby. Feeling a bit excited to finally assess my star witness, I identified myself to the person who answered my phone call and wrote down the room number with nervous anticipation. Slowly I entered the elevator and pushed the number four. Once the elevator delivered me, I walked to the room whose number I had been given and then gingerly knocked on the door.

Suddenly the door jerked open, but only a few inches, as it caught the inside door chain. The cold steel barrel of a .357 magnum pressed against my forehead. "Who the f--- is it?" echoed in my ears.

"It's Richard Jaffe, the deputy district attorney," I stuttered in shock.

"Show me some ID and your badge."

I fumbled anxiously for the items. The mystery man continued to point the gun at my head. I produced the identification and then one of the agents opened the door wide enough to pull me into the room quickly and slam the door shut. "Relax," he said after locked the door behind me. "I am Investigator Smelley and this is Nick Jameson." He also introduced me to the other two agents on the case.

My hand was a bit shaky as I extended it to each man. The four men sat at a card table playing poker and sharing refreshments. I tried to relax and began my trial preparation, interviewing Nick to see if he would be consistent with the recorded statements and interviews he had given as well as with the circumstances surrounding his wired meetings with Neal Rogers. Quickly I grew impressed. Nick was about five feet nine inches tall and weighed around 230 pounds. He had a deep southern drawl and a wide beer belly and his brown, wavy hair was short-cropped. With his easy smile, he appeared relaxed.

After about forty-five minutes of going over the questions I would ask in court, I then role-played my cross-examination with Nick. He answered every one of my harshly worded questions with consistency.

We were ready for trial.

On the opening morning, the Honorable Joe Colquitt inquired as to whether any pretrial motions lingered and were in need of being addressed. I turned and looked directly at Don Holt, the ever-confident and fiery trial lawyer, who declared, "No, Your Honor, the defendant is ready to proceed." There was still no mention of outstanding discovery and lingering issues. It was as if Don was lying in wait when, in fact, the taped conversations provided by State's witness Nick Jameson would soon surprise the courtroom—most especially Neal Rogers and Don Holt.

Still utterly satisfied that no discovery requests had been filed, I decided to put Nick on the stand without asking him about the recorded conversations.

As expected, the trial proceeded smoothly. I had made no mention of the tape in my opening and said little about the post-robbery conversations, other than Rogers admitting his involvement, which we would prove beyond a reasonable doubt.

Don's cross-examination of Nick began as well as I could have imagined. He attacked Nick's credibility, accusing him of saying anything to get out of the charges of robbery and other crimes as well. Don depicted Nick as a robber and liar and questioned why anyone would ever feel comfortable accepting his word without any proof.

When it was time for re-direct, I asked the judge if we could approach the bench. Don and I stood in front of the judge. "In response to the cross-examination," I informed the court, "we intend to play a recorded conversation between Nick Jameson and Neal Rogers as a prior consistent statement to rehabilitate the attack on Mr. Jameson's credibility."

Don Holt's anger exploded.

The judge recessed the jury while Don vehemently argued the statement as inadmissible. The judge did not hesitate to let us play the recorded conversation, first outside of the jury's presence and then for the jury, loud and clear.

No defense lawyer could do much of anything to avoid a guilty verdict from that point on. The jury sentenced Neal Rogers to twenty years, which might be viewed as a victory for Don since the jury could have sentenced him to life.

The Neal Rogers trial brought justice to one of the defendants, but I still had two to go. Wayne Williams immediately informed me that we would both try the second defendant, Stanford Jenkins, the most notorious of the three. Don Holt promptly filed a discovery motion to obtain the wired conversations between Nick Jameson and the other two codefendants.

These cases continued to surprise me. Neither Don Holt nor our office made mention of a plea bargain, despite the incriminatory admissions made by Stanford Jenkins on tape. In fact, Don did not even file a motion to suppress. Unlike Rogers, Jenkins projected the persona of a successful businessman from a small town. If Jenkins gave any real thought to a jury possibly convicting him, he hid it well.

Of stocky build and sporting a very expensive tailor-made suit, the prosperous-looking and handsome Jenkins exuded an aura of unfailing confidence. He seemed much more relaxed than I felt as he joked, smiled and conversed with Don. My tension was well-founded. A few months had passed since Neal Rogers's surprise conviction. This time, Don Holt would be taking nothing for granted, which propelled me into further uneasiness.

The jury selection took only an hour or so. When I delivered my opening statement, I described the recorded meeting between Nick Jameson and Stanford Jenkins and the damning admissions Jenkins had made on tape.

After I concluded, a fired-up Don Holt bolted up from his chair and assured the jury that he would demonstrate that everything I had promised them would prove false—that Jenkins enjoyed a sterling reputation as a fine businessman and was not present at the country club. Besides, Don contended, Jenkins had no financial need to participate in a robbery. Don boldly promised the jury that his client would testify freely and voluntarily and affirm his innocence under oath. According to Don, Jenkins was a family man who had never met Nick and didn't know why Nick had fingered him.

I had no idea how Jenkins intended to explain the recorded conversation. Would he say that the word *"robbery"* was never used? I waited with much suspense, as I'm sure the jury did, for Don's client to take the stand.

First to the stand, though, was Nick. During his testimony, Nick spoke unpretentiously and credibly. Then during Don's ferocious and effective cross-examination, Nick admitted that he expected never to serve a day in prison. Don's questions implied that Nick was just another desperate snitch who would say anything to avoid the penitentiary. Almost effortlessly, Don made it seem that lying came as easily to Nick Jameson as committing robbery. Don pointed out that Jenkins was a perfect target and the kind of respected businessman that some prosecutors would love to capture rather than another cheap thug.

However, Nick kept his cool. If Don felt frustrated, he showed no expression other than a fiery contempt for a perjurer who seemingly would trade anything for freedom.

The next day we rested. Don called a number of character witnesses attesting to Jenkins's good reputation and his veracity in the community. Then the wiry, ever-cagey and always confident defense attorney boldly announced his next witness: the impeccably dressed and polished Stanford Jenkins. As Jenkins slowly strolled to the stand in his silver suit, all eyes followed him. He slid into the witness chair, where he took the solemn oath to tell the truth.

Jenkins looked easily toward the eagerly perched jury, where Don stood ready to deliver the direct examination. As Jenkins testified, I noticed his lips did not seem to be moving very much. It was as if he had some material stuck in the back of his throat, like a wad of chewing gum or taffy. And then Don Holt dropped a bombshell: "Mr. Jenkins, would you turn and look at the fine ladies and gentlemen of this jury and tell them if you recognize the voices on that tape?"

Obligingly, Jenkins turned to his left, looked at the jury and then answered, "Well, Mr. Holt, I think I recognize one of the voices, because it sounds like the man I just heard testify, but the other voice…no, sir, I don't recognize it at all."

"Mr. Jenkins, is that your voice we just heard on that recording?"

"No, sir, Mr. Holt, that's for sure not me."

"Mr. Jenkins, do you swear before God and give us your solemn word that that is not your voice on that recording?"

"That is not my voice, Mr. Holt."

"No further questions."

Don Holt confidently looked at the jury and then to me, "Your witness."

I pondered for a moment before rising to cross-examine. *Should I or should I not ask Stanford Jenkins to open his mouth wide for the jury to inspect it?* Slowly I peeled out of my chair to face a slightly snickering Stanford Jenkins, who seemed ready to take me on. I began cautiously. "Mr. Jenkins, you claim that is not your voice we just heard?"

"That's not my voice."

"I would like you to say the words: 'There ain't no damn other money. You got your entire share and more.'"

Don Holt jumped upright. "Objection, Your Honor! The prosecutor is badgering the witness."

"Overruled," declared the judge. He then gave me a curious, perplexed look.

I reiterated my request. Mr. Jenkins dutifully repeated the words. When he did, I believe the truth became clear. He could not feign the tone and texture of his voice, in spite of the gravelly nature of his words. Still, his lips hardly moved.

I knew the next twenty minutes of my cross-examination would reveal whether or not the jury believed Stanford Jenkins. I was not at all sure of where I stood. Apparently neither was Don, whose shoulders visibly relaxed when I passed the witness back to him. He declined to redirect.

I started our closing statement by summarizing the State's evidence and then calling upon the jury to use their collective common sense. All of the poker-playing businessmen testified that the robbers wore ski masks and robbed them effortlessly and efficiently, making off with more than thirty thousand dollars. One of the robbers fit Jenkins's physical build: the man who clearly projected the persona of the leader of the robbers. I asked the jury if Stanford Jenkins' voice as spoken from the witness stand sounded the same as the voice on the tape, except when he mumbled his answers.

Don Holt then delivered his closing argument to the jury. His face turned redder and redder, more so than his reddish hair, as his voice rose. This fiery, six-foot two-inch lawyer projected his courtroom presence with a booming voice, both passionate and persuasive.

Finally, Wayne Williams closed the case. Quiet in his initial approach, the district attorney asked the jury to return a verdict of guilty and sentence Jenkins to thirty years.

In less than half an hour, the jury did just that.

Now there were two defendants sentenced for the crime and one left to go to trial. The third robber was also caught on tape in the same admissions of guilt, discussing the robbery proceeds and the way they were divided with Nick Jameson. The jury had already sentenced Neal Rogers to twenty years and Stanford Jenkins to thirty. Don's third client entered a guilty plea and was given twenty years.

After languishing for several years on the Tuscaloosa criminal trial docket, the country club cases were now closed.

5

LOST, BUT NOT FORGOTTEN

The last of the historical cases from the previous district attorney's administration still lingered in our office. This was not due to a lack of sympathy for the victim. Instead, the case held many challenges that resided not in the facts or the proof, but in the dynamic realities of the time. While I was still in law school, the DA who preceded Wayne Williams persuaded a grand jury to charge Bobby Thigpen with second-degree murder for recklessly causing the death of a fifteen-year-old African-American boy named Bennie Rae Jones, who was riding his bicycle when Thigpen's automobile struck him. Thigpen was severely drunk at the time and had a long record of DUIs. In the office, we discussed the fact that nobody could recall that any Tuscaloosa County jury had ever convicted someone of murder arising out of a DUI vehicular homicide. The case file sat in the clerk's office but never reached the trial docket. Now I had inherited it.

Sadness enveloped me when I studied the hopeful grin and the bright but gentle eyes of the now-deceased teen in the high school photographs stapled to the office file. I placed one of the photos inside my wallet and carried it throughout the trial of this case, almost a year and a half. From time to time, I took the young man's photograph out and stared at it for a minute or two, long enough for me to remain

committed to seeking justice for this boy, who lay in the ground forgotten by all except his grief-stricken family.

Finally, the court set the trial date.

When I realized the complexities and technical nature of this
trial, I asked the exceptionally bright Jerry Hudson to sit second chair.
One day, he accompanied me as we drove to the scene of the fatality. It
occurred fewer than six blocks from the boy's home, where his parents
and older brother still lived. After we viewed the scene and took some
photographs, we then drove to his parents' home, a run-down, brown
wooden structure. After we knocked on the door, the deceased teen's
humble parents politely and deferentially invited us inside.

Inside it was clean and tidy, consisting of a small kitchen, two
tiny bedrooms and a sparse "living room." We immediately noticed a
large, framed picture of the teen on the fireplace, an enlarged version of
the picture I'd been carrying in my wallet.

Something gripped me after we left: Not once had this poor
family called our office to complain or ask about a trial date. More than
likely, they assumed that because a white man had killed their son, it
would be Southern Justice as usual.

My father, who a few months before the trial had suffered a mild
heart attack, attended the trial with my mother. Unfortunately for everyone, scorching heat swept into the courtroom after the air conditioner broke
down. Although Judge Claude Harris allowed the lawyers to try the case
with their shirtsleeves rolled up, even the open windows provided scant
relief. Everyone in the courtroom was drenched in sweat as justice crept
along on its long-delayed mission to convict Bobby Ray Thigpen.

The most challenging part of the trial occurred during our
scientific expert's testimony in regard to his reconstruction of the fatality. He had calculated the speed of the defendant's automobile using
data provided by the investigating officers who had examined the
roadway, bicycle and automobile. At that time, the rules of evidence
required scientific opinion to be extracted through a series of hypo-
thetical questions posed to the expert. I stuttered and floundered my
way through this technical process and finally the court admitted the
expert's conclusions: Thigpen's driving speed was excessive. This was

exacerbated by the amount of alcohol in Mr. Thigpen's blood at the time, which they were easily able to verify, because he was injured in the accident and taken to the hospital.

After my closing argument, I sat down to discover a handwritten note from Jerry Hudson. He wrote that during my choppy examination of the experts, he was a bit underwhelmed. But after he heard my closing argument that tied it all together, he wrote that he realized how much it took to persuade the jury to return a verdict for murder. It is always nice to receive such compliments from a colleague at trial, because sometimes lawyers are long on criticism and short on praise. But what meant the most to me were the looks on the faces of the young man's parents. They did not seek revenge, only the same justice a white person's child would receive. Their tears were filled not only with sadness but also with gratitude.

During the trial, I felt the defense relied too heavily upon racial dynamics and history. As it was, the nearly all-white Tuscaloosa jury heard enough to convict Thigpen of second-degree murder, at that time an unprecedented victory in a DUI homicide case. But it was even more of a victory for racial justice in a small southern town. The jury sentenced Thigpen to a minimum of ten years, but the message they sent was far louder: times were changing, making room for the memory of an impoverished black child to be honored rather than desecrated. The jury's verdict also established that a DUI homicide for a repeat offender could result in a murder conviction.

This case was my final one as a deputy district attorney. At one time I was conflicted about the ultimate punishment: the death penalty. My conflict ended when, as deputy district attorney, I prosecuted someone who could have received it. He made a plea deal and was sentenced to life without the possibility of parole. Shortly after that I decided to leave the DA's office and move to the other side, to the defense, in part to avoid having to participate in prosecuting anyone facing death.

The senior defense lawyer on the Thigpen trial approached me after the verdict and asked if he could have a word with me. He offered me a job as a litigator in his firm. However, I informed him that

I had already taken a job in Birmingham, Alabama, and soon would be moving home. I would miss Tuscaloosa, Wayne Williams and the people with whom I worked, from the lawyers and secretaries in our office to the probation officers, such as Cynthia McGough, to Mike Everett and many other detectives, some of whom I worked with and befriended.

Thus my career as a prosecutor ended with an explosive quietness. I had no idea that Birmingham, the place I'd gotten my new job, suffered from one of the worst murder rates in the country or that a huge part of my practice would involve defending hundreds of people who were accused of murder—and over sixty people who were facing the death penalty.

6

PRIVATE PRACTICE AND "JACK'S LAW"

Having resigned my position as a deputy district attorney in Tuscaloosa, I moved to Birmingham to try my hand as a criminal defense lawyer. Birmingham seemed like the right place to begin a career with no clients, no name recognition and no money, since there were only a few truly accomplished criminal defense lawyers there at that time.

As the newest associate of a small law firm and at the direction of my superiors, I reported to the District Criminal Court of Jefferson County, Alabama, the Honorable Jack Montgomery presiding. Many other lawyers, including my bosses, had previously warned me about Judge Montgomery, but not nearly enough.

While at the district attorney's office and before then as an assistant attorney general for the State of Alabama, every time I strolled into court I brought with me all of the power and resources of the great State of Alabama and its seal of approval. Everyone on the right side of justice honored the designation.

But on my first day as a criminal defense attorney, I walked in alone, apprehensive and unsure. I soon saw how quickly things had changed in terms of how I was viewed.

In spite of all I had heard about Judge Montgomery's antics and colorful histrionics, I thought I could extend my hand and create a favorable impression. "Good morning, Judge. My name is Richard Jaffe," I uttered, trying to sound cheerful and competent. I then identified the law firm that had trusted me to come before him on my first day.

The good judge looked me up and down as if I represented some piece of cold, volcanic crud and replied, "So?" He turned around and walked away, leaving my outstretched hand dangling in the air amid the not-too-surprised attorneys standing around. I had been welcomed to the private practice of law and to the world of Jack Montgomery—to "Jack's Law."

After a brief time, I decided to leave the law firm that hired me. Having little money, I approached my parents and asked them to co-sign a loan at a local bank. My mother earnestly asked, "Open a law practice? Have you lost your mind? Who is going to come to you?" Although it pained me deeply, it was actually a very good question. I replied, "We'll see," but I entreated them to help me and my pleas proved successful.

People without money to retain a lawyer can receive a court-appointed attorney to represent them at State expense. These people need attorneys and young lawyers need clients, even if the State paid only the sum of ten dollars per hour at the time. To make matters worse, no matter how much time an attorney spent on a case, the State capped the maximum allowable compensation at five hundred dollars for even a major felony. So if the trial lasted three or four days and the attorney did a moderate amount of investigation and legal research, the compensation rate could end up being barely a couple of bucks an hour. I could have made better money in lesser jobs.

Within that world, however, opportunities abounded to sharpen trial skills, to fight for clients, to become known in the legal community, among judges and lawyers and in criminal circles. Also, high-profile cases generated publicity.

For a long time, the empty spaces of the office suite I rented after obligating myself to a three-year lease were filled with lonesome echoes. I had plenty of room and a full-time secretary but no clients. Maybe my mother was right—where would they come from?

In order to be appointed to represent an indigent defendant, a lawyer had to arrive at the courthouse by 1:00 P.M. for the initial appearance or arraignment docket. Judge Montgomery then decided which attorney to appoint to represent a defendant from among the lawyers who showed up for the docket. Recently arrested defendants sat together in the mahogany wood jury box to the attorneys' left and to the judge's right. Most of them were African-American men. All wore the orange jumpsuits recognizable as prison garb. On the first occasion I attended the arraignment docket, only four of us begging young lawyers showed up, hoping to be chosen to defend a man's freedom for a few dollars an hour. We waited patiently to see what kind of mood Judge Montgomery would bring with him as he walked out of his chambers' doorway and onto the bench. This six-foot-two-inch, two-hundred-pound, broad-shouldered man in his mid-forties more closely resembled a retired running back or linebacker than a judge. Although he never wore a robe, he always packed at least one pistol. His handsome but gruff face was normally red and when he got angry, he looked as if he would explode.

When he entered the courtroom that day, Judge Montgomery was in a jovial mood, clearly rambunctious and carrying an edge. The courtroom had filled with spectators, defendants who had made bond and lawyers early for the 1:00 P.M. docket. In addition, there were family members, friends and witnesses for both sides, court personnel and a few bondsmen. Anyone who had practiced in Montgomery's court anticipated that he would put on some kind of show at someone's expense, often the lawyers, sometimes the criminal defendants.

"Alright, court will come to order and that goes for everybody but me, because I'm the judge. I run this place. Anybody who doesn't believe that can deal with me. Anybody can't handle that? I thought so." The judge had quickly warmed up to the idea that everyone had focused on him and so he gladly performed.

"Alright, I'm going to see who over here needs a lawyer." He pointed to the first defendant. "You got a lawyer?"

"No, sir," the prisoner responded.

"Can you afford one?" asked the judge.

"No, sir."

"Are you working?"

"No, sir."

"Why not?"

"I can't get a job," the defendant responded.

"Bullshit. You expect me to buy that crap?"

"No, sir. I mean sir. I mean Judge." The rattled prisoner stumbled over his words. "Yes, sir. I got laid off last month. I've tried, Judge, I really have," the prisoner pleaded.

Judge Montgomery began to taunt him. "Well, take a look out there. See all those hungry lawyers looking like vultures, begging to represent you? Well, take your pick. Any one of those stars you want? It's your choice."

The befuddled prisoner stammered, "I don't know, Judge. They all look fine to me. I wouldn't know…"

His Honor's face seemed to brighten and the corner of the left side of his mouth curled up slightly as he reached into his pocket and pulled out a coin. "Well, then, if you can't decide, we'll let Lady Luck decide for you. See those two guys on the second row to your right?" The judge pointed to the two lawyers sitting on either side of me. "Heads, it's the big guy. Tails, the curly-haired one who's trying to keep from smiling."

The judge flipped the coin. The already riveted courtroom spectators watched with mild astonishment as though lined up at a casino craps table.

"Heads," the judge cracked. "Oh, well, you can't win them all. You get the big guy. Better luck next time."

The judge called the next case and then the next. Finally, each of the other young lawyers had two clients apiece. One defendant remained and one lawyer: me. With hesitation and a slight snarl, the judge appointed me to represent Juan Carlos Rodriquez. Juan was my first client. He was charged with shoplifting from a store. He swore he didn't do it. He could not speak English well. We filled out some paper-work and I told him that I would see him later that day at the jail.

When we met in the jail, Juan seemed more relaxed. His lack of English skills and my deficiencies in Spanish prevented him from inquiring as to my experience—or lack thereof—in the Jefferson County criminal justice system. I knew enough to tell him that his preliminary hearing was in two weeks. "We will be ready," I assured him with more confidence than I felt.

The next time I saw Juan at the county jail, he told me that he had given my name to his roommate, also in need of a criminal lawyer. I asked Juan how his friend would be able to pay my legal fees, the appropriate amount of which I had no clue. Juan explained that his roommate, Gabriel, played the saxophone and was very good. He was willing to sell or pawn his instruments to get the cash to make bail. He would then get a job and retrieve them. I listened intently.

The next day, my secretary could hardly contain her excitement when she announced, "Some guy who doesn't speak much English wants to see you." Gabriel waited patiently in the lobby until she escorted him into my office. He opened cases displaying a violin and a saxophone. Both seemed to be in very good condition.

Like Juan, Gabriel was charged with shoplifting at the same store but on a different day. I took the case for $350 to handle the pre-liminary hearing, which was in two days. We then left to pawn the instruments.

Just two blocks east from my office stood several pawnshops. I started with the most distant shop. We walked in, me dressed in a dark pin-striped suit and Gabriel wearing clothes fit for the homeless. As soon as we entered, I recognized the business owner as a man in his mid-sixties who knew my father. He wanted nothing to do with us and suggested we leave. The second pawnshop owner treated us rudely. Since he also came from the Jewish community in which I grew up, he no doubt recognized me. The third proprietor, however, proved the charm. We walked out with $445. I had my fee and Gabriel had some pocket money.

At that time, Jefferson County employed three district judges to handle preliminary hearings, misdemeanors and traffic cases. The judges rotated, so we never knew which judge would be assigned to our cases until we arrived in court. Judge Red Stewart was so kind and compassionate he gave probation to almost every female, almost any young person not charged with murder and almost anyone with a mother who could cry for her son or daughter. Race didn't matter. Judge Robert Gwin was tough. Then there was Judge Montgomery, who was all over the board, depending upon his mood or other factors yet to be revealed.

I was able to get Gabriel's case continued for a couple of weeks so I could concentrate my efforts on preparing for my first preliminary hearing for Juan Rodriquez. I felt he had a good defense since the store clerk described someone completely different from Rodriquez, who looked foreign for these parts. I felt that the judge would have to dismiss the case in Juan's favor after a thorough cross-examination of the store clerk. Unfortunately, the judge selected to handle this case was Judge Montgomery.

When he saw me, he was not happy. "You're not going to make me hold a hearing for this scumbag, are you?"

"Yes, Your Honor. I need a hearing." I tried to act as if I wasn't scared.

The judge glared at me and then told me to shut up while he reviewed some paperwork. "Mr. Jaffe…that is your name, right?"

"Yes, sir, Judge."

"You don't need a hearing. Hear me when I say this. You don't want a hearing."

Before I could respond, the judge looked at Juan, who must have thought His Honor had purposely selected the worst lawyer in America to represent him. "Look, hoss," the judge deadpanned to him. "I'm only going to say this once. I have a report on you. Jail records show that you have been defecating in your jail cell and then smearing it on the wall. Is that true?"

Juan looked over at me as if he had no idea what the Judge was saying. "I doubt Juan knows what the word 'defecate' means," I stated.

The judge looked back at me. "I don't give a shit what you think and I don't care what he understands. You go tell him that he is about to get a 'Montgomery Special.' I am going to take his guilty plea today and I am going to put him on spot probation and as a condition of that probation, he has got to leave the city—no, he's got to leave the state and never, ever return. Do you understand that? *Capisce?*"

"I understand that, Judge. Let me have a moment with him."

But Juan didn't need a moment. He looked up at the judge and with a sly meekness squeaked, "Señor Judge, I never come back. I leave tomorrow."

"No, hoss, you leave today."

We walked out together. My client acted happy, even more so relieved. I took him to the bus station that night and I am quite sure he never returned. Gabriel, on the other hand, ended up pleading guilty and he, too, received probation. At least on that case I didn't have to put up with any abuse, because the judge assigned was Judge Stewart. Hopefully, Gabriel retrieved his instruments from the pawnshop.

Then I worked my first jury trial. I represented Greg Walkerson, who was charged with armed robbery. I was prepared, but the prosecutor was not and presiding Judge Wallace Gibson did not put up with unprepared attorneys in his courtroom. Unlike some judges, who help an unprepared prosecutor and team up with him or her to marginalize the efforts of an unskilled defense lawyer, Gibson took it as a personal affront when any lawyer was unprepared, unethical or incompetent.

In this case, Walkerson was mistakenly identified. Gibson knew it, I knew it and so did the jury. I heard for the first time those soft, sweet, caressing words: "Not guilty." I would hear them many more times over the next three decades. Those words always sounded as fresh as spring.

That summer I defended three first-degree murder cases, each high-profile and resulting in guilty verdicts and life sentences. I also lost each on appeal. In all three cases, the court appointed me to represent a poor person who could not afford to retain counsel of his choice.

Over the next three years, I tried a host of cases, in several of which my clients received not guilty verdicts. My reputation as a fighter grew, but before I would be truly effective I would have to gain mastery and control over my fiery temper. A jury will not respect someone who loses control. If you can't control yourself, you can't persuade the jurors. That is the key.

7
MONTGOMERY
UPS HIS ANTICS

Over the years, the shock value of Judge Jack Montgomery's bizarre behavior and courtroom antics continued to magnify. He seemed to relish the moments when his shadow loomed larger than life. He acted as he pleased, daring others to challenge him. Various complaints to the Judicial Oversight Board proved meaningless. Judge Montgomery appeared as a popular weekly guest on an Alabama early morning show and his shoot-from-the-hip one-liners made him a pop star in the eyes of his television audience.

Consuming more and more alcohol after leaving the courthouse each day, Judge Montgomery continued to ignore his insulin-dependent diabetes. He flew into rages while on the bench. Judge Montgomery detested lawyers who insisted on holding preliminary hearings. However, due to the restrictive discovery rules in criminal cases, particularly in Alabama, the preliminary hearing provides a crucial opportunity to obtain information about the prosecution's evidence at an early stage of the litigation. In this way the defense can obtain an idea of which direction the case is heading and what type of investigation to conduct.

Even after an indictment, in some jurisdictions the government does not have to disclose the lay witnesses it may call at trial or what the witnesses may say or have said against the accused. However, the government must disclose information that could have a favorable bearing on the defense, including information that might discredit a government witness. The government must also share the results of any scientific testing. If the government cuts deals with witnesses, it must disclose that information to the defense, and if the accused has made a statement to the authorities, the defense receives this too.

In civil cases, the law provides a mandatory open exchange of information known as the discovery process, the reasoning being that fair trials occur only when both sides can prepare. In other words, trial by ambush skews the truth-finding process and is less likely to occur when both sides discover as much as possible about the facts. In civil cases, if the defendant wants to know something, he or she simply asks in the form of an interrogatory or at a deposition, neither of which exists in a criminal case except in a few states, such as Florida.

In most situations, if I determine early on that a case will probably not be resolved by a plea bargain and is headed for trial, I insist on a preliminary hearing. That was my intent on this occasion.

Deeply desirous of leaving the courthouse by noon, Judge Montgomery's impatience was showing and his eyes were riveted on the clock every few minutes. The State had accused my client, a female police officer, and her eighteen-year-old niece of shoplifting. The officer faced both prison time and job termination if she was convicted. Because I knew my client's case would not be resolved by a guilty plea, I demanded a hearing.

When Judge Montgomery called the case, he expected me to waive her case to the grand jury, just like every other lawyer did that day. His angry, tense mood had successfully served as a strong deterrent to them.

"Ready, Your Honor," I stated.

"Ready for what?" he growled. Judge Montgomery was hungry and needed sugar.

As the last lawyer left standing in the courtroom, I saw the clock tick down to 11:30.

"Your Honor," I started in my meekest and most humbling tone, "we really need a hearing in this case. I don't think the State can prove probable cause against my client."

Suddenly, I encountered the glare of Montgomery's deeply piercing blue eyes and I noticed the redness and swelling in his face. In that ticking stillness, the seconds seemed more like an eternity.

"Damn it!" he screamed. "You're not getting a hearing. Do you understand me?"

"Judge," I began, standing my ground and hiding my fear, "we have to." The words rolled off my lips slowly as my eyes met his enraged stare.

Suddenly, he drew a pistol. All bedlam broke loose as the judge began to wave the gun in the air, pointing it just above my head. A judge's bench sits higher than everyone else in the courtroom, so when Judge Montgomery stood and waved the weapon at me, he was more than eight feet away. Even so, I felt as if the barrel of the pistol swished close to my thinning hair.

However, I had no intention of backing down. "Judge," I quietly insisted, fighting back a simmering fear that threatened to choke me, "I need a hearing."

I felt a hand pulling on my shoulder. Without turning away from the Judge, I recognized the bailiff's voice as his warm breath brushed across my ear. "No, Richard. Please, please, not today. Not today. Please, Richard."

Meanwhile, Judge Montgomery's other two bailiffs managed to get behind the judge and coax the pistol away. As his bailiffs escorted him from his throne toward his chambers, Judge Montgomery turned to face me and screamed, "You're in custody!"

The remaining bailiff asked me to sit where the prisoners normally wait to be called upon by the court. I had no idea what my client may have been thinking, as she remained free on bail while I, her defender, sat under arrest. It must have occurred to her that soon she would be joining me.

No more than fifteen minutes had passed when the judge reappeared, his face less swollen, now pinkish rather than ruby red. A soda and a couple of doses of reality served to settle him. He then granted my client the hearing.

Like clockwork, the deputy district attorney who was handling Judge Montgomery's docket that day sprang up and began to call his witnesses, each of whom had just viewed the entire episode. Quite surprisingly, the judge allowed me to conduct a thorough, unhurried cross-examination. After the hearing, Judge Montgomery found that the case lacked probable cause and dismissed it. No one, not even my perplexed and frightened client, was more surprised than I felt.

Nevertheless, the district attorney's office had no intention of dropping the case. The district attorney maintains the option of presenting a case to the grand jury, even if a district judge throws it out at the preliminary hearing stage. Simply put, grand juries most often serve as rubber stamps for the District Attorney's Office, rather than as a protection for citizens. In fact, the grand jury protects prosecutors. If a prosecutor finds himself with a case he doesn't want indicted, perhaps in fear of losing or of trying a politically charged case, he will guide the grand jury not to return an indictment (to "no bill" it). The prosecutor then hides behind the grand jury's decision.

The grand jury did indict my client. At trial, though, a jury of twelve found her not guilty in a matter of minutes. Judge Montgomery had been right in his ruling. In truth, multiple Judge Montgomerys resided in the soul of that man. I strongly believe that, like most people charged, even those who commit crimes as heinous as murder, no one is as bad as his worst acts or as good as his best. We are all human beings with relative coping skills, flaws and imperfect personalities.

This was not the first nor the last time Judge Montgomery brandished a firearm on an attorney or other person in his courtroom; there were a number of individuals who experienced him wielding one of his weapons in court, including my former partners Rick Digiorgio and Charles Boohaker.[1]

As in the case involving the female police officer, at times Judge Montgomery went berserk in some situations and then minutes later did the right thing. Often he attempted to hide bigotry and racism with humor. On one occasion, he created a national scandal by refusing to allow a person suffering from AIDS to appear in his courtroom.[2] After human rights groups united and called for his impeachment, the

Judicial Oversight Board reprimanded him. He quickly relented and issued repeated apologies. He even attended a local AIDS support group, apologized to them and admitted he was wrong.

Throughout his career, Montgomery taunted female lawyers, ethnic lawyers, African-American prisoners and anyone else he didn't like or he selected to serve as the brunt of an attention-seeking antic. On one occasion a twenty-year-old Caucasian man charged with burglary appeared in Montgomery's court. The parents of the young man made a special request. They asked the judge to please appoint their son a "good Christian lawyer."

Montgomery scanned the courtroom with his hawk eyes and zeroed in on me, the only Jewish lawyer there. His already jovial mood turned gleeful and he milked his appointment of me by continuously referring to me as the "good Christian lawyer." Unaware of the waves of snickering, the three family members seemed quite relieved when I hurried them into a back room. Fortunately, the offense was the young man's first. Judge Montgomery later granted him youthful offender status and probation. For several years the family provided steady referrals to me, their "good Christian lawyer."

DEFENDING
ACCUSED MURDERERS

Darron Burpo, a fifteen-year-old, had loving but uneducated and poor parents who struggled to make ends meet. Although not invited, Darron joined older friends one evening at a high school graduation party at a motel in Birmingham. Around 10:30 that night, Darron and his friends decided to leave. They had been drinking.

As Darron made his way through the parking lot and climbed into the backseat of a car, another intoxicated teen threw a beer bottle at the car. Darron grabbed a gun that sat next to him on the backseat. He stuck his arm out of the car window and fired into the air, intending to scare away the other teen. But the gun must have discharged while his arm was still reaching upward. The bullet hit the chest of an innocent fifteen-year-old girl just as she was walking to her friend's car. She was rushed to the hospital but died en route.

The State of Alabama charged Darron with murder in the first degree. Although Darron was a juvenile, the juvenile judge transferred Darron's case to circuit court to try him as an adult. He faced a life sentence if convicted. The community shock quickly grew into outrage. The attorney appointed to represent Darron in the juvenile court did not want to defend Darron as an adult for murder. The court appointed me to defend Darron. I had no hesitation.

My first questions didn't take long to form: *How can we win this case? What will be the defense? When in doubt, why not try the truth?*

This should not have been a murder one case. Darron did not intend to kill anyone, especially an innocent girl. He committed an unbelievably rash and senseless act to scare the boy who threw the bottle, but it happened so quickly he never had the time nor the inclination to form the intent to kill or injure anyone. Legally, the intent to injure or kill was never formulated. Yet, legalities often mean little to jurors who normally focus on the raw emotion of the human loss and pain emanating from the defendant's actions.

At the trial, Darron testified on his own behalf. Before he took the stand, I told him that his only chance was to tell the truth and speak from his heart. I must have gotten through to him, because his raw emotion clearly connected him to the jurors. They could feel how his remorse extended beyond himself and his fate, which the jurors would consider in deliberations.

During closing arguments, I urged the jurors to convict Darron of negligent homicide, a misdemeanor under Alabama law. I looked at each one of them and stated: "Ladies and gentlemen, no one will ever be able to excuse this senseless and tragic act on the part of then fifteen-year-old Darron Burpo. No one here has tried. All of the promise, the innocence and the dreams of youth were extinguished in the flash of an instant when that bullet, meant for the air only, accidentally struck and killed this innocent, beautiful young lady. And yet those same hopes, dreams and innocence of youth lie bundled up in this young man who sits before you. As much as anything, youth and inexperience caused the death of a young, innocent girl.

"Everyone in this courtroom has committed a foolish, senseless act. Each of us has done that on at least one occasion, probably more. We have all had our near misses. The only difference between him and us is that our near misses missed and his near miss hit."

My hands clutched the post of the jury rail as I delivered the closing of my final summation. My eyes were wet with tears, yet the tears dripping on my hands were not mine, but rather those of the juror nearest me in the front row. A man of about forty-five, he was the foreman and his deep empathy for the young victim had developed into a personal conclusion that a verdict of murder would only create another victim. He correctly intuited that Darron knew the senselessness of his act and the travesty he had perpetrated and that Darron could be rehabilitated.

He and the other jurors returned a verdict of criminally negligent homicide, a misdemeanor.

When the jury foreperson read the verdict to the overflowing courtroom, Darron leaped into my arms, squeezed my neck and collapsed against me. This time, I felt the warm wash of flooding tears and he would not let go. The hope I held onto throughout this case and especially while the jury deliberated exploded into overflowing joy for Darron, his family and myself. No one seemed to expect any verdict other than guilty of murder in the first degree. The media covered this case heavily and I knew that word of the verdict would spread quickly. I am sure that, in this moment, I did not think too much about the permanent pain for the young victim's family. My heart only held enough room at the time to know that my efforts had saved Darron from a life sentence and his parents from losing him.

In later years, I would think about this innocent young lady many times.

The judge sentenced Darron to the maximum penalty for the crime: twelve months in the county jail. He served nine. Even as his lawyer and advocate, I knew that Darron needed to experience life in a steel cage with bars to know that he would never want to return. And, if he chose, he could use some of that time to consider the immeasurable pain he caused and the life he extinguished.

Shocked anger erupted after the verdict became public. It would have been easy to convict Darron, simply because his actions were so senseless and reckless. But this jury felt Darron's remorse and knew that a long penitentiary punishment would surely and permanently ruin his life. They wanted to give him a second chance. A few days after the emotional verdict, *The Birmingham News* reported that a committee had been formed to investigate why the jury did not convict Darron of murder. Our reform synagogue rabbi served on that committee. For months he kept asking, "Who is this Richard Jaffe guy, anyway?"

More than thirty years have since passed, but I still hear from Darron. He is doing well. He is not the only one of my clients once charged with murder to become respected. Darron has three children between the ages of sixteen and twenty-six. One is a twenty-two-year-old girl he tries to guide and protect, knowing well that even the best parenting cannot prevent a senseless act from destroying lives.

No one believed in Darron's victory as I did. No successful trial lawyer ever tries a case unless he believes he can win it. That deep, core belief often separates the winning lawyer from one who goes through the motions with more form than substance. No one senses an attorney's efforts and conviction more than an attentive jury. In every case I have tried, I felt in my soul that either I would or could win it (even those where we actually had no chance and lost).

Defending my next client charged with murder proved no exception. Cleophus "Smokey" Bennett was charged with stabbing an elderly lady over sixty times in the housing complex where he lived with his mother, a nurse at a local hospital. When a neighbor discovered the elderly lady's body, she lay in her bed clutching an Agatha Christie novel, *Anatomy of a Murder*. It took little time for me to see that the authorities had focused on the wrong person, if for no other reason than there were no other suspects and the fact Smokey was seen in the housing complex the night of the murder, heavily intoxicated. A more likely suspect fingered Smokey when questioned by the police. However, Smokey had little money to investigate the case and establish a defense and he had committed some petty theft crimes years ago. In my opinion, this influenced his arrest.

During this time, Birmingham was experiencing one of the highest per capita homicide rates in the country. The housing complex where Smokey and his mother lived was in one of the poorest, most dangerous parts of Birmingham. If you were white and entered the complex, you did so at your peril. Sporting much more drive and ambition than sense, I walked every inch of that complex, investigating every minute detail of the facts and allegations. The homicide investigators on the case, Sergeants Morgan Knight and Charles Melton, found me in the complex, unarmed and wearing a suit. I was questioning desperate people, some of whom were intoxicated or on drugs. The sergeants must have felt sorry for me and their concern for my safety grew to the point that they began to drive me from point to point to make sure that I would not get hurt.

My investigation paid off. The State's case proved weak and without much merit. It depended on the credibility of the person who had told the police that he had seen Smokey running from the victim's apartment around 12:30 A.M. the night of the murder. Yet my investigation revealed that this witness was a drug addict whose criminal record filled several sheets of paper. Neither his story nor his character could withstand vigorous cross-examination. I took the huge gamble of asking Judge William Cole's permission to allow Smokey (who did not testify) to try on a bloody belt that police found just outside the victim's apartment. It was too big for the rather thin Smokey but probably the right size for the person who had fingered him.

During my closing argument, I attacked the investigation vigorously. Sergeant Knight, who sat on the front row, got so upset during my argument that he stood up. Out of the corner of my eye, I thought I saw him first take a step toward me before he quickly exited the courtroom.

Judge Jack Montgomery happened to come into Judge Cole's courtroom at the end of the day when the jury began its deliberation. Montgomery saw me and sneered, forgetting that he was the judge who appointed me to this seemingly impossible case. He inquired to anyone who would listen, "What kind of case is this?" One of the bailiffs responded, "It's a murder case. Jaffe's client is accused of stabbing an elderly lady over sixty times."

"That's a joke," Montgomery quipped. "It can't take long for that guilty verdict."

Just then we heard a knock on the wooden jury door that stiffened every spine. Everyone assembled, including some deputy district attorneys, court personnel, lawyers, family members, members of the press and Judge Montgomery. After barely forty-five minutes of deliberation, the jury foreperson announced a not guilty verdict. I jumped up and down. My client broke down crying and fell to the floor. From the corner of my eye, I noticed the shock on Judge Montgomery's face.

The next day, Sergeant Knight called. At that time, he called me "Junkyard" because of the Jaffe family's junk and automobile parts businesses in the Birmingham area. "Junkyard, I want to apologize to you. I walked out of that courtroom during your argument, because honestly, if I hadn't, I don't think I could have controlled myself from doing something to you. So I thought it was best for everybody that I just leave. And then this morning, I woke up and realized that it really wasn't your fault. You were just doing your job. I promised myself that the next time I have a case against you, I will not only investigate it from top to bottom, but also, after I finish the investigation, I will start all over again. I underestimated you, but I won't do it again."

Morgan Knight now works as an investigator for the DA's office. We have been friends ever since Smokey's case.

For several years, I continued to show up at the arraignment dockets in hopes of being appointed to criminal cases. The way I saw it and still do, every client carries with him or her the potential of thirty or more referrals. That philosophy panned out well over the years. Even today I get referrals from people I represented decades ago—sometimes themselves, other times friends, coworkers, family members or even casual acquaintances. When people genuinely feel that you see them as important, many remember you, sometimes for the rest of their lives—but not everyone.

One day I stood before the bench of the Honorable William Cole after entering a guilty plea for a bank teller who claimed she embezzled money, because her husband didn't take her out enough. As I was walking out of the courtroom, I heard Judge Cole call the arraignment docket. He was appointing lawyers for those defendants without funds to retain a lawyer. I turned to my right and began to walk past the jury box where the prisoners sat, waiting to hear the names of their newly appointed lawyers. I jumped back and froze in my tracks after hearing the name "Julia Mitchell."

"Are you in a position to hire a lawyer?"

The third woman to my left in the back row of the jury box softly proclaimed, "No, sir." Judge Cole appointed someone to represent her.

I walked to the jury rail and focused steadfastly on the dark and languid features on the face of the woman whose name I recognized. "Julia, is that you?"

"Yes, it's me," she shyly responded.

Several years before, as her appointed lawyer, I represented Julia in a murder case. I recalled vividly the image of her standing in the kitchen arguing with her abusive boyfriend. Police photos showed large bruises on Julia's face, chest and back.

The physical confrontation spilled onto the top of stairs that led out of the tiny apartment. Julia had managed to grab a butcher knife as her boyfriend dragged her toward the stairs, probably intending to throw her down them. She forcefully plunged the knife into the middle of the man's chest, fatally splitting it open. The jury quickly saw the case as self-defense and returned a favorable verdict for Julia.

"Julia, what are you charged with?" I asked.

Julia did not hesitate in her reply. "Murder."

"Murder?" I asked with genuine surprise. "What happened?"

Immediately she explained, "Well, my boyfriend was beating me up, so I stabbed him."

For a moment, I thought I was experiencing déjà vu before remembering that this was the same woman but in a different time and a different place. I leaned toward her and blurted out, "Why didn't you call me? I did win your case last time."

Again, without hesitation, she innocently replied, "Because I forgot your name."

9

PLAYING GOD WITH EYEWITNESS IDENTIFICATION

Beatryce Pell wore her jet-black hair short and straight. It hardly reached the back of her neck, so she could easily be mistaken for a man, especially with the hat she often wore. Police pulled over the car in which she rode as a passenger only minutes after a local bank was robbed by a male and a female. Beatryce and the male driver were both African-American. Beatryce was a little over five feet tall, thin and very light-skinned. A witness had described the female robber as having a full face, long hair and dark complexion.

The district court appointed me, still relatively young, to represent Beatryce. An older, more experienced lawyer in his mid-forties was called to represent the driver. The older lawyer waived his preliminary hearing on behalf of the driver. I had mine. But rather than toss my case out due to such a discrepancy, the district court bound it over to the grand jury, which indicted both Beatryce and the male driver.

Most people believe that eyewitness testimony is reliable, although scientific studies have shown that it is sometimes far from accurate and has led to the convictions of innocent people, even some charged with the death penalty. Because of this, eyewitness testimony should be corroborated whenever possible and should be viewed skeptically in any case. At a preliminary hearing, if an eyewitness positively

55

identifies a suspect, the case is going to proceed to trial even if the identification appears ridiculous. The judge does not decide guilt or innocence at the preliminary hearing, only probable cause. Probable cause exists in an identification case if a person positively points out the defendant, no matter how far off the identification or unreliable the witness.

The dangers of any eyewitness identification case have been pointed out by psychologists, scientists and the legal community. People truly believe that eyewitness testimony offers the most reliable evidence when, in fact, it is the least trustworthy and the most subject to human error.[1]

How many times have we failed to recognize people we have known for years or accidently walked up to a stranger we thought we knew? Then there's the unreliability of eyewitness identification within the circumstances in which the original viewing took place. Criminals usually surprise a victim of crime, who becomes so nervous and shocked that his or her brain fails to register accurate images. Then the authorities intervene with photos or lineup procedures that contain people who may resemble the perpetrator. The victim, however, often believes that the real perpetrator must be one of the five or six presented in the lineup and selects the one who looks most like the person he or she thinks he or she recalls seeing. More and more states today are enacting laws to allow defense lawyers to be present when the police conduct lineups.[2]

If the victim selects one of the individuals portrayed in a photographic or live lineup, then that person will appear in court to face the victim again. It is unlikely the complainant will fail to pick out the same person in court when the prosecutor asks, "Do you see the person who robbed you in the courtroom today?" The complainant will not have a difficult time choosing the only person seated next to the lawyer at the defense counsel's table.

Studies are replete with misidentifications, especially with individuals of a different race.[3] It is much more difficult for us to distinguish people with the facial characteristics of another race unless we have constant exposure to them.

DNA testing has now confirmed the dangerous unreliability of eyewitness testimony, especially when uncorroborated by objective facts or forensics.[4] Sometimes, the more certain a person claims to be of his identification, the less reliable it is.[5] Many people have endured long prison terms and near-execution until DNA testing disproved former positive in-court identifications. In fact, many of these identifications would not have occurred except for overly suggestive methods injected into the process by untrained or inexperienced police officers.

The court set both Beatryce's case and her male companion's case for trial on the same day. The prosecutor offered a twenty-year plea bargain deal to both because of the prior eyewitness identification. It didn't matter that the descriptions were not even close to their appearances and the white bank teller said at the lineup, "That looks like them." Even that identification was not truly 100 percent.

The older, more experienced attorney and I met in the attorney's conference room thirty minutes before his client's trial. He looked at me with eyes soaked with defeat and said, "Richard, I am going to take the twenty years. You know this case is unwinnable. The teller identified them both and they were pulled over less than a mile from the bank."

I listened intently to the more experienced lawyer. The resignation not only saturated his eyes, but also hung in the tone of his voice and the way he carried his entire body.

"But," I protested, "the identifications aren't even close. At the preliminary hearing, the descriptions she gave were even different from those in the police report and both descriptions are miles away from our clients' actual appearances. Here, let me show you the preliminary hearing testimony."

"But she will identify both of our clients in court. We are going to lose. I believe my client is innocent. I've been down this road before. I've been doing this for fifteen years and you just don't win ID cases. Nobody does. I'm pleading him."

And he did, after which the court called Beatryce's case for trial. The prosecutor approached me and once more asked if Beatryce would plead guilty. This time he offered ten years, since she was alleged to be the passenger. He emphasized that she might even get probation. I asked for fifteen minutes to speak to Beatryce.

She followed me to the conference room. I peered into her frightened eyes and clutched her cold palms, almost dripping with nervous sweat. Then she spoke. "Mr. Jaffe, I didn't do that robbery. I can't go to prison, especially for something I didn't do. What would I do with my children? What would happen to them? What should I do?"

She began to cry softly in confused whimpers. She wanted me to make the decision for her. She had no clue as to how to make it herself.

Normally I do not gamble with my clients' lives. Presenting a client with options and steering him or her toward what I think is most appropriate is one thing, but making the decision is more responsibility that I care to take. At times, though, some clients may be too challenged to make the decision. In those cases, they need more than a little guidance. Beatryce had no way of assessing the situation, no experience in these matters. There was no framework from which to draw and no one else to whom to turn.

I strongly felt she should go to trial, but what if I was wrong? The judge might well give her probation if she pleaded guilty. But the two of us faced another obstacle. The judge would expect her to admit her guilt, especially if he was going to give probation. However, this was something Beatryce adamantly refused to do.

I summoned up my courage. "Beatryce," I quietly counseled, "there are no guarantees, but this is a winnable case. If you are truly innocent and want to go to trial, I will do everything in my power to win your case."

Beatryce stood silent, then softy uttered, "I am innocent and I do not want to plead guilty to something I did not do."

I swallowed hard and then notified a shocked prosecutor and the court to "go get the box" (of jurors).

The female teller, who had seen the robbers through the bank's drive-through window, sounded convincingly positive upon direct examination, but so do many people before they are adequately cross-examined. Her testimony, however, simply could not stand up to not only the original identification, but also the other description she had given at the preliminary hearing that differed from both the police report and her in-court testimony.

I saw no reason to put Beatryce on the stand to testify. The bank teller's testimony revealed that she simply thought she had to pick someone out of the live lineup and to her, Beatryce looked the most like the passenger in the car that had pulled up next to her teller window.

After hardly an hour, we heard that familiar rapping sound against the wooden door separating the jurors from the courtroom. As we made our way toward the defense counsel table, Beatryce's knees buckled and she clung to my arm as if she was hanging from a cliff. I practically carried her to the seat next to mine and carefully placed her there. I could almost feel the fog that obscured all her thoughts other than those about her children. When we rose to hear the verdict, I felt her clammy palms as her fingernails cut into the skin on the top of my hand.

The jury returned a not guilty verdict. I felt not only elation but also relief. A guilty verdict would have probably netted Beatryce a twenty-year sentence in prison.

After many trials I have often replayed my decisions on many sleepless nights. While those kinds of sleepless nights had come in the past and would come again, not this time. Instead, the jury's verdict validated my deep-set belief that criminal defense lawyers must not become defeatists. With preparation and skill we can win cases that seem stronger on the surface than justified by the evidence and quality of the witnesses.

Our mindset makes such a difference. Almost no case predetermines its result. "Liberty's Last Champions" is the slogan of the National Association of Criminal Defense Lawyers (NACDL), the largest and most prestigious organization in the United States for criminal defense attorneys. If we call ourselves liberty's last champions, we must always act like, think like and be champions. Daring and creative warriors never give up and prosecutors and judges must know that we are not afraid of battle, regardless of the odds. Still, we cannot succumb to the temptation of playing God, which is merely a trap for fools. In this case, if Beatryce had pleaded guilty, the judge still could have sent her to prison and denied her probation.

There is an enormous responsibility we often assume when defending another person's life and liberty. Our clients find themselves twisting in the nightmare of a confusing "criminal justice" system. The best we can do is form relationships with them and communicate honestly. That takes time and effort. However, it builds trust and can serve to give our clients the tools to make the right decisions for themselves.

In this case, I felt the need to guide Beatryce in the direction I believed we should take. Fortunately it worked out.

10

THE TRUTH HURTS

Anthony Grantford had been stalked by a man who threatened to kill him on several occasions in their disputes over drugs. We located a police report that Anthony and his family had filed, complaining that the man fired shots at him the day before Anthony killed him. The next day, the man followed Anthony into the apartment complex where Anthony lived. There, a shoot-out occurred in a final confrontation. Anthony had had enough; he shot the stalker multiple times with a shotgun.

By the time the family of Anthony Grantford hired me, I had either prosecuted or defended many major felony cases at trial. A number of these trials were homicides, many of which turned out well for my clients. Some did not.

However, Anthony faced a difficult set of facts. Several eyewitnesses claimed they saw him take a shotgun and discharge it into his stalker. According to these eyewitnesses, after emptying the shotgun, he reloaded it, stood over the victim and emptied it again.

Additionally, either at the scene or at the autopsy, the victim's entire arm had become severed from his body. Over my most strenuous objections of prejudice, Judge James Hard allowed into evidence some of the goriest photographs I had ever seen, including one clearly depicting the severed arm. To make matters worse, Anthony, a large, tall man, looked gruff and severely street-worn. The deceased, although he was a street drug dealer, was small in stature.

Faced with such a horrible fact scenario, I did everything I could to plea bargain this case. I begged prosecutor Bob McGregor to work out a plea deal with me along the lines of manslaughter and twenty years—anything other than a life sentence for murder. Bob could see no reason to plea bargain his strong case; as the defense, we had no choice but to try it.

Impossible cases, sometimes known as "lay downs," present their own unique challenges. Sometimes the prosecutor may feel some hidden pressure, in the sense that no one in the world would ever expect him to lose a "lay down."

From the defense standpoint, a "lay down" may actually ease the pressure. When everyone feels the defendant will be found guilty and expects the defense to lose, defense lawyers sometimes take risks they otherwise might not take in a closer case. This case, however, seemed rather hopeless.

Nevertheless, after our investigation and in spite of learning about the extra shots Anthony Grantford fired, I still planned to argue for an all-out acquittal and hope for a manslaughter verdict.

I strongly believed that my argument that my client's actions resulted from a seizure of fear and terror, which was very true, could get us out of a murder conviction. His fear was heightened by ample doses of alcohol and drugs. In support of our defense was an autopsy report that revealed that the deceased had been drinking heavily and using cocaine. We could show that drugs fueled his stalking of Anthony.

At the end of the last day of testimony, Anthony, who was free on bond, anxiously followed me into the courtroom corridors. We stopped to talk so he could ask me questions and express his concerns.

Some lawyers fill their clients with false hope and expectations for several reasons. Some clients won't hire an attorney who won't assure them of victory. Notwithstanding the absolute uncertainty of accurately predicting what twelve strangers might do collaboratively on any given occasion, some lawyers will continuously promise their clients acquittals, then shrug their shoulders as court personnel cart off their convicted clients in handcuffs.

When he asked for my assessment of his chances, I told him the raw truth, including the penalties for manslaughter, which carried a maximum sentence of twenty years. The parole guidelines at the time were such that it was possible he could get out after roughly a third of the time if in fact the jury returned a verdict of manslaughter and if his behavior proved exemplary while incarcerated.

Anthony seemed satisfied with my explanations. We said our goodbyes and I asked him to arrive early the following morning so we could talk again before the closing arguments began. He assured me he would.

That night I stayed up late to hone my closing argument, outlining the points and the order of presentation. Over the years I have found that imagining and visualizing my actions and comments beforehand helps me deliver them with much more power in the courtroom. I anticipated the prosecutor's arguments and memorized certain passages and phrases. As always, I went over and over the close in my mind, visualizing many of my gestures, hearing my inflections, seeing the suit and tie I would wear, picturing the judge's and jurors' faces.

I envisioned myself approaching the jury rail at certain points during my close, at just the right moments. I felt all the emotions I would convey, including Anthony's fears and helplessness, the fruitless efforts of him and his family to seek the law's protection against a crazed drug dealer who died because of his own violence and drug consumption. I watched in my mind's eye how I would portray the real pictures of the jungle of violence created and inhabited by the deceased.

The following morning, I sizzled with anticipation, excitement and nervous energy. I was ready to give all of myself to defend the life and freedom of my client. I wanted the jury to feel those moments of combat during which Anthony could only focus on preserving his own life. Any additional shots resulted from fear, panic and a recognition that the law had already failed to protect him.

There is an old maxim: "The truth shall set you free." Well, I had given more than an ample dose of it to Anthony, much more than he could handle. It set him free all right. Rather than appear to face his likely lesser punishment, he had fled for parts unknown.

Sitting in the courtroom, I now had an empty chair for a client. Judge Hard would start the trial at 10:30 A.M., with or without Anthony. I would be arguing on behalf of a client charged with a violent killing who decided to flee rather than face the jury's decision. I would have to modify my presentation, but how?

Even a prosecutor less skilled than Bob McGregor would press this advantage. But Bob was impressive as he evoked the absent Anthony and his empty chair. The jury returned a murder verdict.

The judge directed some of his ire toward me, since early in the process I had successfully convinced him to reduce the bail. His rationale for lowering bail could be second-guessed. What if Anthony got into more trouble, maybe even of a violent nature? I knew that since Anthony had just been convicted of murder, the judge did not relish this potential worst-case scenario looming above his head like the blade of a guillotine.

I feverishly began to search for my client before sentencing. Perhaps it wouldn't help, but I thought it might. I knew one tie Anthony wouldn't break: that with his family. I put out the word that I needed him. Finally, a few days later, I learned that he had caught a bus to Indianapolis and sought shelter with his grandmother. His family gave me the phone number and I called him. Ultimately, Anthony returned and turned himself in to the Jefferson County jail to await sentencing.

I truly hoped that the judge would not give him the maximum sentence of life (with parole) for the murder conviction, but he did. I asked myself if I should have been less candid and more guarded in my depiction of Anthony's probable outcomes. What if I had just responded, "We'll see"? I'll never know.

11

FUGITIVE FROM JUSTICE

The family of Donald Underwood asked me to assist them in the prosecution of Bobby Lee Ward, who had killed Donald during an affray more than ten years earlier. After the grand jury indicted him, Bobby Lee pulled a "Roman Polanski," running off to New York, where he married and lived an exemplary life for over a decade.[1]

Bobby's past caught up with him when local authorities pulled his vehicle over during a routine traffic stop near his home. When the patrol officer ran Bobby Lee's name, his social security number and his driver's license number through the National Crime Information Computer (NCIC) system, he discovered that Bobby was wanted in Alabama for an outstanding murder charge and that he was a fugitive from justice. Bobby waived extradition. Alabama authorities then flew to New York and brought Bobby back to Birmingham. He would finally face Lady Justice.

With sad but determined eyes, Donald's mother looked at me in our conference room. "Mr. Jaffe, we don't have much money, but we are a close family and we will pay you. Please help us with this case. My son was not perfect, but we loved him. He was unarmed and did not deserve to be shot and killed by a coward. And that coward should not be rewarded, because he fled the state."

"I agree with you. And I will help you if I can," I said. "But unless the Jefferson County DA's Office agrees to my appointment as a 'special prosecutor,' I won't be able to get involved. I will call the DA, David Barber, who is a very fair and understanding man, and see what I can do."

In England, the criminal trial barristers in any particular case can serve as either prosecutors or defense lawyers. In the United States, the system clearly divides the two. For lawyers, this is a major career decision.

Only in rare, unique circumstances does a criminal defense lawyer find himself in the role of "special prosecutor," such as when the Department of Justice appoints special prosecutors in exceptional circumstances. Famed trial lawyer Gerry Spence agreed to serve as a special prosecutor in his successful prosecution of the Wyoming multiple murder case *Hopkinson v. State* after the family of one of the victims hired him.

The family of Donald Underwood retained me to special prosecute Ward, because they felt the Jefferson County DA's Office lacked sufficient motivation to prosecute this particular ten-year-old case. A family of modest measure, they possessed the passion to do all they could to bring Bobby Lee to justice.

After I talked to the family, I met with David Barber. He agreed to recommend my appointment to the court, with the condition that the DA's office participate in the case. I agreed.

The deputy district attorney assigned to the case had attended the University of Alabama Law School one year ahead of me. I had met her there when she served as one of the leaders of the Moot Court Competition.

After David approved my appointment, I called the deputy district attorney. She suggested an offer of probation to Ward on a manslaughter plea. I explained to her that we intended to proceed to trial, as my clients would not agree to an offer of probation. A local legend, Arthur Parker, and his then-partner, former Chief Deputy District Attorney Tommy Nail, represented Bobby Lee Ward. They realized the case would go to trial upon learning that the family had hired me to special prosecute their client.

Local lawyers considered defense attorney Arthur Parker, five feet seven inches tall, thin, gray and affable, to be the smartest, most experienced and cagiest criminal defense lawyer in the state. Arthur normally stayed two steps ahead of his adversaries, while judges feared him, because he knew the rules of evidence and law better than many of them.

Arthur loved trying cases. Even when he initially lost one, he relished winning an appeal on some technical aspect of the law. Arthur fought fearlessly for every client. He practiced law in the bushes, like a hissing snake under a rock; his opponents always felt his presence but never knew when he would unleash and strike.

Tommy Nail employed his own lethal weapons. A ferocious fighter with a fiery manner from the Jefferson County countryside, Tommy began his career as a prosecutor before joining Arthur's small law firm, where he added much to Arthur's legal talents. I had faced Tommy many times when he served as a prosecutor.[2] Now I faced him as a special prosecutor while he was an attorney for the defense.

In my review of the case file, I realized that the incident occurred during the time when juries, not judges, set the sentences, if they convicted the accused. So the dynamics of the trial would revert back to these standards. Due to docket overcrowding, Judge Robert Aderholt, a retired visiting judge, was assigned the case. Aderholt enjoyed a fine reputation for evenhandedness.

The trial began on a typical Monday morning. We called two eyewitnesses who testified that Bobby Lee Ward, during an argument and confrontation, shot the unarmed Donald Underwood. We then proved that Bobby Lee fled the scene and shared the circumstances of his capture nearly ten years later in New York. When the defense put on its case, they showed that Bobby Lee lived flawlessly before the routine traffic stop that resulted in his arrest and voluntary extradition.

Like most skilled lawyers in these kinds of cases, Arthur and Tommy did not call Bobby Lee to testify in his own defense. They chose to assert self-defense by cross-examining the witnesses, arguing that Bobby Lee feared for his life, which justified both the shooting of Underwood and fleeing.

With closing arguments about to begin, the deputy district attorney asked for a word with me. Prior to that, she had not taken an active role in the trial as far as examining witnesses and making legal arguments. Perhaps she could taste the scent of victory.

"Richard, I would like for us to split up the closing argument."

My shocked mind recoiled. From the moment she got the case and throughout all the proceedings and the entire trial, I had shouldered most of the court work. Now she wanted to be part of the crucial summation. *What is going on?* I wondered.

"Well, I am surprised," I responded, "but I suppose it could actually help if the real deputy district attorney asks the jury to convict the defendant. So why don't you take the second part of the summation? I'll set you up to hammer home a conviction for murder in your close."

She agreed.

Since the prosecutor has the burden of proof, the prosecution argues first and last and the defense closes in between. Knowing the case intimately, I debated in a way that I felt foreclosed any credible claim of self-defense. That was my argument as I closed to the jury.

Tommy Nail closed for the defense. Tommy traveled down an age-old, time-honored path employed in trials since the beginning of the system: "When the facts don't help you, argue the law; when the law fails you, attack your opponent." Tommy did just that. I understood his approach and did not take offense. In his passionate, aggressive way, he scoffed at the need for a special prosecutor and practically yelled that this was "justice bought and paid for, which is no justice at all."

Then my co-counsel assumed the mount. She planned to rebut a few points made by the defense and, clothed with the awesome power of the State, urge a conviction for murder, with a hefty sentence to boot. As she began to discuss the facts of the case, she uttered the words a prosecutor must assiduously avoid, as they could be interpreted to infringe on the defendant's constitutional right to remain silent.

"Did you hear one voice," the deputy district attorney said, "one voice from that witness stand say, 'I thought Donald Underwood was going to hurt him'?"

Although she was referring to the witnesses and not Mr. Ward himself, my heart pounded. Horrified, I could only listen as if a firing squad was aiming its rifles at the center of my chest.

Jumping up, Arthur Parker protested: "Objection to the statement, Your Honor, please. The jury is not to consider that statement. That statement violates the Alabama Constitution."

"Ladies and gentlemen," Judge Aderholt declared, "do not consider that statement in your deliberation of this case."

"Next, I will move for a mistrial," Arthur continued, "because that statement has so prejudiced this proceeding that we are entitled to another trial on this case."

The judge simply said, "Overruled."

I already knew beyond a doubt that it wouldn't matter how the jury voted at that point. Even if the Alabama Court of Criminal Appeals did not order a new trial (which it did not), the Alabama Supreme Court or a Federal Appeals court would. It is indeed axiomatic that no one can comment in any way, shape or form whenever a presumptively innocent defendant asserts his right not to testify under the Fifth Amendment.

The jury deliberated hardly an hour and a half before it convicted Bobby Lee Ward of second-degree murder. Because the offense occurred before the law changed to judge sentencing, the jury was required to sentence the defendant upon conviction.[3] Though confident all along that I would obtain a conviction, I never could have foreseen the jury's punishment for the defendant: thirty-five years in prison. The bailiffs immediately took Ward into custody and he began to serve his sentence.

As I had expected, Arthur and Tommy appealed the case. The Alabama Supreme Court unanimously ordered a new trial.[4]

The visiting judge was no longer available. So the computer randomly assigned the case to the Honorable Richmond Pearson, who would preside over several cases of mine over the years.

A man of great stature, Judge Pearson appeared to loom larger than life. The judge loved to travel and enjoyed good meals. The most charming and best conversationalist I have ever met, this man had forged difficult trails as a pioneer in the civil rights movement. He had worked his way from poverty to the top. Brilliant, savvy and insightful, his intelligence spanned the range from book-smart to street-smart. His instincts about people approached perfection; he seemed a human lie detector. If a defendant in front of Judge Pearson at sentencing or at a probation hearing did not readily admit the truth, that defendant would pay a price.

After the judge received the case, he set a pretrial status conference. The deputy district attorney from the previous trial had left office and Chief Deputy District Attorney Roger Brown inherited this case. Roger seemed unimpressed, as most lawyers would, to take over a case this old and worn from twisting through the criminal justice system.

The second trial began and proceeded as before, but this time Arthur Parker and Tommy Nail knew better than to keep Bobby Lee Ward off the witness stand. They probably could not have kept him from testifying this time even if they wanted. On the stand, Bobby Lee attempted to convey his fear and explained why he hid for over a decade. Most importantly, he talked about his life as a parent since he left Alabama and how he had matured as a man. My cross-examination could do little to deflect the impact of his direct testimony. Bobby Lee's testimony favorably impressed Judge Pearson as well.

In most instances, as with the first trial, the judge allows both murder and manslaughter to be decided by the jury. But Judge Pearson, within his judicial discretion, took the decision of murder away from the jury, leaving only a count for felony manslaughter, a count for misdemeanor manslaughter and a not guilty decision as potential verdicts.

I was shocked, hardly knowing what to say. The closing arguments began with me taking the first part; Roger would argue the second part. However, when it was time for Roger to begin and ask the jury to convict the defendant, Roger sat in his chair like a stone.

"Roger, what are you waiting for?" I quietly but frantically whispered.

"I'm not arguing," he deadpanned.

"But you agreed to argue the second close."

Roger turned to face me. His narrowed eyes looked into mine. "Look at my hands. I'm Gordon Liddy." Slowly, he pretended to place his index finger into a flame of fire. He had made his decision and did not fear the consequences.

I slowly forced myself to my feet and meekly asked, on behalf of the State of Alabama, for the jury to convict Bobby Lee Ward of felony manslaughter. I resumed my seat next to my trial partner.

The jurors debated for several hours before returning a verdict of misdemeanor manslaughter. For the sentence, they recommended a six-month probated sentence. That's a far cry from thirty-five years.

Bobby Lee Ward walked out of the courtroom a free man. My clients, Donald Underwood's surviving family members, had sought justice for over thirteen years. Had they not hired a special prosecutor, they may not have seen much. At least Bobby Lee Ward served around three years in state prison during the period leading up to and including the two trials.

Yet, in this bizarre scenario, I asked myself, *How much justice was served?*

The Bobby Lee Ward trial only highlighted something that I never forgot after reading New York trial lawyer Louis Nizer's book, *My Life in Court.*[5] In that book, Nizer emphasizes the importance of every single word a lawyer utters in court. Especially in front of a jury. He discusses how he once made a major mistake in one of his cases, when he told the jury he would prove the case for his client when his side had no burden of proof. If trial lawyers try enough cases, each will make that mistake probably more than once. I know I have.

BRINGING THE SCENE
TO THE COURTROOM

O ne evening, Tyrone Robinson arrived home several hours earlier than expected, his disc jockey gig canceled at the last minute. Upon arriving, he laid his gun in the kitchen, located on the first level between the finished basement and the upstairs bedrooms. He walked down to the basement, where his wife Lucinda joined him to do some laundry.

The resonant voice and energetic persona of Tyrone Robinson were familiar to many of the million or so people residing in the greater Birmingham metropolitan area. The handsome six-foot-two-inch, 225- pound bodybuilder was an especially popular DJ. In addition, he worked as a court bailiff for Jefferson County. On many nights, he performed at private parties and did not get back home until the early morning hours.

While in the basement, Tyrone heard footsteps much louder than those of his five-year-old daughter. He immediately rushed up the basement stairs, grabbed his gun and looked into the unlit living room. Suddenly, a dark figure darted toward the front door. Tyrone fired twice, thinking he was shooting a burglar. Within a second or two, the door at the top of the basement steps opened, knocking him back against the hallway wall. When his elbow struck the wall, his gun discharged again.

Suddenly he saw his wife Lucinda, who had run up the basement steps. She extended her arms then crossed them across her chest. "Oh, you shot Ken!" she exclaimed.

She ran back down the stairs.

Tyrone immediately rushed to his daughter's bedroom on the second floor. Finding her safe and awake, he called his mother and 911 and then began to look for Lucinda. He found her in the washroom of the basement, bleeding profusely. He had unknowingly shot her in the chest. In sheer panic, he rushed upstairs to get the first aid kit and he heard the Birmingham police department enter the house and announce themselves.

Tyrone sat in dismal shock in his living room, waiting for the paramedics to arrive. Nearby lay the mortally wounded, moaning man he had shot twice. One bullet had entered the man's side and the other the top of his shoulder. His wife lay dead in the basement.

When the detectives arrived, they noticed blood splatters on the wall leading down the basement stairs. Police photos showed a picture that had been knocked off the wall at the top of the stairs, which seemed to have fallen when Tyrone's elbow hit the wall and he accidentally discharged his gun—as he would consistently maintain. Robinson told the truth to the first officers who arrived at the scene, but who would believe it? Two people were dead, his wife and her visiting coworker, Kenneth Simpson. It didn't look good.

The police secured the crime scene and transported Robinson to the police station to wait for detectives to finish viewing the scene and begin the interrogation process. The four-hour tape-recorded statement of their interview began at 2:34 A.M.

Although exhausted, in shock and terrified, Tyrone never wavered in his recitation of what happened and his insistence that he thought he shot a burglar and he accidentally shot his wife. The police did not charge Tyrone that night. Nevertheless, within a couple of days, he and his family met me in my office to discuss the case and retain my services.

The Robinson family was deeply supportive and close to one another. They hovered around a worn, despondent Tyrone as we sat in my conference room. I wondered if the District Attorney's office would decide to charge him with capital murder, which carried the possibility of the death penalty. Many people do not realize that, in several states, murder is not a death penalty offense. In Alabama, for a murder charge to carry a possible death sentence, it must be accompanied by an aggravating factor such as robbery, rape or burglary. It must also be proven beyond a reasonable doubt that the defendant intended to take the life of another person. Otherwise, the person is not "death eligible."

However, in this instance, the authorities could charge Tyrone with capital murder, because he killed two people in one chain of circumstances, making him "death eligible." A prosecutor could exercise "prosecutorial discretion" in deciding whether to charge Tyrone with manslaughter, murder or capital murder. Or nothing.

The atmosphere in my conference room grew chilly as we discussed my concerns. The looming prospect of the death penalty seemed almost too much for the family to absorb and yet it highlighted one of the numerous reasons why the death penalty is so unjust and unfair. One prosecutor might charge someone like Tyrone with a death penalty offense, while another might not. It could be easier to obtain a death penalty verdict in one jurisdiction than another. The complexion of the jury panel always makes a huge difference.

Tyrone Robinson's fate rested on a spinning roulette wheel that some prosecutor would have to stop on red or black. Thankfully, in Tyrone's case the prosecutors chose not to pursue the death penalty.

Still, we had our work cut out for us. In court we would have to confront whether Tyrone intentionally killed his wife and Kenneth Simpson, his wife's coworker, since the media and many in the public had already decided his guilt. With two people dead, rumors flying and the press sensationalizing, Tyrone Robinson needed a perfect trial strategy for any chance of success.

As I carefully studied the transcript of four hours of intense police interrogations in the time following the incident, I noticed several striking features. In spite of his state of shock, a grueling questioning process and being awake for twenty-four hours with no sleep,

Tyrone's version of the events and adamant proclamations of innocence remained consistent. In addition, I found clear violations of his constitutional rights, which required that if at any time he invoked his right to counsel before or during the questioning process, he was given an opportunity to stop the questioning and obtain a lawyer. His requests for counsel were not just ignored; they were obliterated.

The interrogating lead detective appropriately advised Tyrone of his Miranda rights: the right to an attorney to represent him before any questioning; the questioning would stop at any time if he decided he needed one; a lawyer would be appointed for him if he could not afford an attorney.[1] However, when Tyrone tried to discuss the prospect of retaining an attorney before answering any questions, the detective asked Tyrone if he knew of any attorneys he could roust and get to the station in the wee hours.

Instead of complying with the intent and mandate of the United States Constitution, the detective's response directly discouraged, if not foreclosed, Robinson's ability to assert his right to counsel. There was no doubt in my mind that, no matter what Tyrone said, the detectives intended to charge him with these two killings.

The four-hour statement contained inadmissible hearsay and the prejudicial opinions of the detective. It was obtained illegally and should not be admitted into evidence. But I predicted that the prosecutors would convince the judge to permit it anyway. If it was admitted and if the jury convicted him, I did not think that the conviction would hold up on appeal. I felt we had a chance at trial, but I still hoped to keep the illegally obtained statement out. I knew the law carried no certainties, especially when twelve strangers were determining innocence or guilt.

We thoroughly explored every aspect of the case. I directed my investigators to talk to everyone even remotely near the crime scene. I hoped to confirm that the sequence of shots, as heard by neighbors, coincided with what Tyrone told the detectives. I wanted to know everything possible about the relationship between Tyrone's wife and her visitor that night. Further I wanted to know the state of the Robinson marriage, any life insurance policies that might have existed and other such details that might have provided a motive the State could seize on.

As the trial date neared, I became satisfied that Tyrone was truthful and that he had no motive for killing his wife. I believed he reactively shot the man whom he believed to be an intruder. The reason that the intruder tried to rush out did not matter, since Tyrone couldn't see him in the darkness anyway. Eventually, we obtained statements from every neighbor who heard the sequence of shots, all consistent with Tyrone's description to the detectives.

Everyone, that is, but one particular neighbor. Her house was next door to the Robinsons' house. I repeatedly insisted that my investigator obtain her statement, to no avail.

The Robinson case had been assigned to the Honorable William Cole, former FBI agent, civil litigator, domestic judge and circuit court judge who would continue to influence my life profoundly. He was the same judge who insisted that "Lucky" Jaffe represent death row inmate Bo Cochran. After extensive pretrial hearings, Judge Cole denied our motion to suppress the illegally obtained statement. However, he took under advisement our motion that the jury be allowed to visit the crime scene. We felt it would be helpful for jurors to walk through the home and feel Tyrone's experience when confronted with what he perceived to be a life-endangering circumstance.

When Judge Cole ultimately denied this request, I filed another motion. Since Tyrone still owned the home, I proposed that the entire staircase and hallway be removed and reconstructed in the courtroom. The large ceilings of the huge, dark wood, baroque-styled courtroom could contain it without a problem. The judge agreed to our unorthodox request.

With only a few days until the trial, I still did not have the next-door neighbor's statement. My concern dwelled in a cold, uncomfortable chamber deep in my gut. Then, during the weekend before the trial, my investigator brought me a tape-recorded statement from the missing neighbor. In direct contradiction of my instructions, he'd secretly recorded it. While it is legal in Alabama to record someone secretly (as long as one party to the conversation consents to the recording), as opposed to many other locales, I feared what a jury would think if I had to use it.

A skilled prosecutor would take great advantage of such secretive tactics, implying them to be unsavory, even though law enforcement surreptitiously records people every day. Because a lawyer's credibility can be pivotal in many cases, I always urge my investigators to bring me consensual recordings and/or signed statements.

After some delay due to the precisely measured staircase reconstruction, the trial began and seemed to go well for Tyrone. I felt a connection to the jurors and they appeared not to wince when stealing glances at my client. The packed courtroom contained many Robinson supporters and family members.

Then the prosecutor stunned me by calling the one neighbor who had resisted speaking with my investigator. In her testimony, she relayed a description of the gunshots different from the other neighbors and different from our recorded conversation with her. Her testimony had devastated our defense. Would it be necessary to use the tape, which contained a recollection of the shot sequence more favorable than the one she testified to on direct exam?'

I had no choice. I had to gamble and use the tape.

During closing arguments, Bob McGregor, one of the two experienced prosecutors, pounced on my use of the tape, spinning it back to me: "How dare the defense allow such deception?" His tactic worked. The jurors would not look at either my client or me during closing arguments or when they returned verdicts of guilty—a murder conviction for the death of his wife and a manslaughter conviction for the death of the intruder. Judge Cole sentenced Robinson to forty years in prison: thirty for the death of his wife plus ten for the death of Simpson.

The loss sunk me into a deep depression that descended below the typical gut-wrenching feeling of losing. I had lost my share of cases before this one. It hinged upon the fact that everything might have been completely different had we obtained the neighbor's statement immediately after it happened, when it was fresh. Then I could have dealt with whatever the neighbor said in my opening statement and not lost credibility by using a secretly obtained recording.

For the next fourteen months, the case lingered in the appellate courts. Then the Alabama Court of Criminal Appeals affirmed Tyrone's conviction. Following that, I appealed to the Alabama Supreme Court, which reversed the conviction and ordered a new trial. The court cited several substantial errors that effectively robbed Tyrone of a fair trial, including the admission of the illegally obtained four-hour statement that contained the prejudicially inadmissible comments of the detectives.

Tyrone learned the news in his prison cell. We began to prepare for the new trial.

No one looks forward to the second trying of a case. Hundreds of pages of transcripts must be studied, not to mention relocating and preparing witnesses. Sometimes, no matter how identical the information or the people on the stand, things may not turn out the same way the second time around. Lead prosecutor Bob McGregor had recently left to become an Assistant United States Attorney, leaving lead counsel duties to the very capable Jeff Wallace, who had prosecuted the first trial with Bob.

I began to negotiate with Jeff, who would have to prosecute the case without Tyrone's now-inadmissible statement. The State's case had grown weaker, yet retained its high profile. Like all high-profile cases, it was politically sensitive.

My negotiations with Jeff Wallace stood at an impasse. I negotiated for Tyrone to receive probation on two manslaughter counts and receive credit for the time he had already served in prison. We could agree on the manslaughters but not on the sentence. Then, three days before the Monday trial was to begin, while seated at my desk in our old Georgian office building, I glanced out the huge windows onto the avenue. I questioned my sanity. As if in a dream, I saw Judge Cole nimbly limping along as if his compromised knee did not hurt at all. He bounced up the concrete steps to the front door.

Astonished, I managed to untwist myself from my frozen position in my chair and meet him at the door.

"Lucky." He noticed my obvious discomfort.

"Yes, sir, Your Honor?"

"You're going to sit down with me and settle this Robinson case right now and I'm not leaving until it's settled. Do you understand me?"

Not waiting for an answer, he walked hurriedly into the foyer.

I had never heard of a trial judge making an unannounced visit to an attorney's office, especially to settle a case. It appeared that he intended to make sure he would resolve this matter. That was Judge Cole. He had a great sense of humor, but he took things seriously. If it took him personally making a surprise visit to my office to get this politically sensitive case resolved, he would do it.

I pulled up a chair for him, normally reserved for nervous clients. The judge immediately sat down. I swiveled my desk chair to face him squarely. He leaned up, eye level with me, both hands on his knees. "You're asking for too much, Lucky," he admonished. "I am not giving him probation. I can't. He killed two people, no matter what his intent was."

"But, Judge," I gently but firmly, postured, "I am ready for trial. Jeff and I have tried to settle this case, but we can't agree."

"I know. I have spoken to Wallace and we are going to settle this case today. The case is too big, too much press for probation. It wouldn't look good. Can't do it. Not going to do it. And you know what I will do if he is convicted again."

I did know. Murder with a weapon carried twenty years to life. Tyrone faced two counts. Every count of manslaughter carried up to twenty years apiece. He could get forty years if convicted at trial, even of the lesser charges of manslaughter. Or he could wind up with twenty years if convicted of only one count.

This case needed to settle. The judge knew it and I knew it. In federal court, judges are specifically prohibited from participating in negotiations.[2] In some state courts, they may involve themselves but always with both parties present.[3] However, Judge Cole had a mind of his own and could not often be denied. The judge made it clear to me that he had already told Jeff his intention. He expected a guilty plea and would sentence Tyrone Robinson on two reckless manslaughter counts.

He would give Tyrone probation on each case, but he expected Tyrone to serve another year in prison. Tyrone had already served twenty-six months in prison while waiting for his appeals to end and his second trial to begin. I listened attentively to Judge Cole and then he departed, leaving my head spinning.

In spite of our good odds at favorable verdicts, Tyrone wisely decided not to take any chances, as he needed to return home as soon as he could to continue fathering the daughter he and Lucinda shared, as well as Lucinda's daughter from another relationship. On Monday, we entered the pleas, just as the judge had outlined. In entering his guilty pleas, Tyrone was adjudged to be innocent of any form of murder or of any intentional killing. His pleas to reckless manslaughter meant that his conduct was just that: reckless. Not intentional.

I would encounter Judge William Cole many more times, notably with the Bo Cochran death penalty case he had placed in my lap several years before, a case that was still pending. Judge Cole had his unorthodox ways, yet he believed in our system of justice—even if he utilized his own ideas on how it should work.

13

THE DEATH PENALTY AND JUVENILES

One evening, Jermaine Robinson was hanging out with several of his older "friends" at a fast food restaurant in the Western Hills area of Birmingham. Jermaine Robinson had experienced some behavioral problems in high school but had no history of violence. The fifteen-year-old African-American football player had no criminal history. Jermaine's parents were divorced. Both his mother and father had time-consuming, responsible jobs but they did their best to be present and active in Jermaine's life. On that tragic evening, Jermaine allowed his friends to persuade him to walk over to a local bank's automatic teller machine (ATM) located near the restaurant where they had all been drinking beer. They lent him a .25 automatic that he did not know was loaded. Outside the bank, he saw a man in the process of withdrawing cash from the ATM. The innocent, unsuspecting forty-year-old white male had left his wife and child getting hamburgers nearby while he went to the bank. My soon-to-be client pointed the gun at the man's head, demanding the man's money as he was completing his withdrawal. In doing so, Jermaine gestured nervously, accidentally pulling the pistol's trigger.

The video camera at the bank caught the encounter close-up. It vividly captured the gun discharging a bullet into the man's head.

The local television stations aired the security camera footage over the next few days and called-in tips led authorities to several of the young adults who were with Jermaine that night. Five days later, detectives questioned him. Jermaine admitted it was him in the security video and that he had shot the man but tearfully maintained that he was so scared during the confrontation he accidentally discharged the weapon. No one believed him except perhaps his parents and me.

It is never easy when a family member gets in trouble, particularly a teenage son or daughter. Often far more mature in body than mind, they can cause as much or even more devastation and destruction than any adult. They can lie. They can steal. They can even kill. Over the years, ever-younger teenagers and children have committed and been charged with crimes of violence, destroying lives of victims and families far beyond their abilities to perceive or appreciate during their acts.

In the past decade, the second leading cause of deaths among youths aged ten to nineteen was homicide.[1] Economically deprived urban areas are most fertile for such violent criminal activity. For example, in New Castle, Pennsylvania, an eleven-year-old was charged with killing his father's pregnant fiancée.[2] Authorities in Pensacola, Florida, arrested a fourteen-year-old boy for firing multiple gunshots into his father and killing him.[3]

In both of these instances, the prosecution attempted to try these juveniles as adults. There remains a fierce debate over whether children who commit acts of violence should be treated, tried and incarcerated as adults rather than as juveniles. If the juvenile court handled these cases, it could incarcerate the teens in juvenile facilities geared toward treating as well as punishing them. It has been recognized in the scientific community and ultimately by the courts that the brain of a human being does not fully form until past the age of twenty; many studies find the age range to be between twenty-two and twenty-five.[4] More specifically, the area involving the frontal lobes that controls "executive functioning," or judgment and decision making, is the last part of the brain to fully form.

I've defended many death penalty cases. Of all the types of clients I've represented, nothing troubles me more than working with teenage defendants. These clients and their families can be exceptionally challenging to defend. Emotions rarely turn more intense for lawyers than when dealing with the families of juveniles facing time. Jermaine faced death.

This case tore at the community's feeling of safety. Well over twenty years later, I've still not used an ATM and will not even walk by one at night if I can help it. It challenged my long-term commitment to take these cases, but I had to save this teen if possible. I believed his version of the events. As a parent, I couldn't fathom his mother and father witnessing their son's execution. But the State intended to pursue the death penalty in spite of constitutional prohibitions in many jurisdictions against executing juveniles.[5]

The prosecution had to convince Family Court Judge Sandra Ross to transfer Jermaine's case to adult circuit court, rather than try him as a juvenile. I stood little chance of convincing Judge Ross to keep this case in juvenile court. The severity of the crime was the only real argument the prosecution could use under Alabama law, since Jermaine had no criminal record, was of good character and had not been treated in a youth facility before. If incarcerated, he could receive social rehabilitation treatment.

As I expected, Judge Ross ordered Jermaine be tried as an adult. I appealed her ruling on the basis that the severity of the crime alone was not enough to justify adult treatment. The next day, headlines in the *Birmingham News* read, "15 Year Old Could Get the Electric Chair for Lucia Murder." The prosecution began to make plans to present Jermaine's case to the Grand Jury and I began to investigate the case and prepare for trial. At the same time, I pressed the appeal of the family court decision.[6]

Judge Richmond Pearson, the only African-American Circuit Judge in Jefferson County at the time, received the assignment as the trial judge for Jermaine's death penalty trial. The judge knew what it was like to grow up poor and he knew the community, the surrounding area and the challenges Jermaine faced. The judge knew the dark and dismal Birmingham streets from which he rose through sheer determination, courage and talent.

One of the first motions I filed was that the death penalty be removed due to Jermaine's age at the time of the tragic shooting. Judge Pearson granted my motion and removed the death penalty as a consideration, agreeing that it would be a constitutional violation. However, he denied my motion to delay the trial until after the appeals courts ruled on whether Jermaine should be tried as an adult rather than a juvenile.

Still, if the jury convicted this young man of capital murder, he would spend every day for the rest of his life in an eight-by-ten-foot cell without the possibility of parole. He would live but never get out of prison, a just and proper sentence had he intended to kill Mr. Lucia—but not if he shot the gun accidentally.

My defense reflected the truth as I saw it: If Jermaine intended to kill this man, he would have taken the money and ran. Instead, when the gun fired, his own surprise and shock caused him to flee the scene without the money.

As the trial neared, our defense team faced another daunting obstacle: our client was inarticulate and devoid of outward emotional expression. Terror caged his true remorse and pain. We had to bring it out of him, but how could we help him relate to jurors, many of whom were unaccustomed to our client's background and speech? We had to break his pattern of habitually speaking his words as if he had gravel in his mouth while staring at the floor. We began to videotape him while we simulated the courtroom dynamics and did mock direct examinations and then cross-examinations using questions that we anticipated the prosecutor would ask.

With just days remaining before trial, we had not yet heard from the Alabama Supreme Court on my motion to delay the trial until the Supreme Court could consider my other appeal on the family court's decision to try Jermaine as an adult. Then, the weekend before the trial, I received an order from the Alabama Supreme Court. At practically the last second, the court agreed that American Bar Association (ABA) standards be followed, which stated that a juvenile should not be tried as an adult until the court decided the appeal.[7]

Judge Pearson granted our motion that Jermaine be given a $50,000 bond conditional upon his attending school outside of the county. This outraged many; however, Judge Pearson had done nothing but follow the law in this regard. I also knew the strain on Jermaine's family and friends, for his future looked as bleak as it did uncertain.

Eventually, the Supreme Court of Alabama ruled that Jermaine could be tried as an adult. I was disappointed but not surprised, given the magnitude of his actions, even if he did not intend to shoot anyone. Yet, no matter which way we went at trial, we could not escape the images from the surveillance video clearly showing our client with his arm outstretched, gun in hand, shooting and killing an innocent father, whose arms were spread apart as he refused to give up his money.

A trial in which the prosecution can show a video of the actual shooting is intimidating for the defense, to say the least. I utilized psychologist Allen Shealy, a jury selection expert I would use in some of my most challenging cases. In my opening statement I told the jury that the case came down to one question: that of intent.

I was convinced that Jermaine needed to testify honestly from his heart if we had any chance of escaping a capital murder conviction. Fortunately, the tedious videotaped rehearsal sessions with our client paid off. Jermaine made a compelling witness—believable, sympathetic and remorseful. He never denied that he did the shooting nor that he planned to rob someone. He did not ask for a lawyer or one of his parents to be with him when he originally spoke to the police, although he had those rights.

Just before closing arguments, a bailiff discovered that some of the jurors had been playing the word game "hangman" on the chalkboard in the jury room. The image of a partial stick man hanging by a noose was on the chalkboard during lunch break. I moved immediately for a mistrial. The judge promptly made an inquiry. After he learned which juror had initiated the game, he dismissed that juror. The others were allowed to stay, over my objection.

Prosecutor Roger Brown, the chief deputy district attorney, forcefully argued his case. He reminded the jury that after the shooting Jermaine ate a hamburger. But the jury knew that Jermaine's tears on the stand were real and he felt badly for the victim and his family. The victim's family would always feel life's deepest wound from Jermaine's senseless conduct. My heart swelled with sympathy every time I saw the widow in court.

Abraham Lincoln, a famous trial lawyer who unsuccessfully ran for many public offices before becoming one of our greatest presidents, once said that a skilled lawyer will concede most of his case, only to focus the jury on the most important points that he can vigorously contest. In our defense, we conceded 98 percent of the prosecution's case, except for the intent to kill.[8] In my argument, I stressed that Jermaine had no motive, no criminal history, no reason to fire that gun; it must have discharged accidentally.

However, would a jury really consider finding Jermaine not guilty amidst all the sadness and pain of his foolish actions? Would they acquit him when, thanks to the surveillance camera, they too stared down the barrel of Jermaine's .25 automatic, just as the victim had done? Even if the jury believed Jermaine had panicked and accidentally fired the gun, he could still be guilty of felony murder, which carried a sentence of twenty years to life in prison. If a person even accidentally kills someone during the course of committing a felony (robbery in this case) he is guilty of felony murder. I pleaded with the jurors to accept that Jermaine shot the victim accidentally: "Tragic? Yes. Foolish? Yes. Intentional? No."

After hours of deliberation, the jury found now seventeen-year-old Jermaine Robinson not guilty of capital murder. That spared the judge from imposing a life sentence without the possibility of parole. Given only two other options—not guilty or guilty of felony murder—the jury convicted Jermaine of felony murder. With its verdict, the jury sent a note requesting leniency from the judge. At that time probation was not an option.

Judge Pearson sentenced Jermaine to twenty-six years in prison. He would get his life back one day, but he would have to live always knowing that his foolish actions created irreparable and unimaginable devastation to an innocent family and an entire community. It also was a very sobering reminder of the often incalculable and permanent cost of succumbing to peer pressure. Jermaine tried to impress his "friends" and they let him think they would be impressed. Sadly, classes on resisting peer pressure are not taught in schools and juveniles do not understand the consequences of blindly following such influences. These are not excuses, just realities. Even as adults, we sometimes allow ourselves to act or think based upon the expectations of our friends. Loneliness and ostracism are fearful possibilities for most of us.

No verdict could undo the irreparable wake of devastation. Even if Jermaine served the entire twenty-six years, he would leave prison when he was roughly the same age as the victim had been. The rest of his life was up to him, a lifetime more than the victim and his family would share together.

14

ALL KILLERS ARE NOT ALIKE

I heard a routine buzzing sound on my office intercom and my legal assistant alerted me: Carol Downs wanted to speak with me about a coworker. "Richard," Carol began. "It concerns someone who works at the school where I teach. He has always been soft-spoken and gentle. He is at the Jefferson County Jail. They have charged him with killing his wife. I was not at the school yesterday but my coworker told me that Daniel got dizzy and sweaty while he was at work yesterday, after going to the doctor. I was thinking you could check on him, as he may need medical attention and I don't know if he will get it at the jail."

A pause offered us both a chance to catch our breaths, yet the urgency lingered for a few moments.

"Carol," I inquired, "has he been arrested?"

"Yes. Last evening, shortly after a coworker drove him home from work."

"Do you know if he made any statements?" I asked, hoping to mask my anxiousness with calmness.

"No. From what I have observed about Daniel it does not seem to me that he would intentionally hurt anyone and he would be honest with everyone." She spoke with a degree of certainty. "Will you meet with Daniel's family? I could have his brother call you right away."

"Yes, Carol, have him call me. I will do all I can."

"Thank you, Richard. I feel better already."

Fifteen minutes later, I answered the call from Daniel's older brother, a lieutenant in a nearby law enforcement department. We set up an appointment for the next day. When the lieutenant arrived at my office, he brought his mother, Daniel's three young children and several other close family members. An air of heaviness permeated the conference room. Except for the young children, the faces that stared at me could not hide their gloom, fear and sadness. They shook from the shock of how their lives were suddenly turned upside down.

"Mr. Jaffe," the lieutenant began, "Daniel and Denise were truly a loving couple and practically inseparable. When Daniel wasn't working, he and Denise were together. He all but worshipped her and, Mr. Jaffe, during their fifteen-year relationship I never heard him utter one unkind word to Denise. He treated her with such respect and tenderness. They really loved each other a lot. They had fun together. Daniel would never dream of laying a finger on her, much less of hurting her."

I listened attentively and patiently, all the while mindful of the couple's children cushioning themselves into Daniel's mother's arms, no doubt too young to process the current tragedy that would follow and influence them indelibly.

The story of Daniel's relationship with Denise, coupled with the family's closeness to this usually quiet and lamblike man, created quite a contrast to the reality of the murder charge he faced. The discord resembled a pleasant dream suddenly morphing into a destructive nightmare—like a Sunday morning family drive that ends when a drunk driver crashes head-on into the car.

I wanted to know more about how, why and when Daniel and Denise ended up in Birmingham from the Northwest. I wanted to know what the family knew about any problems Daniel may have experienced growing up. I wanted to know what Daniel had told the detectives.

Most of all, I wanted to meet Daniel, who sat in the Jefferson County Jail charged with murdering his high school sweetheart.

The following day, I visited my sullen and depressed client, informed him that Carol Downs had asked me to represent him and told him that his family had hired me. I wanted to make sure he agreed with his family's intentions. I found him to be as quiet and soft-spoken as his family members portrayed him and just as much in shock as his family.

In his mid-thirties, Daniel was about six feet tall, weighed around 220 pounds and had closely cropped hair. He was clean-cut and mild mannered. He did not appear to be a weightlifter, but he was built sturdy and strong, with broad shoulders. He slumped over in his chair and would hardly meet my probing eyes as I tried to learn his version of the tragedy that led us both to the Jefferson County Jail. Nothing about this man resembled a killer. It seemed the gravity of the situation had not yet penetrated the shock, which, thankfully, had still not turned into hopeless despair. If anything, Daniel remained in the midst of a nightmare and had not yet awakened to something all too real.

Daniel's main concern was his children, whom he knew had moved in with his mother and continued attending school. As I carefully explained the steps through the legal process, Daniel stared blankly at me, trying to absorb my words, unable to make sense of his predicament. He was still too stunned to understand that he would never see his deceased wife again. Perhaps he would only see his children through the windowpane of a wired cage in a prison.

I left the jail that day feeling perplexed and a bit lost, yet instinctually knowing that the answers might be hiding somewhere in the Northwest. I would also have to know what exactly happened on that fateful day. For now, I would leave Daniel to process what happened. In time, the shock would burn off like coastal fog in the midday sun and he would come to grips with the consequences of his actions and the prospect of facing life in prison.

When I returned to my office, I instructed my assistant to enter my notice of appearance as Daniel's lawyer and set up another meeting with his mother and brother. I also contacted the DA's office, only to learn that one of the toughest prosecutors had been assigned to handle

Daniel's case. The deputy district attorney assigned to the case lived to fight and was a tenacious prosecutor. He was short and stocky, like a prize fighter. He sported a pleasant disposition, friendly yet firm, easy to talk to but somewhat uncompromising. He confirmed for me that Daniel had indeed confessed. With confidence, he read the police report to me over the phone and gave me a summary of the case.

According to the prosecutor, Daniel had come home from work that day a little after 4:00 P.M. and gotten into an argument with his wife about a planned trip to visit family out of state. During the course of the quickly escalating argument—and with an impulse that seemed to be strikingly uncharacteristic to me as I got to know him better— Daniel suddenly grabbed Denise. Tragically, he grabbed her throat at its weakest point. She immediately collapsed onto the bedroom carpet.

Not knowing what to do with his wife's lifeless body, Daniel called his mother, who called police. Within minutes, officers arrived at the scene to find him cowering in a fetal position on the corner of the couch in the den, softly whimpering as if he were the mother of a fawn that had just been shot by a hunter. The police read Daniel his Miranda Rights. He admitted to all the details of the argument leading to Denise's death. To the police, this crime appeared straightforward and airtight, a brutal, unprovoked killing of an innocently demure mother of three children.

The deputy district attorney had a killing and a confession.

However, I longed to know: Why?

At my next meeting with Daniel's mother, she told me he grew up quiet and shy. He got along with friends and family. He did not argue with people. He did well in school. His mother could not remember even one single incident of violence, any fights or disciplinary actions at school. Daniel always walked away before arguing. According to Daniel's mother, that placid temperament carried right into Daniel's marriage. He and Denise never argued, to her knowledge. On the contrary, he longed to spend his free time with her, their children and their extended family.

I told Daniel's mother that this tragedy made no sense to me.

"It makes no sense to us either, Mr. Jaffe," she uttered with disbelief.

"Tell me more about Daniel's childhood. Did he play sports? Did he have many friends? Was he a happy child growing up?"

"Daniel mostly kept to himself," she replied. "He didn't play any sports. He did have some friends back then, but he was always on the quiet side."

"But would you consider him to have been a happy child?"

"He did seem to be happy most of the time. Except there were times, as he got older, in his twenties, when he got especially quiet, as if he were depressed. And these bouts just seemed to come out of nowhere, Mr. Jaffe."

A flame of realization lit up inside of me, ever so slightly. "Did he ever seek any mental health treatment for his depression?" I asked patiently.

"Yes, when it got really bad and he just couldn't seem to come out of it, we had him treated in Chicago. On several occasions the doctors prescribed him medicine and he took it. After he began feeling better, he stopped taking it. One time they actually hospitalized him for a few days."

Later that week, I called Carol Downs and asked her to tell me anything else she may have heard about Daniel's last day at work. Carol related that a coworker of hers had seen him just before he left the school. During the school day he had grown dizzy, thrown up and fainted. The coworker said Daniel had been to see a doctor and may have been on medication. I thanked her for the information.

I drove back to the jail to visit Daniel. It had been a week since his wife's death. He still seemed lifeless and withdrawn. "Daniel," I asked, "tell me what you remember about how you felt on your last day at work."

"I was feeling real bad, so I called my doctor and told him how I was feeling," he flatly stated.

I asked him for the name of his doctor. "What was wrong with you that day?"

"I had just been feeling bad, so I called the doctor. He has one of those, you know, little clinics and I went in there once without an appointment. He asked what was bothering me and he gave me some medicine."

"When in relationship to your last day at work?"

"It was the day before."

"What medicine did the doctor give you?"

"I don't know, but I took one of the pills around ten o'clock at work and then I began to feel dizzy and I got sick. I remember being on the floor and then I felt a little better and drove home."

"Daniel, Carol told me she heard you may have called a doctor."

"Yeah, I called to tell the doctor how I was feeling. He told me to take another pill, so I did."

"Did that help? Did you feel any better after taking another pill?" I asked.

His face remained expressionless and listless. His depression had not dissipated a bit and the sadness of his wife's death had begun to sink in deeply.

"I don't know. I hardly remember driving home and then the next thing I remember Denise and I started arguing about going on the trip. I had the tickets in my hand. She and I were both holding them and they tore. Then I grabbed her and she fell and I told my mom. I said, 'I think something happened to Denise. She is on the floor. Won't move. '

"And then my mom came to the house and the police came and I told them what happened. I don't know why I grabbed her. I didn't mean to. I didn't mean to hurt my wife. I would never hurt her. I love her more than anything."

Daniel hung his head low. His shoulders collapsed. "I'll do all I can to help you," I told him. He signed medical releases for the mental health records from Birmingham and the Northwest. I left my despondent client alone at the jail.

The next step in the legal process was the preliminary hearing. Fortunately, Daniel's mother had possession of the pill bottle and she brought it to my office. The bottle contained an antidepressant. Three pills were missing from the quantity on the prescription label.

At the preliminary hearing, the deputy district attorney exuded complete confidence. He called only two witnesses, the first officer on the scene and the lead detective who questioned my client. My cross-examinations focused on the fact that Daniel's mother called the police, who found her son listless and curled up on the couch. I argued that he answered all of the police's questions as best he could. He did not want a lawyer. He cooperated fully. Next, my questions centered on his demeanor. I could see some sneering from people in the courtroom as if my questions made no sense, almost as if I had given up.

Even before the preliminary hearing, the only real and true defense leaped out at me like a racehorse when the gate opens. I thought of the police reports, Daniel's statements to the detective and the first officers on the scene, his history of depression and his uncharacteristic behavior that day. Everything in me felt Daniel was not guilty by reason of severe mental disease or defect, otherwise known as insanity.

However, like most jurisdictions, Alabama carries no laws on the books for temporary insanity. Finding a reputable psychiatrist to diagnose a defendant properly and explain the diagnosis to a jury posed its own challenge. Nevertheless, Daniel had no motive to destroy his loving, innocent wife, nor his own life and especially the lives of the children he adored.

Several months after the preliminary hearing, the grand jury returned an indictment for murder. During the time leading up to the trial, I endeavored to learn as much as I could about the relatively new antidepressant Daniel was taking. I began my incessant search for a psychiatrist without tight relationships with the drug companies, one who could understand this darker truth within Daniel and articulate his defense convincingly to twelve strangers.

Jurors and prosecutors detest and disbelieve insanity defenses. To the average person, an insanity defense represents a legal "Hail Mary," the desperate final act when the defendant has nothing else to offer. To some juries, insanity defenses signal loopholes through which the guilty can slip; for that reason, jurors will reject them without giving them much consideration. Although insanity defenses rarely work, many people remember that John Hinckley was found insane after his unsuccessful attempt to assassinate President Reagan. Many fail to consider that three decades later, Hinckley remains under the supervision of a psychiatric institution, where he belongs.[1]

Ironically, it was because the Washington, D.C., jury correctly found Hinckley insane at the time of the shooting that legislatures nationwide immediately changed the law. At Hinckley's trial, the prosecution carried the burden of proof. They had to prove that Hinckley was not insane. After that case, the laws changed so that the law presumes a person sane and the *defendant* bears the burden of proving his or her insanity by "clear and convincing evidence."[2] That's quite a shift from many years of legal precedent.

In my preparations for the trial, I learned more about Daniel's antidepressant, along with its risks and side effects, which were rare. Only the smallest fraction of users experienced adverse reactions to the drug. To my dismay, I found that the antidepressant possessed few dangers and only rarely created a dangerous condition for someone who experienced a negative reaction.

Then I looked at the side effects. To my utter amazement and encouragement, I discovered that if a person truly experienced the worst adverse reaction from taking the antidepressant, he or she could experience violent tendencies and present a real danger to self and others.[3] Daniel's coworkers confirmed that his symptoms on the day of Denise's death mirrored those of an adverse reaction: dizziness, light-headedness, confusion, vomiting, fainting, uncontrollable sweating and violent propensities.

The doctor who treated Daniel had only seen him once and was not a psychiatrist, even though he was licensed to prescribe antidepressants. These records also revealed that Daniel had said he had felt depressed for a week and it kept getting worse. When Daniel called the physician to complain about his symptoms—*the exact symptoms of an adverse reaction to the medication*—the doctor simply told him to take another pill. This compounded the severity of the adverse reaction. Having confirmed the truth of what caused him to behave in a way he'd never acted before, especially toward his wife, I still needed to locate a reputable psychiatrist to examine and test Daniel—and hopefully testify in support of our defense.

Everywhere I turned, I hit a dead end. Most psychiatrists wanted nothing to do with this case. The companies that manufactured such drugs would not look kindly toward a physician who testified negatively about a very popular medication. However, during my search, I kept hearing the name of a highly respected psychiatrist in the area. I called him and convinced him to meet with me. I hoped that this doctor would agree to review the records and ultimately take on the thankless task of testifying in a murder case in Birmingham. I knew that I would have but one chance to convince him that the door of justice needed to be opened so a jury could consider the truth.

As I drove to the psychiatrist's office, I mulled over the facts of the case: Daniel's history of depression and his gentle nature, his tender relationship with his wife and children and his family's strong support since his arrest. I also reviewed the issue of the antidepressant and what happened that fateful day when, with one forceful action, Daniel extinguished the light of his loving wife.

The psychiatrist could not have been more engaging and gracious upon meeting me. He sensed my passion and belief in Daniel and my planned defense and I could feel his budding interest. He asked me searching questions regarding the medical records. To my delight, he agreed to testify.

Finally, the trial began. Even though I had entered a plea of not guilty by reason of mental disease or defect at the arraignment months before, the prosecuting attorney knew that insanity defenses often fall through. Accordingly, he did not request that a State-appointed mental health expert examine and test Daniel.

In Alabama and most other jurisdictions, the definition of legal insanity states that if a person is suffering from a severe mental disease or defect at the time of the offense that prevents him from appreciating the wrongfulness of his conduct or otherwise conform it to the requirements of law, then he is legally insane.[4] The psychiatrist who testified for our defense had determined the mental disease or defect to be clinically severe depression that became so much *more* severe from the antidepressant that it caused Daniel's inability to appreciate the nature and quality and wrongfulness of his actions.

In jury selection, the prosecutor and I both focused on the pro-spective jurors' attitudes about mental illness, the insanity defense, depression and antidepressants. Not surprisingly to me, more than half of the potential jurors or someone close to them had been prescribed antidepressants or had been treated for some type of mental or emo-tional problem.

The prosecutor called the pathologist as the State's first witness. He testified about the autopsy he performed on Denise and gave his opinion as to the cause of death. Notably, he admitted that her eyes contained no evidence of strangulation, which was a sure sign of intent to kill. Her neck snapped from one fatal forceful thrust. The medical examiner then showed the gruesome photographs of Denise's body and close-ups of her neck and face.

Next, officers who had reported to the scene testified to their collection of evidence and the photographs of the room showing little disruption of the furniture and Denise's lifeless body lying on the floor. The final witness, the lead detective, testified to the recorded statement Daniel gave him while still curled up in the corner of the couch in the den. I requested that the prosecutor play the entire tape recording itself, so that the jurors could hear and judge for themselves Daniel's true mental state and demeanor at that time. I believed that the jury would know and feel his psychotic state right after the event, along with his bewilderment, already present deep remorse and disbelief that he had actually killed his wife.

My cross-examination of the detective echoed the issues I raised when questioning the first officer on the scene. The detective admitted that before he took Daniel's recorded statement he spoke to the first officer who had interviewed Daniel. That was the same officer who had responded to the call from Daniel's mother.

"It was your understanding, was it not, that Daniel had called his mother and told her that he had grabbed Denise during an argu-ment?" I asked.

"Yes, sir."

"And the officer had arrived at the scene within ten minutes of that call?"

"Yes, that is true," the detective confirmed.

"The officer then secured the scene and called you?"

"Yes."

"And then you arrived at approximately 9:15 P.M., did you not?" I continued my questioning.

The detective nodded. "I did."

"The first officer had already spoken to Daniel, who told him what happened?"

"Yes, that is true."

"And to your knowledge, when you spoke to and recorded Daniel, he remained in the exact position that the first officer found him in, did he not?" I asked.

"Apparently that is true."

"Curled up in a fetal position at the end of his couch, crying softly and in shock."

"Yes, that is how I found him."

I was satisfied that the jury had heard the position in which Daniel was found. Remorseless murderers don't curl up in fetal positions. I pressed on. "When you spoke to Daniel, you read him his Miranda Rights?"

"Yes, that is customary."

"You told him he did not have to talk to you and he could stop at any time and call a lawyer, but he spoke to you anyway and fully cooperated as best he could."

"That is correct."

"In fact, you had to come closer to him as you continued your interview, because he spoke so softly."

"Yes, he did speak softly and I did have a difficult time hearing him."

"And you were within three or four feet of him when he answered as best he could. You did not handcuff him then, did you?"

"No, I did not."

"Nor did you draw your gun, as you were not afraid of him at that time?"

"No, not at that time."

"But, as you testified at the preliminary hearing in district court, you noted his eyes looked red, glassy and glazed over."

"Yes."

The detective further testified that Daniel appeared confused and he saw no evidence of intoxication. He admitted that he had found nothing inconsistent with what Daniel had told him or the first officer on the scene. The detective stated that he had to repeat some of his questions to Daniel but that Daniel answered every question. In addition, the detective testified that he had no reason to disbelieve Daniel, who had made no excuses. Further, he verified that Daniel whimpered softly and cried throughout the interview and repeatedly stated that he did not know what caused him to grab his wife.

"You interviewed coworkers and family members, didn't you?" I inquired.

The detective testified that everyone associated with Daniel expressed shock and disbelief that Daniel was capable of such conduct. The detective also acknowledged that he was unaware of Daniel's history of depression or the effects of the antidepressant. He also didn't know Daniel had suffered an adverse reaction on the day of the fatal incident.

The State rested its case and we began ours. We called members of Daniel's family to testify of the ideal relationship between Daniel and Denise and of Daniel's consistently loving treatment of his wife. Later, our psychiatrist testified to his opinions, which were reflected in his detailed report. In that report, he wrote that Daniel had suffered an adverse reaction from the antidepressant he took, which exacerbated his severe depression, resulting in a severe mental disease and defect on the day of the incident.

For our last witness we called Denise's father, who had traveled from the Northwest to testify on behalf of Daniel. He told the jury that when he learned what had happened, he did not believe it. He stated that he knew the entire history between Daniel and Denise and how much they cherished each other.

We rested our case. During the closing arguments, in a voice which carried forcefully throughout the courtroom, the prosecutor proclaimed that Daniel was a murderer and that our defense was frivolous.

When it was my turn to sum up, I reminded the jurors of the detective's testimony that supported our insanity defense. I walked slowly to the middle of the jury box and spoke softly: "Ladies and gentlemen, you have heard and seen the unrefuted evidence that my client suffered from a debilitating depression that adversely and severely affected him. The person whom you heard about and now know was not the same person who uncontrollably grabbed his loving wife. You know how deeply he loved and cared for Denise and how much she loved him.

"That proof comes from neither us nor the State. It comes from Daniel's family and coworkers; it comes from a highly respected psychiatrist; most importantly, it comes straight from the one man who hurts the most and who suffers irreparably, whose loss is both immeasurable and irreplaceable: Denise's father, who took off from work and traveled here just to tell you the truth. This leads to only one conclusion: Daniel must have been insane at the time of the unfortunate incident that took Denise's life. And if Denise were here to talk to you and testify, I think you know what she would say…and maybe she is here, speaking from her heart to yours: 'Please don't convict my husband. He didn't mean to hurt me. He would never hurt me and has never hurt me before. He wasn't himself. The drugs that the doctor told him to take made him sick. After he suffered a severe adverse reaction, what did the doctor tell him? He told him to take more. Please know it was an accident. Please help him get well so that my children won't lose both their mother and their father."

After the judge read the Alabama law on insanity, the jurors retired and deliberated. Within fifteen minutes, they came back with a question: Could they find Daniel not guilty as well as not guilty by reason of insanity? Judge Mike McCormick responded they could not.

Within an hour the jury reached its verdict: "We find the defendant not guilty by reason of mental disease or defect."

Appropriately, Judge McCormick sent Daniel to a state mental health facility where he was tested, treated and ultimately released. He was no danger to himself or the public if he continued to receive mental health treatment. It must have seemed evident from the psychiatrist's extensive report that Daniel's depressive condition and adverse reaction to the antidepressant he took created a horrible combination.

Because Daniel's employer felt she had no choice but to terminate him, my law firm hired him to work as an intern and runner until he could find another job consistent with his talents. He has continued to be a present and loving parent to his children. He also remains devoted and close to his larger family.

Twelve jurors gave Daniel and his family a second chance and, in essence, saved his children. Denise's loss will haunt all of them for the rest of their lives, but Daniel is raising their children in a way that would make her proud.

15

DEATH IS IN THE DETAILS

Renard Pruitt, a Birmingham grocery store employee, babysat his twenty-two-month old daughter Tamika one night while her mother, Renard's girlfriend Samella, worked the night shift at a local convenience store. He realized that Tamika wasn't feeling well. Over a six-hour period, Renard tried diligently to feed the little girl, but she couldn't keep any food down. Renard had no car while he babysat at Samella's house. He kept trying to call Tamika's mother to report his concerns but could not reach her.

Then Renard's life changed forever. According to Renard's police statement, at about 10:30 P.M. the baby began to tremble and convulse violently. She started to drift in and out of consciousness. Although he didn't fully understand the perilous situation presented by the baby's symptoms, Renard knew they were serious. Finally Samella returned home. Immediately he told her that something was wrong with Tamika and explained how he had unsuccessfully attempted to feed her.

They drove to the emergency room, where they reported to the doctors what had occurred with Tamika, but she died that night. The autopsy revealed a dilation of the baby's pupils indicating that someone had violently shaken her. In addition, the autopsy showed a tear in the baby's anal and vaginal area.

The State charged Renard with capital murder and sexual abuse of little Tamika.[1]

Although I had taken Renard as my client, I wondered if he was the kind of sick and twisted human being who could possibly extinguish the life of a toddler after sexually molesting her. I wanted to know my client's background and character and what impulses lay within him. Did he have a criminal record? Had he ever been treated for mental or emotional disturbances? What about his family? Was there any history of mental problems there? What did others say about Renard? How did he treat people? Who were his friends? What was he like when he got angry? What was his sexual history? What did his school records reveal? His birth records?

I meticulously studied the autopsy, medical, arrest and offense reports, statements of witnesses, including those of Renard and his girlfriend, and all the literature I could find pertaining to the type of person who could commit such a despicable and atrocious act. I needed to understand the types of injuries consistent with sexual abuse. I delved deeply into medical and legal concepts such as competency to stand trial and mental retardation, both very complex scientific areas. As lawyers, we rely on both the prevailing literature and the experts we locate and obtain to help us learn those aspects.

Every death penalty case involves intricate sociological and psychological factors, especially in regard to the penalty phase. American Bar Association (ABA) standards require capital lawyers to add appropriate mental health experts to the core team and to investigate the entire physical, mental and emotional history and background of not only the client but also three generations prior in regard to the client's development.[2] But the nature of Renard's defense in the first phase—the innocent-guilty phase—required me to explore intently not only the medical features of the case but the psychological factors as well.

All my life I have been fascinated by and studied the fields of psychology and psychiatry. When any case involves mental and psychological issues, I look at all issues that pertain to the case very carefully. I began my work by obtaining the funds to hire a death penalty mitigation investigator to obtain and compile records and information on Renard. After that, I got the records of the toddler, her mother and her mother's family and studied their histories.

As is common in many cases, the investigation may follow an obvious course, but the truth often hides in other directions not clearly visible at first. While Renard was a natural suspect, it did not make sense to me. By all accounts he was respectful, quiet and placid. He worked two jobs, maintained a close relationship with his mother and sister, didn't smoke, drink or use drugs and had no adversarial relationships or broken friendships that I could discern.

People said only positive things about him, cause enough for me to start wondering exactly what happened. He had displayed no violent tendencies during his twenty-eight years of life and had no criminal history, not even an isolated incident of bad temper flaring. His school records revealed no behavioral problems whatsoever, though they did present an issue that made Renard's adjustment into adulthood difficult: He tried to keep pace with his classmates and schoolwork, but a severe learning disability challenged him too much. At best, he read at a second-grade level.

The authorities fixated on the fact that neither Renard nor his girlfriend noticed any symptoms of illness with the baby during the day or in the early evening. According to at least one prosecution expert, they should have.

In my opinion, there were significant problems with the prosecution's case that warranted much more extensive investigation. Most significantly, Samella and Tamika lived in a small dwelling crowded with twelve other immediate and extended family members. Two of the residents were crack cocaine users, one of whom was known to have an explosive temper and showed no tolerance for the baby's constant colic-driven crying. Our investigation revealed the baby had been left home alone with this family member and several of his crack cocaine acquaintances on numerous occasions.

I also learned that Renard had never been alone with the baby except for this one occasion, so he could not have perpetrated the sexual trauma. The mother would have noticed bruising and possibly tearing, maybe even some dried blood, the next time she changed the baby's diaper. Scar tissue takes days and weeks to form, not a couple of hours. By comparing these two profiles—the violent crack user who had frequent access to the baby versus the placid man who babysat only once—I felt the prosecution had a weak case. Not only should capital murder be withdrawn, but any lesser charge as well.

As I uncovered this history, my concern for my client was partially eclipsed by my frustration with the prosecution's seeking the death penalty. When the wrong person is prosecuted in a capital murder case, the real killer remains free, as the investigation normally ceases at the moment of arrest. However, the actual killer, whoever he or she is, poses a real and present danger to society, especially in the sexual abuse and murder of a toddler. Furthermore, if the court *executes* the wrong person, it is dooming an innocent man.

The case was assigned to the Honorable Richmond Pearson. I believed Judge Pearson would truly be fair and impartial; he knew what it was like to overcome social disadvantages. In a case like this, the judge's insights would especially matter. However, the jury would determine the merits of the prosecution's case against Renard.

Contrary to public perception, lawyers do not choose juries. Instead, they "strike" jurors, which means that each side is given a set number of strikes or elimination options. After each side exercises their choices and eliminates the jurors they do not want, those who have not been struck (eliminated) by the prosecution or defense become sitting members of the jury.

In capital cases, such as Renard Pruitt's, lawyers in most jurisdictions also receive the opportunity to question jurors on their views regarding the death penalty and the publicity to which they have been exposed. This affords a much better opportunity to identify potential jurors who cannot reasonably consider both forms of punishment in the event of a capital murder conviction: life without the possibility of parole or the death penalty.

On July 24 we began to select a jury. In every jury selection, capital or non-capital, each side identifies some obvious strikes. When Renard's case began, one of the jurors was an obvious strike decision for us. This conservative Christian did not hesitate to make his biases known. We could tell that he was hostile to us from the way he answered our questions versus the easy way he related to the prosecutor. We rated him as a person to strike due to his general attitudes about the death penalty, even though he claimed that in a rare case he could consider a sentence of life without parole.

After both sides exhausted their strikes, the clerk called those not eliminated to be seated in the jury box. The juror we wanted to strike was one of those chosen. I looked up and could not believe my eyes. I glanced over at my expert jury consultant, who was assisting me in the strike process. *How did he get back into the box?* I wondered. As the man made his way to the jury box, I compounded my error. "Excuse me, Your Honor," I said as I stood up in dismay, "I struck that one."

Judge Pearson's clerk shook her head, conveying that I had not. To my disbelief, after reviewing our lists, we discovered the clerk was right. Somehow, this juror ended up in the wrong column. Even more unfortunate, he clearly had heard my inquiry. Our eyes locked. In my gut, I knew that the climb toward the summit of acquittal had just became steeper.

I understood that the challenge for the defense is even higher in a case where a child has been murdered. If we held back and failed to be just as aggressive in our presentation as we were in our investigation, we would lose before we started. In my opening statement, I did not hesitate to make promises that normally the defense may not want to make since the defense does not have burden of proof: "Members of the jury, I will guarantee you two things: this case will be very emotional, because it involves the death of an innocent child who was subjected to serious abuse in the mere twenty-two months she spent on this earth. And there sits her innocent young father who is hurting and hurting badly—not only because he has lost his child, but also because he is wrongfully accused of it. What fear is greater than losing one's child? Nothing could be worse than being falsely accused of it.

"Before I get into the week of December 13, I want to talk about Renard Pruitt, what the evidence will show you about him and how he ended up being wrongly charged.

"The evidence will be that Renard is a quiet young man who doesn't say a lot. He is soft-spoken, pleasant and passive. He treats people with kindness and respect. The prosecution will not be able to point to any violent actions in his past—no bad temper, no outbursts, no unkindness."

I pressed on. "Unfortunately, Renard is not well educated. When you read his handwritten statement you will see what the testing revealed—that he reads at a second grade level and his IQ is seventy-one. Yet even in that statement he gladly tried to write out for the police, Renard is clear: the baby was already not well when she was placed in his care for those brief hours. Even the detective will admit that Renard was charged because he was the last person with her and that their investigation stopped there. They did not presume Renard innocent. But you do and took an oath to do exactly that. Renard had no motive, no reason and no interest in his daughter's death, only her health."

Despite the significant snafu in the jury selection, the case tried well for us. We had to vigorously cross-examine the State's witnesses, especially its experts, and expose the fallacies in the prosecution's case so we could give Renard a chance at freedom.

Through cross-examination of the lead detective, we showed that crack cocaine users inhabited the house (corroborated by witness accounts) and that one particular addict constantly lost his temper and abused Tamika by screaming at her and striking her. We excoriated the detective for not following that lead and questioning or investigating the drug addict.

Through other witness testimony and school testing results, we managed to show that Renard could not have used the words the detective attributed to him when he typed out Renard's "statement" and that Renard could not have read and understood it. Through cross-examination of the State's pediatricians and pathologist, we demonstrated that Tamika's sexual injuries predated Renard's night alone with the child.

Medical records revealed that the bruises on Tamika's face, forehead and chest occurred four to eight days before the night of her death. The lacerations to her vaginal and anal area were inflicted more than thirty days before her death.

Samella, Tamika's mother, stated under oath that Renard had never been alone with the baby until that night. She confirmed that Renard was pleasant and quiet and she had neither seen nor heard of him ever losing his temper.

Renard could not have committed these vicious acts, because he had never been alone with Tamika until then. After hearing the medical testimony from experts including the State's pathologist, Judge Pearson dismissed the sexual abuse charges but left the capital murder charge for the jury to determine.

As the jury deliberated I felt a queasy feeling in the pit of my stomach that at least one, if not more, of the jurors wanted to convict Renard, likely the juror we wanted to eliminate. In the end, they were hopelessly deadlocked. Nine people voted to acquit Renard, while three voted for a guilty verdict of manslaughter. The juror we were concerned about was one of the three holding out. No juror voted for a capital murder conviction.

The judge called a mistrial. Sadly, Renard would remain in jail to await another trial.

I sought bail for Renard, although he probably would be unable to make even a small amount, due to his poverty. However, I knew the wheels of justice would churn slowly to a second trial date. I had to try.

The purpose of bail is to accomplish two goals. The first is to protect society from a dangerous person. The second purpose is to guarantee the appearance of the charged person for all court proceedings.

Nine members of a jury who had heard all of the evidence voted to acquit Renard and the three jurors who voted to convict settled on manslaughter. The severity of manslaughter is below that of capital murder. I believed Renard was entitled to bail, even though he was charged with a capital offense.

However, Judge Pearson denied bail. We appealed his decision through the appellate courts. Ultimately, the Alabama Supreme Court ordered Judge Pearson to issue written findings by a set date. Judge Pearson ordered another hearing. Before the hearing, I met with the deputy district attorney, Mike Anderton, and requested that he stand silent and leave bail up to the court. He agreed.

At the hearing, the deputy DA honored his word and left the bail issue entirely up to the court. Suddenly, Judge Pearson changed course. In a stunning moment unprecedented in my experience, he announced that not only would he grant Renard bail, but also he would allow Renard to sign his own bail, known as a recognizance bond. For several years since his arrest, Renard had been denied bail completely. Now he was free on bail simply on the good faith of his own signature and his promise to attend all future court proceedings, which he did.

Judge Pearson, as usual, found a way to do the right thing.

I think everyone was tired of litigating Renard Pruitt's case. The prospect of preparing for a second trial was now approaching and one jury, despite the member we'd been so concerned about, had already almost acquitted Renard. After several negotiations, we entered a guilty plea to reckless manslaughter. The court accepted the plea bargain and sentenced Renard to serve a few more months in prison, followed by probation.

Renard entered a "best interest" plea as authorized by the United States Supreme Court Case of *North Carolina v. Alford*.[3] That case allows a person to plead guilty without admitting actual guilt if he intelligently finds it is in his best interest. While confident of our chances at the second trial, one never knows the future decision of the next twelve strangers sworn to do justice. Renard could have ended up with manslaughter and a twenty-year sentence. Or the jury could have hung again. And if things went really wrong, Renard still faced the death penalty. The risk versus reward was simply not there.

The Renard Pruitt case finally concluded. He and his mother stay in touch with our office. My legal assistant, Meredith Gray, calls

Renard periodically to see how his life is going. Since his trial, Renard has married and held the same job for over ten years. He works hard, tends to his family and remains a very grateful client.

I have never forgotten the reason Renard was charged in the first place: He was the last person to be seen with Tamika. Renard had no violent past nor reason to hurt his tiny child, although others did. Renard faced the death penalty. I am not really sure how aware Renard was as to how close he came to it. As with police officers, when a baby is the victim, jurors are looking to punish someone.

I deeply regretted our mistake during jury selection. Fortunately, our investigation kept Renard from the death penalty and saved me from many sleepless nights. Had we not located the records of the baby's prior injuries, we would have had no defense. Had we not learned from witnesses the violent nature of the crack users living in the apartment, the jury would have had nowhere else to look except to Renard. And Renard would have landed on death row.

16

THERE BUT FOR
THE GRACE OF GOD

Larry Whitehead was arrested on charges that he had been stealing from his former employer, a food packager. The State claimed that Whitehead had skipped work for eleven months while someone else clocked him in. Since Whitehead was a habitual offender under Alabama law, he knew the judge could sentence him to life in prison if he was convicted. The State's case depended almost entirely upon the testimony of Detective Andy Whitten, who had extracted pay records and somewhat of an admission of guilt from Whitehead. As the trial approached, Whitehead became increasingly anxious.

Just thirty-two, Whitehead's attorney Shannon Mitchell wore his light brown hair neatly trimmed and possessed an average height and build, along with a pleasant smile. He looked, sounded and acted like a small town guy and was raised by quality parents. When I met him, he had been a practicing lawyer for a little more than five years in Boaz, Alabama, which at that point had a population of around 7,400 people. Mayor Tim Walker described it "as a city of possibilities."[1]

Most of Shannon's practice consisted of real estate closings. However, like most small town lawyers, he accepted just about any case that paid the bills, including minor criminal matters. Newly married to a lovely young lady and respected in his community, Shannon's world appeared nearly perfect. Life clicked along assuredly without any foreboding signs that it would soon collapse.

In an attempt to ease his client's anxiety, Shannon Mitchell explained to Whitehead that the State had no case without Detective Whitten's testimony. Shortly before his trial date, Whitehead recruited two young men, Matthew Hyde, who was seventeen, and Stephen Brookshire, twenty-six, to help him murder Detective Whitten. The three men drove together to the detective's home. Whitehead and Brookshire waited in the car while Hyde knocked on Whitten's front door. As soon as Detective Whitten opened it, Hyde killed him with one shot to the chest.

Whitehead had no means of paying his two young and gullible associates for their part in the senseless killing. However, he told them that once Detective Whitten was dead, he would win his case and sue his former employer for millions of dollars for maliciously prosecuting him. He promised his cohorts that he would split the millions with them. Whitehead also told them that his attorney, Shannon Mitchell, engineered the whole scheme and would handle the lawsuit.

Malicious prosecution cases rarely succeed even when justified. If Whitehead won his case and sued for malicious prosecution, he would have to prove that he was prosecuted *without probable cause* and that it caused him extreme financial and emotional damage. Although the general public would not know the daunting odds of such filings, any lawyer, prosecutor or judge learns this in law school. Even if the doubtful case ever got to a jury, the lawsuit would be totally worthless once it was discovered that Whitehead won his case because someone murdered the lead detective, . No lawyer, even the greediest and most careless, would touch such a frivolous suit. No evidence would exist to prove the original charges were unfounded and no jury would pay a previously convicted felon serious money under such circumstances, especially one who had confessed.

As in many senseless and tragic murder cases, the perpetrators could not keep quiet about their dastardly deeds. Something in the human spirit, maybe a sense of guilt, perhaps some desire to be punished, often creates a need to discuss one's darkest secrets. In this case,

Stephen Brookshire, the least culpable of the coconspirators, bragged to some friends. Word drifted back to the investigators from local informers. The authorities interviewed Brookshire, who had driven the getaway car and quickly began to cooperate with the authorities, and the other individuals to whom he had bragged. The investigation then led to Larry Whitehead, the mastermind, and Hyde, the shooter. The investigators also interviewed Whitehead's brother. However, when asked about who planned it and why, no one could tell the detectives anything other than the preposterous lie that Larry Whitehead told them about Shannon Mitchell and the fictitious potential lawsuit.

The authorities approached Mitchell to learn what, if anything, he knew about Whitehead's involvement. When the authorities informed him of Detective Whitten's death, Shannon found himself in a regrettable "catch-22." The first thing he did was call the office of the Alabama State Bar. Based upon his conversation with an attorney who worked for the bar, Shannon concluded that he could not disclose past communications made to him by Whitehead without facing disbarment for violating the attorney-client privilege.[2] While an attorney may disclose information that a client tells him of a future crime he plans to commit, the attorney cannot discuss communication involving a *past* crime. On the other hand, if Shannon refused to disclose his communications with Whitehead, the investigating officers, who were close with Detective Whitten, would probably not understand Shannon's dilemma and suspect that he had something to hide. They could conclude that he had orchestrated this horrific murder.

Unfortunately, Shannon naively underestimated the intense underlying emotions experienced by law enforcement in regard to police killings. He pointedly told the authorities that the attorney-client privilege prevented him from disclosing confidential communications between him and his client, Whitehead. When Shannon refused to disclose these confidential communications with the authorities, they became furious. With tempers flying and emotions and pain escalating, the investigators focused on Shannon as a suspect, notwithstanding that nothing in Shannon Mitchell's background suggested he would ever take part in such an atrocity.

As law enforcement began to target Shannon as the ringleader, friends, family and associates of Whitehead began to devise a plan to help Whitehead.

Appropriately, the local judges and the district attorney's office removed themselves from the case, as often happens when prominent citizens in small locales are accused of crimes. The attorney general of the State of Alabama appointed David Whetstone, a multi-talented district attorney from a county on the Alabama coast, to prosecute Shannon. Soon after, the grand jury indicted Shannon for capital murder and conspiracy to commit capital murder of a law enforcement officer. An absurd figment of a desperate criminal's imaginative scheme had unleashed an avalanche of devastating injustice and it had come crashing down upon a completely innocent person, his family and friends.

Fortunately for Shannon, Judge Samuel Monk was appointed to try the case.[3] An exceptionally bright legal scholar and respected jurist, Judge Monk accepted the challenge without hesitation. Though such motions rarely succeed, Judge Monk granted our change of venue motion and moved the trial to Anniston from Marshall County.

In most capital cases, the court declares the accused indigent. The lawyer for the accused then must beg judges for expenses to hire experts and investigators to prepare the case adequately for trial. Even then, the defense will often only obtain a minuscule portion of the funds needed to mount an effective defense. In this case, however, Shannon had friends and family rushing to his aid.

Shannon began assembling his defense team. He first retained Doug Jones, a former Assistant United States Attorney and successful trial lawyer. Shannon then hired me, because of my experience in defending capital murders. He also hired Randy Brooks, an experienced and exceptionally talented lawyer, after we convinced the court to change the venue to Anniston, where Randy practices.

Over the years I have represented many individuals charged with violent offenses; many of them carried the death penalty. However, attorney Shannon Mitchell was unlike anyone I had ever represented.

American history contains only a handful of cases in which the prosecution has charged a respected lawyer with capital murder.

Consequently, press coverage quickly mushroomed to an intense level. Much of the press (though not all) assumed the worst about Shannon Mitchell. Some superficial veneer of credibility to these ridiculous allegations apparently stemmed from the fact that the killer had murdered a respected police detective. The State sought the death penalty ferociously. We knew that innocence offered no immunity from Alabama's electric chair, "Yellow Mama."

Our jury psychologist, Allen Shealy, assisted us in the motion for change of venue and worked with us to formulate a mock trial. To assemble mock jurors, we contacted the local unemployment office and hired a group of out-of-work people. We also commissioned law students and their friends to serve as witnesses. At the mock trial, which we videotaped, I acted as prosecutor and Doug Jones was the mock lawyer for the defense.

The mock jury found Shannon Mitchell not guilty in less than fifteen minutes and I questioned my memory of success as a prosecutor. But it wasn't that I performed poorly as a mock prosecutor; rather, the "jurors" saw the absurdity of the State's case. Would a real jury in the actual case reach the same conclusion?

The jury pool in Anniston drew heavily from the local Army base, Fort McClellan. The intense publicity had not yet poisoned the jury pool, although it heated up immensely as the trial approached. After all, someone had murdered a police officer at his home in the dead of night and that case presented enormous problems for any defense. However, the views of each of the potential jurors in regard to the death penalty would be of primary concern in a pool disproportionately filled with military personnel, especially with a highly regarded police detective as the victim.

At jury selection, we posed the question, "How many of you would always vote for the death penalty if you found a person guilty of intentionally killing someone such as a law enforcement officer?" In response, more people in the jury pool raised their hands than I had ever seen. For a juror to be qualified, he or she must be able to consider both the death penalty and life without parole as alternative punishments should the jury convict the accused of capital murder.

After a week of back and forth questions and answers, many potential jurors reluctantly stated that they could consider both forms of punishment. The court qualified them. However, the court disqualified a large number of African-American jurors, along with a few Caucasians, because they could not consider the death penalty under any circumstances. We ended up with what the law calls a "death qualified" jury, as each of the sitting jurors expressed affirmatively that he or she could impose the death penalty. Among the twelve were several former military personnel and those still connected to the Army base.

From the moment opening statements began, the trial erupted emotionally. Like bloody fireworks, it kept exploding. The courtroom atmosphere thickened with each witness, beginning with the escalating sobs of Detective Whitten's widow and then the uncontrollable ones of the lead investigator, who had been Detective Whitten's lifelong best friend. I could understand why he would want to participate personally in the investigation, but that kind of emotional involvement would make it very challenging for anyone to be entirely objective. Not only was Detective Whitten deeply loved and respected in his community, he was also the son of a beloved former longstanding county sheriff. Furthermore, the killers had gone to Detective Whitten's home, where Matthew Hyde shot him fatally with a .380 automatic just as Whitten opened his front door.

Every day, spectators packed the courtroom for this highly dramatic and emotional trial of an attorney facing the death penalty.

The prosecution called witnesses to attempt to prove Shannon Mitchell had orchestrated the murder of a well-respected and honored police detective. We cross-examined them exhaustively. Each witness who offered incriminating evidence implicating Shannon had tried to cut a deal in exchange for his testimony and no witness was able to testify consistently with statements previously made to and recorded by law enforcement. Moreover, some of the witnesses who had cut deals also dealt drugs and sported extensive criminal histories. During Brookshire's cross-examination, he admitted that the prosecution had offered him twenty-five years for a plea to felony murder rather than a capital murder charge and a sentence of life without the possibility of parole. We fought hard to expose the lies or biases we believed existed in the testimony of each of the witnesses.

The prosecution called Larry Whitehead's brother to the stand. He told the jury that he had overheard Shannon plan the murder and explain the lawsuit proposition to Larry. On cross-examination, the brother admitted that he faced twenty-five pending theft charges and wanted the district attorney's office to dismiss those charges in exchange for his testimony. Shortly before trial, we had obtained a letter the brother had written to the DA's office. I showed the brother the letter, which the judge admitted into evidence. In it, the brother not only asked for his charges to be dismissed but also requested other remunerations, including a new car at the expense of the DA's office!

At one point during my cross-examination of Whitehead's brother, he asked me how I knew it was him who had made prior inconsistent statements, since only his initials appeared on the transcript. I asked him if he would like to hear himself on the tape which I had in my coat pocket. He then readily admitted it was him. In fact, he had no compunction whatsoever in admitting all of his past theft convictions except one that involved stealing chickens; clearly offended, he angrily denied that he would resort to that low degree of thievery.

Nevertheless, the problem we continually faced was the charge of conspiracy to commit murder. Conspiracy counts can be conviction traps, because of the dragnet evidence law that allows a prosecutor to use hearsay statements against the accused that he may have known nothing about, nor would have approved if he did. In this case, the prosecution brought in witnesses who testified that they heard other alleged coconspirators make statements that they claimed Shannon had made about planning the murder. Fortunately, Judge Monk limited those statements, but plenty got into evidence and there was no way we could disprove what these liars had said.

When the State rested its case, each juror carried the testimony and emotions from Detective Whitten's law enforcement family, with little sympathy for the young, good-looking lawyer defendant. If the jurors believed that Shannon had told Whitehead that without the detective's testimony he would walk, they might be tempted to convict

Shannon anyway, without fully appreciating the foolishness of this fictitious motive forming the State's theory of intent.

Some would say, "The bigger the lie and the more absurd, the less people tend to question it." Though we felt the State's case consisted of nothing, the lies kept coming. I began to feel an achy fear in the pit of my stomach that the jury would convict Shannon.

David Whetstone's forceful courtroom style suited this prosecution perfectly. After his moving, passionate and eloquent closing, I might have considered a guilty verdict myself if I had sat on that jury. As he so powerfully put it, "words can hurt," and in this case they helped kill Detective Andy Whitten. If the jurors acquitted a young, brash, financially well-situated attorney, they would disappoint the devastated family of a slain police officer. Whetstone's argument rang the sonorous tone of a requiem: dark, appealing and lethal.

Doug Jones and I split the closing argument. We both empathized with the excruciating pain and deep, unexplainable loss inflicted upon the family of Detective Whitten and the entire community. We stressed the fine reputation of Shannon and his family and the fact that each incriminating State's witness was a convicted felon, a drug dealer or a proven liar—in some cases all three. We conveyed to the jury the compounded tragedy that would result from convicting an innocent young man trapped within the confines of the sacred attorney-client privilege. Doug argued that the prosecution had called a patently ridiculous "parade of stars" to convict a well-respected lawyer. I argued that Whitehead was a "drug-crazed con man" whose desperation to avoid prison led to the murder of a beloved and respected member of the law enforcement community.

Following closing arguments, Judge Monk called a "charge conference" to consider whether to add any additional items proposed by the respective sides to his instructions to the jury. We proposed several, but desperately needed one in particular: one legally defining an "intervening cause." Randy Brooks led the arguments to convince the judge to instruct the jury on the law in that regard. We begged the judge to instruct that Shannon would not be guilty if Whitehead and others had devised their own scheme to kill Detective Whitten. Their subsequent scheme would be the intervening cause. Special Attorney General Whetstone vociferously argued against the court giving the jury our requested charge. Judge Monk retired alone to his chambers. After what seemed an interminable deliberation, he emerged from his chambers and announced he had decided to instruct the jury in accordance with our request.

The jury began deliberating early in the afternoon. The defense team of Jones, Brooks and I felt only deep fear and exhaustion. Not only did we represent an innocent man with whom we had grown very close, we felt the grim prospect of facing Shannon's family if the jury convicted him and sentenced him to death looming agonizingly close. How would we ever explain this loss to the many lawyers and legal organizations that would review our work, with the evidence so thin and the State's theory, in our opinion, so weak?

During deliberation, we adjourned to a local fast food restaurant with investigators and support staff. At a large table we tried to eat. Derek Drennan, my law clerk then and soon to be my newest associate, sat to my left. We were sick with fright, much too tense to converse. Suddenly, Derek broke the silence. "I don't see what everybody is so upset about. This case is ridiculous. There can only be one verdict and it is going to be not guilty. I just don't get all of you." All seven of us fixated upon Derek, glaring at him until he shrank back into his chair. We could not believe his comment, as the rest of us were terrified. If looks could kill, Derek would have been another victim at that moment.

Finally, at 9 P.M., after seven hours of deliberation, the jury returned its verdict. From behind, I watched Doug Jones' gloomy, forlorn walk as we filed into the courtroom to await the pronouncement of the verdict. Somehow I refused to believe that this jury would convict Shannon Mitchell of capital murder or any other form of homicide.

The jurors would not look our way but had sad faces. Generally, when jurors will not face the defendant or his lawyers, we expect the worst. The jury had elected a middle-aged career military man as its foreperson. Next to him sat another military man, probably in his late twenties. Lawyers constantly speculate during jury deliberations over which jurors seem to be leaning for or against us. We had been certain that the younger of the two men hated us; he seemed to glare at us and at Shannon throughout the trial.

The foreperson sounded reluctant when reading the verdict, one that softly filled our ears with the world's sweetest words: not guilty on each count. The courtroom erupted into shouts of glee.

Later that evening there was a party at the home of Shannon Mitchell's family. For Doug Jones, Randy Brooks and me, the time allowed us the space to finally breathe with the kind of heart-pounding relief that occurs when waking up from a terrible nightmare. It did not escape any of us that we could not ask the real hero in this case, Judge Samuel Monk, to attend the party. Had he refused to give the jury charge on "intervening cause," it may well have convicted Shannon. The seemingly small, subtle details in many trials form the tightrope between life and death upon which the accused unknowingly walks.

During the weeks following the verdict, we tried to speak to the jurors. Only one would talk to us. Shockingly, we learned that one particular juror, whom we thought had been for us, had voted guilty initially, as did seven others. Meanwhile, the young man whom we thought despised us had held this juror's hand in prayer and taught him about reasonable doubt and the presumption of innocence. He somehow convinced this juror and then the others that regardless of the emotions and deep sympathies involved, the law required a not guilty verdict; no proof or reason supported the prosecution's theory. The evidence originated from desperate killers and liars who cut deals to save themselves. Sadly, the senseless killing of a police officer and Shannon Mitchell's invoking of the attorney-client privilege almost catapulted him onto death row.[4]

Now, over fifteen years later, Shannon continues to practice law in the same community, his home since childhood. He holds his head up but has never forgotten the two years of hell he lived, the forty-five pounds he shed and the loss of Detective Whitten, who, coincidentally, was a distant relative. Every Thanksgiving, Shannon sends me a special handwritten note, saying the same thing he told Doug Jones, Randy Brooks and me throughout our representation of him: "Thank you for being my lawyer."

17

MONTGOMERY
MEETS HIS MATCH

After staking out a motel for several days, narcotics officers stormed two of the rooms and arrested Nathaniel Jones for drug offenses and being a fugitive from justice in Texas. No one suspected for an instant that politics, money and mysterious deaths waited in the wings of an upcoming, panoramic parade of explosive events.

After posting bail, Jones was transferred to Jefferson County, Alabama, to await action from the State of Texas. He was charged with being a Texas fugitive. As is customary, the judges in Jefferson County refused to set bond in the case of a fugitive from justice.

Jones tried to reach me by phone from the county jail, but I was deep in the middle of a capital murder trial forty-five miles north of Birmingham.

My then-partner, Roger Burton, took the call and began to focus on the client's utmost concern: getting out of jail on bond. However, my normally smooth, easygoing and persuasive colleague could not get Nate out in spite of repeated requests. The presiding jurist, Judge Jack Montgomery, told Roger that nothing could make him change his mind; Nate was not going to get a bond in his court.

Unexpectedly, the following morning Nate called Roger and told him that bail was no longer a problem, because arrangements had already been made. When Roger inquired how Nate had arranged for bail after his own persistent yet unsuccessful attempts, Nate replied that bail bondsman Warren King, along with another lawyer, had contacted Judge Montgomery, who agreed to set a reasonable bail as long as Roger showed up in court that morning.

When I heard this, all I could think was, *Is this the real Jack's Law?* This time his antics surpassed his erratic conduct on and off the bench over the years. The scenario that unfolded demonstrated how far one can stray once one walks an inch down the path of corruption.

Roger had no idea what to think. He had never heard of such a development in his thirteen years of law practice, but he showed up, as requested, in Judge Montgomery's court. The judge treated Roger differently from before. He set bail at the low amount of five thousand dollars and told Nate Jones to "stay in close touch" with the bail bondsman. Nate was free to go. A memo Roger wrote for the case file revealed that he detected something suspicious.

When I first met with Nate Jones at my office, I was taken aback by this huge man, apparently a former football player in his thirties, over six feet tall and weighing close to 250 pounds. He was dressed in a brown leather jacket, gold silk shirt, blue jeans and expensive shoes. Upon my prodding, he related the events of the past two weeks. As I listened to the unusual saga, I felt a cold, sick sensation in my stomach and I grew sad and scared. My sadness grew from my conclusion: I now believed that Judge Montgomery was "on the take." His sudden change of heart hinted at the depths of his corruption. I was scared, because if our suspicions were correct, we were representing a person who had bribed a judge.

How would we proceed? Should we withdraw as Nate's attorneys? Should we confront our client? What if he denied it? What if he *admitted* it? We would then be in possession of confirmed information that Birmingham's most well-known judge had accepted a bribe from our client, which is public corruption, not to mention a federal criminal offense. If, in fact, Nate had bribed the judge and admitted it to me, professional ethics would prevent me from disclosing anything he said to me because of attorney-client privilege. Recall that an attorney can be disbarred and lose his license to practice law if he breaks attorney-client privilege.[1]

The philosophy justifying the attorney-client privilege also resonates at the core of our criminal justice system. A client has to be totally confident that he can trust his attorney, without reservation or hesitation. The government, with all its resources and power, threatens to destroy the client's world. A person facing this awesome onslaught can only receive adequate representation and an opportunity for a fair trial if he feels safe to disclose fully every detail, even the sordid or less flattering ones, to the lawyer who defends him.

The proof that the system is far from compromised by the attorney-client privilege can be found by examining over two hundred years of trials and corresponding statistics: over 90 percent of those charged with criminal offenses either pleaded guilty before trial or were convicted outright. Questionable cases do not result in an initial guilty plea and are tried before juries in the courtroom. There, the conviction rates at trial are also very high: more than 90 percent in federal courts.

However, as previously noted, the attorney-client privilege does not prevent an attorney from revealing client's secrets if the client discloses he intends to commit a *future* criminal act. When that happens, the attorney may disclose such information for the protection of future crime victims and society.

Nate Jones and I went over the particulars. Officers arrested him after they searched the two motel rooms he had rented in his name, as well as automobiles parked outside the motel. The officers found cocaine in one of the rooms. Agents seized eighteen thousand dollars in cash from one of the automobiles. Whether Jones could get this money returned would depend on whether it came from a legitimate source or the fruits of unlawful activity.

Large amounts of cash indicate possible suspicious activity. When found in conjunction with illicit substances, the law requires that the owner demonstrate the money came from legitimate sources. That can be difficult. If Jones could show that the money came from his clothing business or the athletes he supposedly represented as a sports agent, he'd likely get it back.

Our meeting lasted around an hour and a half. At this point, I still did not fully understand the strange circumstances that had led to Judge Montgomery's sudden decision to reverse his ruling and set such a low bail amount. On five thousand dollars bail, a bail bondsman would charge only five hundred dollars (10 percent) to arrange a client's release, a paltry amount for being an alleged fugitive from justice. I was convinced, though, that Nate possessed a razor-sharp mind, was very articulate and showed no fear about anything, including the criminal charges he faced.

Nate's next court appearance was scheduled for January 6. I appeared for the first time on behalf of Nate in Montgomery's court. After court, I often write memos to the file. That day, I wrote:

> It was clear that something was up in Judge Montgomery's court. When he found out I was representing Nate Jones, he said he wanted to see Jones' face. He then allowed Jones to get very smart with him, in a way that he normally did not let anybody act. He said at least three times—and laughed when he said it—that Nate needed to see his bondsman and square him up since Nate had already paid large amounts of money. This sounded very strange. Montgomery also backtracked regarding the bond, trying to say that it wasn't he who set that five thousand dollar bond but, ultimately, the magistrate. In my opinion, this is a bunch of hogwash. Montgomery set Jones' fugitive case for June 30 at 10:00. He acted and made statements that he really wanted this to go away, which is strange.

"Strange" would be an understatement. Montgomery never let anyone show him up in his court. Also, judges typically have no reason to concern themselves with the bail bondsman's fee. My burning instinct that Montgomery was on the take was fueled by the way he looked at Nate, followed by an odd-sounding laughter I'd never heard out of Judge Montgomery's mouth in thirteen years of appearing in his courtroom.

Over the next several months, I only saw Nate Jones once or twice. The only way I could get in touch with him was through his ex-wife. However, one day, after leaving a court hearing, I headed to the elevator and came face-to-face with Warren King, the bail bondsman. Flashy, loud and boisterous, King normally decked himself out in silk shirts and loaded his fingers with huge diamond rings and his wrists and neck with gold chains. Over six feet tall and above two hundred pounds, he oozed with energy and confidence. He was quite a contrast to his deceased father, a mild man whose integrity no one ever questioned. King's father had started the bail bondsman business that Warren took over upon his father's death.

"Hey, man." Warren King stopped me in my tracks. "I need to talk with you."

"About what?" I knew it could only be about Nate Jones.

King held the elevator door open for me with his hand. Instead of walking into the elevator, I asked him to wait for a moment. I noticed an empty attorney conference room a few feet away. I stepped into it quickly, yanked open my briefcase and found a handheld recorder I carried for preliminary hearings, in case a court reporter did not show up. I placed it in the breast pocket of my suit jacket and pressed the "record" button. Quickly I returned to the elevator. King had moved to a corner of the hallway.

"Now, what do you want to talk to me about, Warren?" I inquired.

"Your client, Nate. He owes me five thousand. Tell him he needs to pay me. I want to help that boy, but he's got to get right."

"Five thousand dollars?" My surprise was evident. "For what? How could he owe you five thousand if his bail is only five thousand in the first place? If he owes you anything, it shouldn't be over five hundred dollars—ten percent."

King mumbled something about a loan. He ended the conversation by telling me to make sure that Nate called him, as his court date was not too far away.

Back at my office, I placed the small cassette in an envelope and attached it to Nate's case file. The time had come for me to press Nate Jones.

Shortly before the June 30 court date, I confronted Nate with the guts of the conversation between King and me. I told Nate that I felt a strong need to go to the FBI, as I had information that I felt concerned a continuing criminal act. Nate dispelled that notion, stating he had no intention of paying one more dime. He knew the scope of the attorney-client privilege and how it protected his conversations with me, as long as they pertained to past acts. If he had no intention of paying King and Montgomery in the future, he had no plans to commit a future criminal act. I could not ethically report his conduct to the bar association or the authorities. My hands felt uncomfortably tied.

As the hearing loomed closer, I grew increasingly more uncomfortable, as if a vise had seized my brain, squeezing it tighter and tighter. The only way for Nate to protect himself was to record King asking for more money. Then I could convince him to go to the FBI. Unbeknownst to Judge Montgomery, he had met his match in Nate Jones, a more stubborn, smarter and brasher man. I felt in the middle of the standoff between these two men as Nate's court date grew closer.

Nate left town and did not commit to recording a conversation with King. Judge Montgomery postponed Nate's case until sometime in September, probably at King's request. True to his word, Nate never intended to pay the rest of the bribe money. He had engaged in a high-stakes game: Montgomery and King wanted the rest of the bribe money and they held over Jones' head the possibility of revoking his bond, even though no legal justification existed. In the meantime, I hoped that Nate would either capture King's implication on tape or give me permission to visit the FBI.

Shortly before the next hearing, at Nate's request, I called Judge Montgomery's secretary and asked that she approach the judge to continue the case. She said it should be no problem. However, only a few minutes after my call, she called back apologetically and reported that Judge Montgomery "went ballistic" when presented with my request for a continuance. She expressed real surprise, not understanding the judge's explosion when he heard my request.

In denying Nate's motion to continue, Judge Montgomery had created a showdown. Someone would blink or be shot down. But Nate had no intention of blinking. Instead, he waived the attorney-client privilege and authorized me to go to the FBI. Judge Montgomery had pressured the wrong man; Nate would expose the judge, no matter the personal consequences for himself.

The potential implications of knowing that a judge was actively engaged in improper conduct made me want to be anywhere other than involved in this case.

Doug Jones arranged for me to meet the assistant United States attorneys already working the investigation. That meeting was perhaps the most nervous and scared I have ever been as a lawyer, including fifteen years earlier, when I gave my opening statement in my first murder case as a prosecutor in Tuscaloosa. When I met the team of government prosecutors, I was almost trembling. Would they understand that the attorney-client privilege had prevented me from going forward until then? Fortunately they all knew me and understood the pressure and constraints I faced. And I was relieved to discover that another lawyer had already come forward with his client, as had a local police officer.

Nate agreed to cooperate with the FBI investigation, headed by veteran Birmingham FBI agent Steve Brannon. Over the years, I'd dealt with Steve often and grew to admire him, professionally and personally. Nate trusted no one, including me. However, he learned to trust Steve Brannon.

That was the beginning of the end of Jack Montgomery's history of corruption.

A few days after Nate decided to cooperate with the FBI, I happened to be walking into the Jefferson County Jail to see a client in the late afternoon. As I made my way toward the sign-in cage, I came face-to-face once again with Warren King. As before, I excused myself, this time to go to the bathroom, and returned with my recorder turned on inside the breast pocket of my suit. Apparently still unpaid, King seized another opportunity to urge me to put Nate in touch with him. King talked doggedly and loudly about his urgent need to contact Nate. During his monologue, I noticed a person whom I did not recognize within a few feet of King, one who could clearly hear our conversation. I terminated it as quickly as I could, assuring King that I would get Nate to call him.

Too ruffled now to meet with my jailed client, I rushed out of the door to the courtyard and headed toward my car. That's when I noticed two men in a green sedan. One of them waved me over. As I walked to the car, I recognized the driver: the FBI's Steve Brannon. He motioned for me to get in the backseat and we sped off.

I began to tell them what had occurred inside the jail and that I had caught King on tape. Brannon looked at me and said he had heard the whole conversation, as the man near King was a government informer and was wearing a wire. I gave the agents my tape of the conversation. After cruising around for a while, Brannon drove me back to my car. Brannon told me, confidentially, that something "big" was going to come down within the next few days.

18

THE END OF JACK'S LAW

As a result of the information gained from an informant, Jones and the recorded meetings between them and King, the government obtained a court order authorizing a wiretap on Judge Montgomery's home. The wiretap captured at least two lawyers closely associated with Judge Montgomery allegedly discussing bail for bribes. One of these attorneys had already been convicted years before and sent to prison for allegedly lending his client a gun to obtain the attorney's unpaid legal fees. After five years and time for rehabilitation, he convinced bar association officials to reissue his license to practice law. The other lawyer told Montgomery during the wiretap that the judge had "five thousand good reasons" to help his client get out on bond. Ultimately, the government successfully prosecuted both lawyers and sent them to federal prison, along with the lawyer who originally arranged Nate Jones' bond.

But Brannon, not yet perceiving an airtight case, devised a plan to wire Nate Jones, mark thousands of dollars with invisible ink and have Nate pass it to King. Agents would then follow King, hopefully, to the judge's upscale home, and obtain a search warrant. If the search netted the marked money, the case would be practically airtight.

On October 22, FBI Agent Steve Brannon and other local and federal agents knocked on the front door of Judge Montgomery's residence.

After the judge invited them in, they displayed the search warrant. Judge Montgomery voluntarily opened his wall safe; the marked money and other cash were inside the safe and Judge Montgomery all but confessed to bribery.[1]

The news that the FBI had busted Judge Montgomery traveled fast. I viewed the local news that evening on at least three stations and saw reports on Montgomery on each. I was shocked as the stark reality of Judge Montgomery's resignation splashed across the airwaves. I could not escape from the thought that his actions had collectively sunk the legal community to which I belonged to his low level. For years we all had allowed the outrageous outbursts and antics of this irrational man to escalate, what we referred to as "Jack's Law."

Out of either fear or complacency, we unwittingly supported his seemingly intolerable behavior. Thus, we acquired some ownership that we now had to face in the remnants of his infamy. The distance we tried to place between him and us did not shroud our knowledge that we had allowed it to happen. We had shirked our duty to police our own. We had created a protective shield of encouragement that empowered the monsters and demons swirling inside Judge Montgomery.

Montgomery's lawyers wasted no time in strategizing an insanity defense. One psychiatrist diagnosed the judge with post-traumatic stress disorder, perhaps associated with trauma from serving as a prisoner of war. Judge Montgomery had often told people that he had escaped from an enemy prison camp where he was tortured. However, I do not think that any military records revealed that information and no one could be found to verify his war story.[2] In the meantime, the lawyers for both Warren King and the attorney who had negotiated Nate Jones' bail readied themselves for their individual trials in federal court for conspiracy, bribery, money laundering and a host of other related charges.

This saga had just begun.

Following Judge Montgomery's plea of not guilty by reason of mental disease or defect (insanity), the government responded by asserting that Montgomery was faking mental illness and that his bond should be revoked, as he could be a danger to society and to himself.

Federal Judge Sharon Blackburn presided over Montgomery's case. A former federal prosecutor, Judge Blackburn had established herself as a tough-minded, fair and thorough judge. She held a hearing on the government's motions to revoke Montgomery's bond and send him to FCC Butner, the main medical facility for the Federal Bureau of Prisons (BOP), for a mental and psychiatric evaluation.

Montgomery's lawyers argued that there was no reason to send Montgomery to Butner, since he was neither suicidal nor a danger to the community. Instead, they convinced Judge Blackburn to allow Montgomery to be evaluated as an outpatient and remain at his home in the care and custody of his wife. Judge Montgomery had recently married an attractive young lawyer who had appeared in his court on a number of occasions.

Not too long after the hearing, police officers found a ragged looking male crawling naked on the side of a road near Montgomery's home. It took only a short while for the officers to realize the man was Judge Montgomery himself. He appeared incoherent.

Meanwhile, the two lawyers associated with the bribery scandal were indicted, tried and convicted for charges involving the bribery of Judge Montgomery.

Ultimately, to almost everyone's surprise, Judge Montgomery decided to enter a guilty plea. The court set his sentencing for February 14. Two days before the sentencing hearing, Montgomery's wife left their house for a few minutes to go to the grocery store. When she returned, she discovered her husband dead in their basement. An autopsy revealed one shot to the chest.

No one could explain why the weapon was never found.

19

A STRIKINGLY SIMILAR MURDER

Warren King, the bail bondsman who was charged with bribing Judge Montgomery, had been cooperating as a government witness against the judge and others. Known as "the King," as prominently displayed on his customized car tag, he could be electrifying with his energetic persona, flashy clothes and expensive jewelry. Just before his father, who founded the family bonding company, died, he had asked Judge Montgomery to "take care of my son." For that reason, Warren often called the judge "Dad."

However, once the FBI raided "Dad's" home and discovered the marked bribe money, King could not help but see his prospects of beating the rap diminish. He had agreed through his attorney to plead guilty and testify against Judge Montgomery and others in exchange for receiving a non-binding prosecution recommendation for a twelve-month prison sentence. Accordingly, after King entered the guilty plea, the court put off his sentencing hearing until the Judge's case had been concluded.

Now that Judge Montgomery was deceased, Warren King was in the hot seat. But King did not want to serve any time in federal prison. As King was leaving one night to go bowling, a regular Wednesday night routine for him, his longtime live-in girlfriend Regina Gratton heard him talking to his lawyer on his cell phone. As she was getting ready to go out to meet friends, the last words she heard Warren saying were, "What if I could give them some more names?" A pause followed and then he said, "You mean I may not have to do any time at all?"

With that, Warren King walked out the door, got in his car and headed for the bowling alley.

King and his girlfriend had been living together for several years. King presented an imposing figure as he ran adeptly between the court-rooms and the clerk's office, making bail for defendants and arguing for extra time with judges when someone did not show up for court in viola-tion of the bail agreement. If that person could not be found, the bonding company owed the amount the company guaranteed in exchange for the person being "free on bail," rather than waiting in jail for a trial or plea that might not take place for a year or longer.

As she entered the house after returning from her evening out, Regina noticed that the iron grill covering the front door was not fully shut. Understandably, King never left the front door unlocked. When Regina quietly slipped in, she noticed King apparently sleeping in his burgundy love chair, as he often did, with the TV on.

Minutes later, the phone rang and Regina answered it. It was a part-time employee of King's bonding company. The night before, King had planned to pick the man up at the bonding company, only a few blocks up the street. Someone had jumped bail and they had made plans to track the client and deliver him to the jail. Still on the phone, Regina nudged King to wake him up. He slumped over from his sitting position. She noticed "something shiny" on the left side of his head.

Looking closer, she recognized blood. She yelled into the phone, "Something bad is wrong with Warren. He's bleeding. Get over here!"

Regina hung up the phone, called 911 and then dialed her father, a very successful and respected man in the community. It only took a few short minutes for Warren's employee to arrive, along with King's mother, who often worked at the bonding company.

When the employee walked in, he fell to his knees. "Warren, Warren! Why? Why did you do it, man? It wasn't going to be that bad. It was only twelve months."

But Regina never believed King had taken his own life.

Soon the police and medics arrived. Like Warren's girlfriend, they suspected that Warren King had not committed suicide. Regina believed that King had allowed some person or persons he trusted into their home. That person shot him execution-style.

An autopsy confirmed that King was shot point-blank. The coroner fixed the time of death at approximately 1:30 A.M. Just as with Judge Montgomery's death hardly a month before, the police found no weapon at the crime scene. In addition, King's unique four-barrel "stacked" pistol could not be found.

The similarities between the King and Montgomery killings were striking. It still had not been determined if Judge Montgomery killed himself or was murdered. And Judge Montgomery, like Warren King, knew plenty about plenty of people.

Because both Montgomery and King faced federal charges of bribery and money laundering among other accusations, the FBI, the Birmingham Police Department and the Jefferson County Sherriff's Department conducted a joint investigation into the shootings. When the investigation revealed that Regina had actually pawned some of King's jewelry for crack on the night of his death and again a week or so afterward, she became even more of a potential suspect than a significant other naturally becomes in a possible homicide of his or her partner. Prompted to action by the intense publicity, Regina's father sent her to stay with family out of state to get away from the mounting pressures.

A few months after King's death, the authorities obtained a capital murder warrant for Regina. They brought her in the back of a paddy wagon to the Jefferson County Jail in Birmingham, where she would await trial. Her potential punishment? The death penalty.

Regina's father hired Doug Jones to represent her. Doug selected me as co-counsel due to my experience in death penalty cases. We faced an uphill battle, but we were already struck by the similarities between the Montgomery and King deaths. Both were shot once in their homes after guilty pleas were entered but before sentencing. Both were discovered by their significant others. No weapons were ever found.

There were several people with reasons to be concerned over what King and Montgomery could have told the FBI. During our subsequent investigation, we learned of King's efforts to provide additional information to the government about other individuals in the hope of avoiding prison entirely or at least sweetening his deal. Before he had the opportunity to sit down with FBI lead agent Steve Brannon and Birmingham lead detective Ken Glass and offer this supposedly new information, King was found dead, just like Montgomery. We also learned that prior to King's death the FBI had warned King's girlfriend that she (and possibly Montgomery's wife) could be in danger, based on threats that the FBI picked up on the street. Regina often stated that if she had not been out that night, she might have been killed too, because she would have been with King when he returned from bowling.

At first, King's mother refused to believe that Regina killed her son. Warren and his girlfriend had always seemed to get along fine in their several years of living together. Lately they'd talked about making it official and getting married after Warren returned from the expected twelve months he would serve in a federal prison camp. Regina would remain in their home until his release. In fact, King's girlfriend and mother were close and genuinely cared for each other.

Judge Alfred Bahakel set Regina's case for trial. She was now free on bond, because she had no criminal record, no history of violence and considerable family and community ties and support. Regina worked for her father and brother in the family's popular restaurant in downtown Birmingham, famous for its chicken wings. Regina always had a lucrative job there. But, motive or not, Regina pawned King's jewelry while on a crack binge. She left the state shortly after the murder. Upon her return, she gave four tape-recorded statements to law enforcement, full of lies about the missing jewelry as well as her whereabouts on the night of the murder.

She told law enforcement she did not know when King was shot. She tried to give herself an alibi for part of the night, when the simple truth would have served her better: that she was out on a crack binge and not home when someone with a real motive murdered King. Unfortunately, Regina's only alibi witnesses were crack addicts who had no inclination to testify on her behalf or about their drug-selling activities, which included exchanging crack for a man's jewelry of questionable ownership. They must have figured out it was King's after they learned someone had murdered him. None came forward voluntarily.

Regina told conflicting stories. For example, she told Agent Steve Brannon, who was working the case along with Birmingham lead detective Ken Glass, that she was with a wheelchair-bound girlfriend that night. The problem: she described an evening that had occurred several weeks before the murder. The agents found the woman and dispelled that lie.

Because state and federal authorities jointly investigated the case, we argued that the prosecution had an obligation to turn over FBI memos that we strongly believed would connect the Montgomery and King murders. Our theory of defense was that both Judge Montgomery and Warren King were killed because of information they could reveal to ensnare some prominent people. The deaths were just too similar in timing and method.

Finally we convinced the court to order that we be given the FBI memos. These files contained records of documented threats on King's life that were quite specific. One memo confirmed King's desperation to avoid prison and willingness to provide additional information about the corruption scandal. Other memos noted reported threats against certain people, including Regina, by contracted hit men. Another documented a call from a lawyer representing Judge Montgomery's wife to report a death threat that she had received.

Within a week of trial, the prosecutors provided a memo written by a senior official in the state prison system. It chronicled a conversation between the prison official and an inmate, Roger McCoy. This inmate told the prison official that he was in the neighborhood when King was killed and saw a guy he knew as "Cowboy" run from King's home after he, the inmate, heard a shot. Cowboy was running with a weapon wrapped in a towel. McCoy told the prison official that he saw Cowboy put these items in the trunk of his car. In his statement to the prison official, McCoy stated that he, Cowboy and Cowboy's girlfriend conversed briefly by Cowboy's car before the three left the scene. Subsequently, we subpoenaed both McCoy and Cowboy to testify.

McCoy was serving a twenty-five-year prison term for murder. He did not know Regina but did know and like King, who had made his bond before and was a family friend. He came forward with this information, because he claimed to know the real killer and it was not Regina. McCoy had no reason to lie or provide information that would require his testimony. Testifying had no upside for him but carried quite a downside. People in prison who testify in criminal cases risk their lives. He also knew he might jeopardize his chances for an early parole.

The prosecution and prison officials would also not be happy that he was testifying for the defense. There was nothing for him to gain and much to lose, which made him, in my mind, a very credible witness. Yet I worried about whether he could hold up to a vigorous cross-examination due to his mental limitations.

In our opening statements, we told the jury that Regina had no motive to kill Warren King, above all because of her love for him and reliance upon his financial support. We told the jury that Regina had pawned the jewelry because, at the time of the murder, she had been on a crack binge. We told them to expect the prosecution to play the recordings in which she had lied about her drug activities, which the prosecutors later did. They also produced a neighbor, a college student home for the summer who heard the shot from his home. He testified that the shot was so loud he went outside to investigate and saw three people standing next to his driveway, but they kept on talking as if nothing was wrong. He said he did not call the police, because shots were commonly heard in his neighborhood.

When it was our turn, we called Roger McCoy. He had graduated high school from a special education program but could neither read nor write and suffered from some mental problems. On direct examination, McCoy told the jury that after hearing a loud shot he witnessed Cowboy come from behind King's home. He saw Cowboy place the towel containing the weapon in his trunk. According to McCoy, Cowboy then told him, "You didn't see, hear or know nothing." McCoy testified that Cowboy was there with his girlfriend and described their clothing. He had also heard King's dogs.

I began to wonder if it was McCoy, Cowboy and Cowboy's girl-friend that the neighbor saw moments after the murder.

Unfortunately, our concerns about McCoy undergoing the cross-examination proved justified. McCoy possessed limited intellectual abilities. Along with his criminal record, that made him an easy mark for a skilled prosecutor to discredit. Prosecutor Laura Petro cross-examined him perfectly and discredited him, capturing minor inconsistencies between the statement he had volunteered to the prison official and his courtroom testimony.

The prosecution then called Cowboy to refute McCoy's testimony. Cowboy did not suffer from any intellectual deficits and made a very convincing witness for the prosecution in spite of his extensive criminal record, lengthy hair and street-worn clothes. He also possessed a likeable and somewhat charismatic personality. I am convinced that had we called him, he would not have been so believable. I have noticed for many years and said many times that jurors seem much more inclined to believe a State's witness than one called by the defense.

As it turned out, the jury believed Cowboy, although he had no alibi for the night of King's death. We also learned Cowboy had a close relationship with one of the lawyers caught on the wiretap of Judge Montgomery's home phone—the lawyer who told the judge he had "five thousand good reasons" to approve a bond for his client.

The jury deliberated for several days but was unable to reach a unanimous verdict. Judge Bahakel declared a mistrial. The case would have to be retried.

Afterward, our investigator conducted interviews with the jurors who would agree to talk to him. We learned that no juror voted to convict Regina of capital murder or any form of intentional killing. They were divided between not guilty and manslaughter. Apparently, several jurors believed that other people held much greater motive to kill King. To our dismay, several really liked Cowboy!

On April 14 of the following year, we began jury selection for Regina's second trial, but my eighty-nine-year-old father, who had been sick, was rushed to the hospital that morning. Judge Bahakel asked me if I wanted to postpone the trial by a continuance. I did not, since every time a case is reset, you have to prepare it all over again, because it ceases to be fresh. However, I felt that my father might not make it this time, so Judge Bahakel dismissed the jury panel and reset the trial. My dad died in my arms at the hospital two days later.

Finally, a few months later, we started Regina's second trial, the prosecution's second attempt to convict her and subject her to the death penalty. As in the first trial, we used jury consultant psychologist Allen Shealy and a jury questionnaire. Again, it took nearly a week to obtain a jury that we thought would view the evidence fairly and consider the alternative punishment of a life sentence without the possibility of parole if the jury convicted Regina of capital murder.

After Regina's first trial, we reassessed our defense. From the juror interviews, we learned they did not believe the mentally challenged Roger McCoy, who came forward for no other reason than he considered it the right thing to do. Since the prosecution in the first trial discredited him, we decided not to call him again as a witness. Nonetheless, we still presented our theory linking the Montgomery and King killings but without McCoy as a witness. The prosecution also refrained from calling Cowboy to refute him.

The second trial went well for Regina. The jury began another long deliberation. While they deliberated, we stayed on the edge of our seats in the courtroom for several days, nervously questioning our decision not to call McCoy as a witness. We also fretted over our decision to advise Regina not to testify in her own behalf. Doug Jones and I had hotly debated that point many times, with Doug leaning toward calling her.

For a couple of days the jury continued to deliberate. While it is not unusual to hear loud voices during a long deliberation, we heard continuous screams that never seemed to let up, like a torrential rain unmercifully beating on a tin roof. Although we heard some female voices, we could readily identify the loudest as coming from two or more males. We felt things were not looking promising, so we began speaking to Judge Bahakel about declaring a mistrial. We did not want the very aggressive males to overpower jurors who conscientiously viewed the case as lacking proof and, therefore, had reasonable doubt.

But Judge Bahakel seemed determined that this jury continue its deliberation. The prospect of trying this case a third time, which would be necessary if the jury hung again, appeared dismal.

Voices quieted within the jury deliberation room. Suddenly we heard a loud knock on the door. One of Judge Bahakel's bailiffs opened the door to ascertain if the jury had reached a verdict. Instead, he returned with a note and brought it to the judge, who shared the note with the lawyers. Two jurors were holding out for not guilty. One wrote a note urgently asking the judge to summon his personal lawyer immediately, respected former prosecutor Kay Laumer. Having declared himself gay during jury selection, the juror said that his life had been threatened by several of the other male jurors to change his vote to guilty.

Judge Bahakel summoned Kay. We made motions for a mistrial. Any verdict the jury reached now could only be a product of coercion. Ultimately, the female juror who was holding out folded. But this courageous man told the other jurors that hell would freeze over before he changed his vote. He believed the evidence simply wasn't present for a conviction on any charge, including manslaughter. For a second time, the jurors were split between a manslaughter conviction and a not guilty verdict.

No one wanted to try this case a third time. Nevertheless, Judge Bahakel had no choice but to declare a mistrial and set a third trial. Meanwhile President Clinton had appointed Doug as the United States Attorney for the Northern District of Alabama. With that, Regina lost one of the two lawyers who knew her case intimately.

Since I never try a capital case alone, I then approached Emory Anthony, one of the best trial lawyers I had ever worked with in a courtroom. Emory assessed the situation and agreed to represent Regina. I also filed a motion to dismiss the case on the grounds that a re-trial would violate the double jeopardy clause of the Constitution as it related to the murder charge being considered by the jury. Our argument was that two juries already had unanimously found Regina not guilty of any degree of murder, as their division arose between manslaughter and not guilty. We also held affidavits from jurors in each trial to prove it. However, Judge Bahakel denied the motion. Regina would face a capital murder charge and the death penalty for the third time.

The long process began of educating Emory on the nuances of this complex case and its many alternate theories and strategies. I also launched an intense lobbying program of plea-bargaining. Finally, prosecutors Laura Petro and Laura Poston, faced with another two-week trial and knowing that neither of the past juries had voted for capital murder in the first place, agreed to allow Regina to plead guilty to reckless manslaughter with a sentence of probation, under the condition that she serve four months behind bars. The actual sentence was fifteen years, with four months to serve if she successfully completed a probationary period. Regina did not have to admit her guilt but instead entered an Alford ("best interest") plea to one count of reckless manslaughter.

Regina understood that gambling on another trial did not necessarily present her with the best option. I informed her of documented cases where one jury had hung up eleven to one to acquit a person and then a second jury found the same person guilty of capital murder and sentenced him to death. Still, she did not want to plead guilty, even if offered straight probation. She refused to admit guilt to something she did not do.

After six years of litigation and two long trials, Regina's case was finally finished. Judge Montgomery and Warren King were dead and three lawyers were in federal prison for bribery, conspiracy and money laundering. Regina readied herself to serve four months in the county jail, complete her probation and then face the world drug-free, having committed to a successful rehabilitation program. Today, more than seventeen years after King's death, she remains happily married, gainfully employed and drug-free.

In this headline-grabbing case, the lady of justice eventually lay down in her bed and went to sleep quietly, with no fanfare and just a whimper. However, the mysterious deaths of bail bondsman Warren King and Judge Jack Montgomery must still trouble her dreams. Of that I have no doubt.

Richard Jaffe
in the 1980s

The "Lucky Jaffe"
phone message from
Judge Cole

Bo Cochran with Richard
Jaffe at Jaffe's office in 2009

Photo courtesy of Linda Jaffe.

Judge Jack Montgomery looking dapper in the early 1980s

Judge Montgomery shortly before his death

Fifteen-year-old Darron Burpo, being tried as an adult

Tyrone Robinson,
on trial for
shooting his wife
and her coworker

Tyrone Robinson's
staircase is reconstructed
in the courtroom

A still image from
the ATM video
in the Jermaine
Robinson case

Richard Jaffe advocates
for Jermaine Robinson
during jury selection

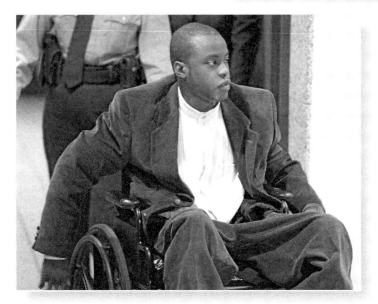

Ardragus
Ford enters
court in his
wheelchair

For the first time in five years, Randal Padgett celebrates the holidays at home with his daughter, Heather, and son, Micah

Gary Drinkard
leaves jail
a free man

The New Women All Women
Health Care Clinic in
Birmingham, after the bombing

Eric Rudolph in custody after
evading capture for over five years

Richard Jaffe introduces
attorney Johnnie Cochran
as the keynote speaker
at the Miles Law School
Annual Law Day
Celebration and Banquet

Photo courtesy of Chris McNair

BIM
WITNESS:
6-02 185 830-11TH ST
HANGS OUT: CHURCH OF RECONCILER
STATED THAT HE OBSERVED
2 WIM SUSPECTS AT 1525-
8TH AVE, N, (IN-N-OUT). THE
SUSPECTS WERE IN A GREEN
SUBARU STATION WAGON.
SUBJECT ON THE PASSENGER
SIDE HAD SHAVED HEAD.

Richard Jaffe, Che Swindle and Derek Drennan study an enlargement of Swindle's cell phone log

Officer Parks' handwritten note describing Dickinson Walters as a witness to Carlyle Hall's murder

Sister Helen Prejean, author of *Dead Man Walking*, with Richard Jaffe in Chicago in 2003, when Illinois Governor Ryan commuted all death sentences to life without parole.

Photo courtesy of Andrea Lyon.

Invitation to a
United Nations
performance
of the play
The Exonerated,
based in part
on the testimony
of Bo Cochran and
Randal Padgett

THE EXONERATED

Monday, 11 December 2000 at 6 P.M.
Dag Hammarskjold Library Auditorium
United Nations

Richard Jaffe with Stephen
Bright of the SCHR after
Bright successfully argued
Snyder v. Louisiana before
the US Supreme Court

20

FIGHTING FOR BO'S LIFE

I had not seen Bo Cochran since our meeting at the Jefferson County Jail the day after Judge Cole had sentenced him to die in Alabama's electric chair. We lost his appeal to the Alabama Court of Criminal Appeals, so we promptly appealed further to the Alabama Supreme Court, hoping to obtain a new trial for Bo—and a fair one.

A few years later, with the case in the hands of the Alabama Supreme Court justices, the United States Supreme Court issued one of the most far-reaching decisions in its history, in the case of *Batson v. Kentucky*.[1] Our highest court recognized that race exerts a fundamental influence on our criminal justice system. The justices determined that, historically, racial bias and prejudice had overwhelmed the presumption of innocence, resulting in unjustified jury verdicts. Further studies would show that, in cases in which a black person was accused of killing a white person (as opposed to the opposite scenario), the black person was 80 percent more likely to receive a death sentence.

In the *Batson* case, the United States Supreme Court held that a prosecutor violates the Constitution whenever jurors are excluded from serving due to their races. Morris Dees, John Carroll and Mike McCormick, the original attorneys who represented Bo, had filed a motion objecting to the racial composition of the jury and the manner in which the State struck potential jurors of color. Like many judges would have, Judge Cole denied this motion, resulting in two practically all-white juries that convicted Bo and then sentenced him to death. Because of the prescient efforts of Dees, Carroll, and McCormick, they were able to set up the *Batson* claim that we utilized more than a decade and a half later.

While we had already submitted our briefs to the Alabama Supreme Court when *Batson* came out, we had not included this issue. Since the court had not yet issued an opinion, we wrote a letter requesting they consider that historically the district attorney's office had systematically struck black jurors from cases, including this one.[2]

The Alabama Supreme Court turned us down. We had one more possible avenue within the state court system. We would file a post-conviction appeal, then known as a Rule 20 Petition.[3] In the Rule 20 Petition, we would specifically outline our racial claims and raise the question of whether Bo received a fair sentencing hearing, since virtually no investigation into his background and childhood (mandated by the United States Supreme Court in death penalty cases) was conducted for his third trial.

I had no experience in this hyper-technical, esoteric and intricate area of post-conviction law in which a case is challenged through filings in both the state and federal courts after the appeals process is exhausted in the state court system.

Knowing I needed help, I called Tuscaloosa attorney Joel Sogol, one of the most knowledgeable criminal defense lawyers in Alabama. Sogol possessed both brains and heart. I felt confident he would help and, like me, do it without thought of being paid. Joel did not hesitate for an instant to assist Bo and me.

Sogol and I felt we could establish that the bankruptcy attorney appointed as co-counsel in Bo's last trial was ineffective, because he completely lacked any training in the area of mitigation. We also knew that to obtain a new trial, we had to establish and prove our racial discrimination claim in the jury selection process. How would we prove that, well over a decade ago, the Jefferson County District Attorney's Office had struck blacks because of their race? How could we prove the exact racial composition of the jury panel and resulting jury without the strike sheets, which were not part of the court transcript nor in the materials we had received from Bo's previous attorneys?

The fog within which Sogol and I brainstormed lifted as I recalled who had prosecuted this case. District Attorney David Barber, who prosecuted Bo in both trials as a deputy district attorney, was as honest as he was careful to retain all relevant documents. I believed he would still possess these strike sheets and felt confident David would give them to me. Sogol believed it to be a long shot.

I met with David the following week. As I thought, he had kept the strike sheets and graciously made me copies. As is customary, the race and gender appeared prominently next to each juror name. A reconstruction of the numbers proved us right: It was virtually an all-white jury. The State had used practically all of its strikes to remove potential jurors who were African-American.

Our hopes brightened. We now had the evidence to back up our Rule 20 Petition claim of discrimination in the jury selection process, which had resulted in an unfair and constitutionally defective trial. We attached the strike sheets obtained from David to our petition.

That February, Judge William Cole held a hearing and promptly denied all of our claims. When we read his detailed written order the light of earlier hope turned into a faraway dim flicker. Judge Cole found that we were procedurally barred from raising the racial claim, because we did not include it in the original appeal. He found that the State had not racially discriminated against Bo. Judge Cole did not have to reach the merits of our claim, but he did. Because he made a factual finding that there was no racial discrimination in the jury selection process, we had a better chance that it would be considered when the federal court petitions were filed.

Sogol and I appealed Judge Cole's denial of our petition through the Alabama appellate courts. The Alabama Court of Criminal Appeals again turned us down. So did the Alabama Supreme Court. We then filed with the United States Supreme Court but it turned us down as well.

We had gone as far as we could. We had exhausted all state appeal alternatives. Bo's death sentence stood. Now Bo would have to find other lawyers to take him through his final steps of appeal: the federal courts. If the federal courts refused his appeal, he would have nowhere else to turn. The State would shave his head and strap him into "Yellow Mama." Twenty-one hundred volts of electricity would surge through his body. Witnesses would see, hear and smell his burning flesh but would not observe his eyeballs popping out, as a blindfold would cover them.

Sogol and I received virtually no compensation for the hundreds of hours we expended just pressing the Rule 20 Petition, but that is not the reason why we had to leave Bo's case. This difficult decision was premised on our belief that Bo needed lawyers with the resources and ability to master constitutional law as well as federal post-conviction procedures. Through those legal lenses they would freshly review the case, the performance of Bo's trial lawyers and our work as well.

Bo's new lawyers would allege, as we did, that Bo's previous trial lawyers were ineffective by not investigating and presenting any meaningful mitigating evidence. They could also allege that I had been ineffective in my representation of Bo on the appellate level if they found that any mistakes were made. This would give Bo another possible argument before the State could throw the switch.

But there were no funds to pay even a paltry amount to an attorney to file a petition in federal court. In 1963, in the famous case of *Gideon v. Wainwright*, the United States Supreme Court held that the Constitution requires that any person charged with a crime in which incarceration is a possibility has an absolute right to be represented by an appointed attorney at State expense.[4] Clarence Gideon was convicted of theft and received a new trial after being denied an appointed attorney to represent him. At his second trial, represented by an attorney at State expense, the jury acquitted him.

However, there is no requirement that a person facing the death penalty be given an appointed attorney once his direct appeals have run out, and the State of Alabama does not supply these funds. So Bo had no right to be provided with an attorney to assist him in the complex litigation ahead.

Bo's options seemed to have run out. Fortunately, he turned to the Equal Justice Initiative (EJI) located in Montgomery, Alabama. Bo contacted its founder, Bryan Stevenson, whose small group already had many more cases than they could possibly handle. The lawyers at EJI worked tirelessly, day and night, but could only take limited cases, since they were the only attorneys in Alabama both capable and willing to fight the thankless fight to stop death's crushing onslaught.

Bryan and his associates are both brilliant and passionate about the injustices in the death penalty. They work for salaries far less than first-year associates at most law firms, but they perform miracles, just like the lawyers and staff at the Southern Center for Human Rights (SCHR) in Atlanta. Both are nonprofit organizations dependent upon private funding. States fund to carry out the death penalty, but they won't fund to defend against it. Were it not for these organizations, I shudder to think of the countless lives lost and injustices perpetrated upon so many defenseless citizens, including innocent ones. Regardless of the accusation, our Constitution requires that each citizen receive a fair trial. That will not occur without resources and trained, committed and quality lawyers.

Like Stephen Bright, the founder of SCHR, Bryan Stevenson has devoted his life to defending people sentenced to death who otherwise would have no access to an attorney. Brilliant, compassionate and self-less, the Harvard Law School graduate could easily choose to work for any Wall Street law firm, which would pay him many hundreds of thousands of dollars a year.

After receiving a MacArthur Fellowship Genius Award, Bryan donated the large monetary prize to EJI, the organization that he started when the State took away public service funds for people like him who offered assistance to the poor who awaited execution. Sadly, with only voluntary funding and limited staff, they can only help so many. Several people now linger helplessly on Alabama's death row at Holman prison without lawyers to assist them with their appeals. Alabama keeps adding to the death ledger, but the number of lawyers at EJI and SCHR cannot represent all of them.

Meanwhile, Bo was forty years old and facing the end of his life.

Bryan Stevenson wasted no time in responding to Bo Cochran's urgent call. He contacted Lis Semel, an exceptionally bright, seasoned and energetic California lawyer. The American Bar Association (ABA) hired her to recruit large corporate firms to take on cases like Bo's, in which a person sentenced to death was about to run out of time.

Bryan knew that Lis would do everything she could to find a law firm and she did. A nationally prominent Philadelphia firm agreed to take on Bo's case with the assistance and counsel of Bryan Stevenson, Randy Susskind and the other lawyers at EJI.

A memo circulated through the firm requesting a group of volunteers. Three lawyers took on the challenge: Ken Frazier, a partner that a pharmaceutical company would later scoop up as its in-house corporate counsel; Brenda Williams, a gifted, young associate with empathy to match her intellect and Seamus Duffy, another young associate whose father was a successful criminal practitioner in the Northeast.

Duffy spent much of his childhood in his father's law offices, in courthouses in Philadelphia and other cities on the East Coast, watching his father represent criminal defendants. Like my daughter with me, Duffy observed his father fight for those targeted as criminals by the government. The decision to represent Bo Cochran presented Duffy with the unique opportunity to deepen his already close connection to his father, whom he respected and adored.

After reviewing thousands of pages of transcripts and briefs covering two jury trials and one mistrial and numerous appeals and hearings, Duffy and his team formulated an investigation plan. They undertook the monumental task of becoming experts in post-conviction death penalty law, some of the most complex litigation in the American legal system.

Then Seamus Duffy contacted me. We stayed in touch throughout his team's representation of Bo.

The law offers few ways for a death row inmate to receive a new trial. One occurs if new evidence surfaces, such as in DNA exonerations, but this happens rarely. The main avenue is to show that the inmate did not receive the effective assistance of counsel at his trial or on appeal.

Duffy and his team trained their focus on the injustices that the record reflected as they pored through its voluminous content. The

Philadelphia lawyers probably did not envision that they would devote the next six years of their lives to try to save the life of Bo Cochran. They did not foresee how much time, effort and energy they would spend in Birmingham, Alabama and at Holman State Prison, the site of Alabama's death row and home of "Yellow Mama," the infamous metal chair designed as a conduit for over two thousand volts of electricity.

But that's exactly what happened.

21

A GRUELING WAIT

Bo Cochran waited in Holman State Prison for United States District Judge Sam Pointer to make a decision on one of three possible outcomes: a new trial for racial discrimination in the jury selection process, a new sentencing based upon the failure of one of his lawyers to represent him adequately at the penalty phase or a finding denying him any relief. The last option would add one item to the schedule: Bo's execution date.

Seamus Duffy stayed closely in touch with me as he and his team made the arduous journey through the federal courts. I met several times with the team and testified in a crucial hearing in Judge Pointer's court. At that hearing, Duffy and his team presented powerful evidence that Bo neither received a fair trial due to racial discrimination in the jury selection process nor the effective assistance of counsel at the sentencing hearing. The hearing in Judge Pointer's court lasted several days, during which Duffy called numerous witnesses to prove these claims, including then-elected district attorney David Barber.

David offered up truly courageous testimony. When asked under oath if his office, like almost all district attorney's offices in Alabama, had engaged in a pattern of racial discrimination when selecting juries at the time of Bo's original trial, David confirmed that it had. Duffy's team had made invaluable use of the strike sheets David had provided me years ago. Yet without David's totally forthright responses, the strike sheets alone would not have provided enough evidence of the practice Duffy needed to prove. In spite of David's strong belief that Bo was guilty, he did the right thing in this hearing.

Finally, I received a call from Seamus Duffy, a call I will never forget. Seamus told me that Judge Pointer had found that one of Bo's lawyers had been constitutionally ineffective for failing to develop and present sufficiently available mitigating evidence at the sentencing phase of his trial. He ordered a new sentencing hearing but upheld the capital murder conviction.

David Barber's honesty and integrity made him an unsung hero in Bo's marathon quest for justice, in spite of David's personal feelings and beliefs. His testimony had given Bo a final chance at life. Judge Pointer demonstrated heroism as well. He had always been known for his extraordinary intellect and unfailing commitment to follow the law.

When Seamus gave me a copy of Judge Pointer's written opinion to read, I was exhilarated. If the Eleventh Circuit agreed with Judge Pointer's ruling, Bo would receive a sentence of life without the possibility of parole. He would live the remainder of his days in the general population of the prison. Escaping the jaws of death was, in itself, a huge victory. Yet at the same time, Bo's legal team and I believed that he deserved not only a new sentencing hearing, but also an entirely new trial. Duffy decided to press Judge Pointer on the claim that Bo did not receive a fair trial because of a racially defective jury. Duffy's team filed a motion requesting that he reconsider that issue.

When Judge Pointer realized that Duffy and his team were seriously pressing for a new trial, he told Duffy that he failed to understand their reasoning. Since Bo had already been tried twice and both trials had ended in convictions and death sentences, he pondered aloud why anyone would believe that a third trial would net a different result. Yet Duffy and his team adamantly insisted that racial discrimination had poisoned the jury selection and the law required that the judge order a new trial.

Always the scholar and fiercely committed to the Constitution, Judge Pointer then announced that he would reconsider the question of whether Bo deserved a new trial due to racial discrimination. After careful consideration, he then issued a new order: the law required that James Willie Cochran be granted a new trial. The State appealed. The Eleventh Circuit Court of Appeals agreed with Judge Pointer. Bo Cochran would receive another trial.[1]

After almost eighteen years on death row, Bo could glimpse a tiny sliver of sunlight.

When I received the call from Seamus Duffy, I couldn't believe my ears. Victories like this happen so rarely. Not only did Bo receive the opportunity of new life, but also the system now had a chance for redemption. Duffy's team had gone far beyond anyone's wildest expectations. They had performed an unforeseen miracle.

Neither Duffy nor any of his associates had ever tried a criminal case, much less one involving the death penalty. Their corporate law firm had volunteered to do the pro bono work in the federal courts as a public service. Yet they became so attached to Bo that they did not want to abandon his cause. Duffy began to interview lawyers to represent Bo at his new trial. He asked me if I would consider rejoining the team and serving as Bo's lead trial counsel.

We met for dinner to discuss the proposition. At dinner, I looked directly into Duffy's burning, committed eyes. "Seamus, I know one thing," I declared. "Whichever lawyer or law firm takes this case had better perform with perfection. There is no room for error in your eyes, after all you have put into it for the last five years."

Duffy did not skip a beat. "You're right. There is no room for error. We have come too far for that."

A few days after meeting for dinner, we reached an agreement. I would file motions to ask the trial judge to allot us funds for necessary expenses, such as an investigator and a psychiatrist.[2] Duffy's firm would pay all remaining expenses. Fortunately for Bo, the law had changed dramatically in the years since his first trial as it related to the question of a poor person's right to obtain the expenses necessary to mount an effective defense at trial. If we could show it critical and necessary, the court would order those expenses paid.

I was back in Bo's corner as his lead defense counsel.

My newest associate, Derek Drennan, and our investigator, Rick Blake, began to study every word of the trial transcripts. Blake, a twenty-year veteran of the Birmingham police department, was extremely qualified. Several years of his career were spent training police officers in homicide investigation, procedures and techniques. At our first meeting, he could barely contain his enthusiasm to begin locating witnesses, nor his outrage.

"Richard, all the answers are here in these transcripts. From what I can see, the police accidentally shot this man. It's obvious to me. It was pitch dark there in that trailer park and dangerous. It no doubt was an accidental shooting. They just panicked and covered it up."

Blake echoed my original thoughts upon studying the transcript when Judge Cole had first appointed me almost thirteen years ago. Drennan came to the same conclusion after reviewing the case for only a short time.

Still, I wanted his law enforcement perspective: "Rick, what makes you say that?"

"Everything points in that direction. Look at these pictures. The body was found under a trailer, but there were no drag marks or blood spots in the grass. Just look at the photographs. It was not a through and through shot. Where is the bullet?" he asked with incredulity. "They had a metal detector out there for several days. The bullet had to be somewhere."

He paused briefly. His voice grew soft. "Tell me this, Rich: Why did it take forty-five minutes for the police officers to call the coroner? Why did the officers who first entered the trailer park change the frequencies on their walkie-talkies? But what I really don't understand is why, after the shot was fired, did the plainclothes officers leave the trailer park rather than proceed in the direction of the shots? Why didn't they follow the shot? That's how I was trained. You always follow the shot."

Blake's points appeared compelling. "We need to check the experience of these plainclothes officers. I bet they were rookies and had little, if any, experience responding to shootings."

His instinct was right. In fact, one of the plainclothes police officers was a rookie and just twenty-three years old at the time of the incident, the same age as the deceased store manager. Bo had never denied that he committed the robbery of the grocery store, but for almost twenty years he had consistently maintained that he did not shoot the store manager.

When Judge Cole retired, Judge James Garrett became our presiding judge. Hardly a better trial judge could be found in Alabama. Judge Garrett was a member of the DA's office when Bo's first trials occurred. Though he did not know what our investigation had revealed, he knew what he had heard back then. The judge clearly believed Bo to be guilty, but I never doubted he would give my client a fair trial.

The federal courts had ordered new proceedings, not only because of racial discrimination in the jury selection process, but also because they found one of Bo's attorneys ineffective in preparing his case for a sentencing hearing. Both Judge Pointer and the Eleventh Circuit Court of Appeals had found that Bo's lawyer did virtually nothing in this regard. In fairness to the attorney, the defense had lacked the funds to investigate Bo's life adequately.

Seamus Duffy and his team, however, had developed lots of mitigating evidence that they presented to Judge Pointer to show what Bo's lawyers could have accomplished had they been properly funded. Now we would have the opportunity to present this evidence to save Bo's life at a new sentencing hearing if, in fact, the jury found Bo guilty.

While I hoped and prayed that we would never get to a new sentencing hearing, I wanted to have Dr. Prudence Baxter, one of the nation's top psychiatrists retained by Duffy, give her opinions about the effect of Bo's upbringing on his development. She had also spent a great deal of time working on Bo's case and had agreed to come to Alabama for a huge discount from her regular fee.

Dr. Baxter had already examined Bo extensively and relied upon numerous witnesses to detail pertinent developments in his life. He had been the shunned child of a cruel, abusive father. His father had often beaten him unmercifully with his fists, his hands and extension cords. She chronicled the effect of racism on the young Bo, who had grown up in Birmingham.

I filed an *ex parte* motion (a sealed motion when funds for indigents are requested) for funds to hire Dr. Baxter. The Judge balked. He wanted me to employ a local psychologist. But I felt strongly that we be allowed the benefit of years of work by Dr. Baxter, rather than starting all over with someone who had not met Bo nor extensively studied his case and background.

In Judge Garrett's chambers I argued the *ex parte* motion for funds with the hope of reasoning with him. Although a former prosecutor, he had also defended accused criminals for over fifteen years, including many high-profile murder cases.

We began cordially enough. We exchanged pleasantries at the end of a long day as he sat calmly at his desk, leaning back and warmly smiling. Normally mild and easy-going, this handsome, blond, six-foot three-inch, 230-pound former University of Alabama football player was adamant: he would grant limited funds for an Alabama psychiatrist. He would not authorize Dr. Baxter as an expert witness. He had no inclination to change his mind. As the discussion continued, both of our voices escalated in pitch and speed and then over and above one another. I lost myself in the moment. Bo was entitled to those funds! The State would empty the taxpayers' pockets in funding their case to kill Bo. My hiring someone local for an entirely new evaluation of Bo not only didn't make sense, but also placed Bo at a disadvantage.

"There is no reason why you can't use an Alabama psychiatrist. I am not going to approve one from Boston and that's all there is to it!" The Judge had dug in, but still I refused to give up. This was a life or death case.

"But, Judge," I protested in a more gentle tone, "she has already tested Bo extensively, interviewed witnesses and prepared a report. It would be so much more efficient and no more expensive to use her."

The judge's irritation grew more apparent. "Look," he retorted, "I was in the DA's office when the first case was tried. I remember this case. The evidence of his guilt was overwhelming."

"Judge," I said, with the strain in my tone rising, "he is still presumed innocent. And this psychiatrist understands Bo and his background. The State again seeks the death penalty and will spare no expense to kill Bo Cochran. We want a fair chance to save his life if we get to a sentencing hearing."

The volume of our discussion climbed to the point that a bailiff rushed in to find out what was going on. When the bailiff saw it was just me, he left us to continue the shouting match.

Once more I pleaded, this time softy and sincerely, with Judge Garrett. I appealed to his innate sense of fairness and the compassion he had always exhibited as a former prosecutor, defense lawyer and then a judge. I reminded him how hard he had fought in one particularly notorious death penalty case he had tried. I emphasized how important it was to utilize the best experts possible.

To the judge's credit and my great relief, he authorized the funding we needed to hire Dr. Baxter.

It was one small victory for Bo.

22

BO'S JOURNEY ENDS

B o Cochran's first trial was one of the first death penalty cases tried in Birmingham, Alabama, after the United States Supreme Court reinstated the death penalty.[1] Now, over twenty years and two death sentences later, we were getting ready for a new trial.

With just days left to start the trial, Derek Drennan made arrangements for us to inspect all the items from the previous trials that were still in the clerk's office, including the weapon. He hoped to find some answer to the question of what happened to the missing bullet. The autopsy revealed that one projectile had entered the store manager's left arm, then passed through it to the left rib cage. The bullet must have ended up lodged in the inside of his right arm, because his outer right arm showed no exit wound. Also, the store manager was wearing a long-sleeve shirt that night and the right sleeve didn't have a hole where a bullet would have exited. However, no bullet was lodged in his arm. The official police and autopsy photographs showed scrape marks on the inner side of his right arm. It certainly appeared to us that someone might have used a pocket knife to dig out the projectile. If the projectile wasn't dug out of the store manager's arm, where did it go?

Drennan went to the clerk's office and examined the clothes carefully. He confirmed that the store manager's shirt sleeve had a hole matching up with the entrance of the projectile but no exit wound hole anywhere. The projectile must have been removed from the body before the coroner arrived on the scene.

We had another question: How did the store manager's body end up in a position underneath one of the trailers and parallel to it? He could not have crawled twenty-five feet to get under the trailer without leaving drag marks and a blood trail in the grass. It was quite suspicious that he would lie perfectly parallel to anything. Also, we wondered why anyone would crawl all that way to die in the dirt underneath a trailer.

Duffy's team had poured their hearts and hard work into their courageous and tireless efforts. Seamus planned to be in Birmingham for the trial.

We had a list of approximately fifteen people who lived at the trailer park on the night of the incident. We needed to find at least one former resident who was in his or her trailer at the time the shots were fired. We believed we could then show that Bo was nowhere around. The sequence of shots would be crucial.

Within a week of the trial, not one person had been found. Yet Blake would not give up; too much depended upon his investigation. The pressure continued to mount.

Finally, a break: Blake located a former trailer park resident whose mobile home would have rested within feet of where the shots were fired. The former university student was now the director of a clinic in Tampa, Florida. He could be a crucially invaluable and credible witness. However, when Blake finally reached him by telephone, the man adamantly refused to come to Birmingham, insisting that he knew nothing that could benefit Bo or the State.

My instincts told me differently.

Ultimately, the former trailer park resident cut off all communication with Blake and referred him to his attorney. Only days before the start of the trial, I desperately phoned his lawyer. Initially unable to convince this lawyer to urge his client to fly to Birmingham, I asked the attorney, "Do you ever handle any criminal cases?"

"Yes, on occasion. Not often, but sometimes."

"Have any of them been felonies of a serious nature?"

"Yes, a few of them have," he replied.

With that I knew I could reach him. "You know the tremendous responsibility we lawyers assume when representing someone accused of a crime."

"No question about it," the attorney freely acknowledged.

"And, of course, the pressure is even greater when you are representing an innocent person."

"No question about that."

I then appealed to his humanity. "Think about it. I promise you that if you called me and told me that one of my clients had information that could be instrumental in saving an innocent man in a death penalty case, I would do whatever I could to convince my client to do the right thing and speak with us. I need your help."

He paused for a moment. "Why do you think he could help?"

"Because if he remembers the sequence of shots and what was said, that could make a world of difference. It could be critical in this case," I insisted.

After another pause, he responded, "I will talk to my client and do what I can to help."

I believed him.

On the following Monday morning, the first day of the trial, we did everything we could to work out a plea bargain with David Barber and Henry Cornelius, the forceful and powerful deputy district attorney who assisted David at trial. Although we knew Bo was innocent, we had no motivations to become heroes and chance another death sentence if we could assure that Bo could plead to the robbery and be released relatively soon. One never knows how twelve people would view the evidence and decide the case. Even though David's candid and forthright testimony before Judge Pointer had made this third chance for Bo possible, he would not budge. As he rejected my offers to work out a plea bargain arrangement, David looked at me and said, "Looks like we'll make it three in a row."

Jury selection began and lasted throughout the week.

To its immense credit, the clerk's office had maintained the store manager's clothes and all of the physical items, including the weapon introduced by the prosecution at the previous trials. The clerk's office also had kept all of the photographs, including aerial photos and the charts and blowups the prosecution had introduced. That made quite a significant difference, because the trailer park and grocery store no longer existed. Our visits to the "scene" were helpful only to the extent of enabling us to travel the path the robber took before he fled into the dark trailer park as the store manager pursued him.

It took more than a week for the prosecution to present all of its witnesses.

Although more than two decades now had elapsed since the shooting, only one material witness the prosecution had called in the first two trials could not be found. That witness was the officer who had discovered the gun in the brush where Bo had hidden. But the transcripts from the previous trials had preserved his testimony. The prosecution called every important witness they had used in the two previous trials, including the plainclothes police officers, investigating officers and detectives. In addition, they called the eyewitness cashier who was held up and robbed. They even called Haddon Rutherford, who had since moved to Texas.

Rutherford had a date the night of the robbery and murder. He and his date were driving from an apartment complex located behind the grocery store when he saw the store manager following the robber, who was about thirty yards away. Rutherford pulled up beside the manager, asked him what was going on and then assisted him in trying to keep an eye on the robber. The manager walked alongside Rutherford's car. When the robber leapt out from behind a bush and vanished into the trailer park, the manager continued to follow him. Rutherford and his date then left the scene before returning later to speak with the police. Incredibly, we were able to locate Rutherford and interview him with the help of his date from more than twenty years ago, because she still lived in the same apartment complex as she had at the time of the first trial.

We believed that Haddon Rutherford was the key to this puzzle. He and his date had driven to the entrance of the trailer park before actually leaving the scene. He saw the police officers as they arrived at the scene. Importantly, the officers saw Rutherford's car leave the scene before they entered the trailer park. The store employee who had called 911 had reported that the store manager had been chasing the robber. In our opinion, the police must have believed that Rutherford was the store manager; therefore the only person left in the trailer park would be the robber. For that reason the shots fired were meant for the robber when in fact it was the store manager who was killed.

Through our cross-examinations, the police officers established that Bo was searched at the scene several times, but no money was found in his possession. At the police station, a final search allegedly revealed grocery store money stuffed in the pocket of Bo's coat.

The police officers also testified to their discovery of Bo and the location of the weapon that was cold to the touch. Additionally, the position of the revolved chamber had revealed that the last shot fired could not have been the one that discharged the fatal bullet.

The prosecution took more than a week before resting its case.

Finally, it was our turn to present our case.

My general rule is to present as little as possible. If the defense presents too much, a jury may begin to see it as a contest of which side has the better proof. In fact, a trial is not about guilt or innocence or which side presents the best case; it is about whether the government has presented evidence so strong that it excludes every other reasonable conclusion other than the guilt of the accused. If the government fails to present such compelling proof, each juror must abide by his oath and vote not guilty.

The founding fathers of our nation knew full well the incredible advantages the government possesses with its sheer power and unlimited resources. The government can obtain most any information simply by virtue of its authority and, as a consequence, thoroughly and completely investigate a crime. They also knew that the public and jurors tend to believe the voice of authority. In other words, popular belief follows that if the police arrested this person, they have good reason to believe he is guilty. To balance these realities, those who designed our system built in a presumption that anyone accused of a crime is innocent unless the government produces evidence sufficient to rid any reasonable doubt.

Practically every juror wants and expects to hear the defendant say, "I am not guilty. I am innocent. I did not do this. I am wrongfully charged." Naturally, the jurors also want to hear the defendant's side of the case.

I try to keep my clients off the stand. The downside of being cross-examined often outweighs the upside of allowing the jurors to hear the defendant proclaim innocence. Hardly anyone makes a perfect witness. Jurors expect near-perfection when an accused testifies. They tend to judge any inconsistencies in a defendant's testimony harshly. Nerves, fear and frequently a lack of communication skills prevent many witnesses from effectively communicating with jurors in the public setting of a courtroom. These realities are multiplied when the witness is the defendant. Many innocent defendants have been convicted due to stumbling on the stand.

The framers of our constitution designed a system based not upon innocence or guilt, but rather on the question of proof. That is the reason the courts instruct the jury to consider and verdict forms to state "guilty or not guilty" rather than "guilty or innocent." The real question in any trial is supposed to be, "Did the prosecution carry its burden of overcoming the presumption of innocence by presenting proof beyond a reasonable doubt?" If not, the correct verdict that every juror takes an oath to return is "not guilty."

However, in Bo's case, we were forced to take on a huge burden. Our defense theory postulated that if our client didn't shoot and kill the store manager, then it must have been an accidental shooting by law enforcement. We needed our cross-examinations of the police officers and other credible witnesses to solidify that position and exclude Bo as the shooter. The jury must, at the very least, accept and understand that the evidence pointed just as strongly in the direction of the officers accidentally shooting the store manager as Bo doing it.

Finally I got to meet the clinic director who had lived in the trailer park. True to his word, his lawyer had convinced him to come to Birmingham. He was a mild-mannered man in his mid-thirties. We met for an early breakfast at a small restaurant and he did not appear resentful for taking the time and incurring the expense of this trip. After

I inquired, he explained that his reluctance to fly to Birmingham came from his belief he could not have any helpful information for either side, because he did not see the shooting.

Though he did not see the shooting, he heard it and much more. His information would prove invaluable.

The timing worked out perfectly. We would call the clinic director to testify later that morning. He could fly home afterward. Less than an hour remained to prepare before court began.

I went straight to the point: "How clear is your memory of this incident?"

"Mr. Jaffe, I remember it like it was yesterday. I'll never forget that night. I still tense up at the thought of it."

"Why is it so clear?" I asked.

"Because after we heard the shots, my roommate and I and some other residents went outside to see what was happening. All of a sudden I saw two men. One had a rifle or shotgun and the other a handgun. They started screaming at us to get the hell back in our trailer, lie down on the floor and not get up until they said. Mr. Jaffe, I was just a student. We did exactly what they said. We were scared out of our wits."

"Were these two men police officers?" I asked.

"Yes. Right before I heard the shots, I heard, 'Halt! Police!' When we opened the door, there they both were, with their guns out, screaming at us to get back in the trailer."

I perched on the edge of my chair, trying not to appear too anxious. "How long after you heard 'Halt! Police!' did you hear the shots?"

"It was immediate. 'Halt! Police!' Barely a second passed and then two shots."

I could hardly believe my ears. The robber would not have yelled, "Halt! Police!" More importantly, within seconds of the shots being fired, who was standing outside with weapons?

Not Bo Cochran. Just the two plainclothes officers, one with a shotgun or rifle and one with a pistol.

The former student and now clinic director would make an incredibly powerful and unimpeachable witness. Before his lawyer explained to him why his testimony was so important, he truly believed that he had nothing of value to add to this case. His only allegiance was to the truth, but we were convinced the truth could set Bo free.

Throughout the trial Bo projected an angelic presence. He seemed to have reached a peaceful state, sensing that his lawyers had finally investigated his case thoroughly. The people on his side had spent enormous amounts of time, effort and money so that he could receive a fair trial. Finally, his lawyers believed in him and had the evidence to support his mantra: "I did not kill the store manager. I was in the woods, far away and never even heard a shot. The old rickety gun I had wouldn't have worked anyway."

The clinic director surpassed our expectations in his testimony. He could not be impeached. The jury appeared to believe him. They were riveted to every syllable he uttered.

When he was finished, we rested our case.

During closing arguments, the jurors sat on the edges of their seats. First, Henry Cornelius made a very eloquent and forceful close on behalf of the prosecution. Then David, more low-key, delivered a logical and moving closing argument. He had successfully tried this case two other times, obtaining quick convictions and death sentences. Despite the eleven-year gap when he did not try cases, he had not lost his eloquence or his jury appeal.

This time, however, things were different.

We had, we felt, positive proof that the store manager followed the robber into the trailer park. When he was shot, Bo was nowhere around. Instead, when shots were fired, the only nearby people with weapons were two plainclothes police officers. After the shots, they did not turn on their flashlights and go straight to the body…or did they? Did they find the store manager and, overwhelmed with panic, begin to cover up their mistake?

"Ladies and gentlemen," I said, "I want to know where that missing bullet is. I want to know how the store manager's body ended up under that trailer, why it took forty-five minutes before the coroner was called, why there were no blood spots or drag marks, why the store manager's arm had scrape marks where the bullet penetrated it.

I want to know how Bo could be in two places at once, because we know that he was not at the trailer when the shots were fired. We do know who yelled, 'Halt! Police!' less than a second before shots were fired and who stood there with drawn weapons when trailer residents walked outside. And I want to know why the plainclothes police officers, rather than following the shots, changed the frequencies on their two-way radios and then went the other way. I want to know why, the first several times Bo Cochran was searched, no money was found on him. And how can it be explained why Bo's gun was not warm and how a gun that was fired in that position could have fired that night?

"Nineteen years is long enough to pay for a crime that you didn't commit. Nineteen years is a long time to seek justice. The store manager's death will be even more senseless if an innocent person is wrongfully convicted of it. Can you say with any certainly that Bo Cochran shot and killed this man? Can you say it without hesitation? Because if you can't, then that is reasonable doubt.

"I am not here to prove who killed the store manager. That's not my job. But if the prosecution has failed to convince each of you beyond a reasonable doubt, then they have not met their burden of proof and your oath requires you to say so, not only for Bo Cochran, but also for the integrity of our legal system. You see, it's always on trial, in every case. We test it and it only works when we all follow the law and our oaths. The system will break down otherwise.

"Nineteen years is a long, long time to wait for justice. It is now time for you to deliver it, not only to Bo Cochran but to the store manager and the system as well."

As I returned slowly to my chair, I noticed the elderly parents of the store manager sitting in the courtroom and my heart ached for them. Nearly twenty years later, the book was still open on their son's death and so were the emotional wounds. I so deeply hoped for justice for Bo, but I also sympathized with the victim's parents. I knew that Bo had received unfair trials, hampered by a lack of funding to adequately investigate his case and a racially biased jury. I knew that Bo had been on death row for nearly twenty years for a shooting he denied and the evidence supported that he did not do it. But all that had nothing to do with the painful loss of the store manager and the pain in his parents' hearts. I knew I could never do anything about it.

Less than two hours after the closing arguments and the court's jury charges on the law, the Jefferson County jury found Bo Cochran not guilty of all counts of homicide. Every muscle in Bo's face relaxed and his eyes welled with tears before he grabbed me in an unforgettable embrace.

As we walked out of the courtroom and out into the cold sunlight, I found several jurors waiting in hopes of hugging Bo.

He would be released within thirty days.

23

THE WRONG ROAD
TO DEATH ROW

At about 12:30 A.M. on a warm July night, Deputy Sheriff William Hardy walked out of the back door of a Birmingham hotel into the parking lot. Several guests heard shots and immediately looked out their hotel room windows or walked out of their rooms. Deputy Hardy lay sprawled on the pavement, shot twice in the face at close range. Uncharacteristically, he had left the hat he always wore on a table inside the hotel. He must have left quickly; his cigarette was still burning in an ashtray. At least one hotel resident saw a yellow late-model car speeding out of the parking lot. Other witnesses described a similar car. The description of the car quickly made its way onto the police airwaves in the form of a BOLO (be on the lookout).

The murder of a law enforcement officer strikes at the very heart of our system of laws. When the people who have devoted their lives to protecting us lose their own in the process, it is like losing a family member, and the system responds dynamically. That response can turn into a reaction of panic, especially when very few clues exist. After Deputy Hardy's murder, not only did the Jefferson County Sheriff's Department take over the investigation, but one of Deputy Hardy's closest friends became the lead detective.

About ninety minutes before Deputy Hardy was gunned down, Toforest Johnson assisted Ardragus Ford, both then nineteen years old, as they made their way into a local hot spot. Paralyzed from a bullet he took in his spine while protecting his cousin in a dangerous area of Birmingham, Ford had been confined to a wheelchair for several years. Before his injury, Ford stood about five feet six inches. He was handsomely dark with chiseled features, as if his face were some type of sculpture. Despite his physical limitations, he was still pursuing a lifestyle of chasing women, drugs and alcohol. He had not missed a Tuesday or Thursday night at one particular local bar in months. Many of his family and friends frequented it on those nights as well.

Earlier that week, Ford had met Roshanna, a fifteen-year-old girl. The girl rarely spent the night at home with her mother and was planning a night of partying with Ford and Johnson. Her friend Tammi intended to sneak out of her house in the early morning hours and party with the three of them. Around 12:30 A.M., almost the exact time that the shooting occurred, Ford called his new girlfriend from his cell phone while he and Johnson partied at the bar. They had made arrangements to pick her up around 2:00 A.M. She coordinated the arrangements with Tammi.

Subpoenaed phone records revealed the trail of phone calls solidifying all these arrangements, even verifying a call to Tammi at approximately 2:25 A.M. to let her know they were on the way to pick her up.

Once the four were together, they drove to a local motel to find a room. That first motel did not have handicapped accommodations for Ford. The second motel they tried was too expensive.

When someone murders a police officer—for that matter, when any crime occurs—it is important to investigate with efficiency and speed. The evidence of a fleeing felon fades fast and so do the legal requirements of probable cause. On that night, as the police records later revealed, scores of people were pulled over and searched by law enforcement.

The list included Ardragus Ford. When police pulled over Ford and the other three occupants of his automobile, he was driving a *black* car fitted for a wheelchair. Hotel witnesses had given various descriptions of a car leaving the scene but none closely matched Ford's car.

However, it was 3:00 A.M. and they were only a mile or two from the murder scene. No one seemed to question why the killers would have remained in the immediate area.

The police officers explained to the teenagers that the reason they were stopped was because a deputy sheriff had been murdered in the area only a couple of hours earlier. The officers questioned all of them long enough to satisfy themselves that nothing appeared suspicious about the occupants or the automobile to suggest they had any involvement in the murder. The officers thoroughly searched the car and its occupants anyway, finding no blood splatters, weapons or fruits of any robbery or other crime.

When the officers ran Toforest Johnson's name through the National Crime Information Center (NCIC) database, they learned of an outstanding traffic ticket Johnson had not paid. Johnson was carted off to jail. Since Ford did not have a valid driver's license, the police required him to leave his car parked on the side of the road. Ford and the two girls took a taxi to their respective residences. Within a day or two, the police impounded Ford's car and again found no blood anywhere in the automobile.

The next morning, Roshanna had a conversation with her mother, who asked her if she had heard about the murder of Deputy Hardy, who was a friend of the family. Upon hearing the news of Hardy's death, Roshanna exclaimed to her mother, "Oh, I think I know something about that." With these spontaneous words, the investigation of Deputy Hardy's murder took an ominous turn.

A significant monetary award was being offered to anyone who provided information that successfully led to the arrest and conviction of the killer of the police officer. Roshanna's mother retained counsel to represent her and her daughter to collect the award. She also called a law enforcement acquaintance and reported that her fifteen-year-old daughter might have information about the Hardy murder. The acquaintance passed on the message to the lead detectives; soon they were looking for Roshanna.

When the police caught up with her, she had gotten little, if any, sleep. They took her to the juvenile facilities where detectives questioned her. She stated that Ford and Johnson picked her up shortly after 2:00 A.M. on the morning of July 19 and then returned to her friend Tammi's residence at approximately 5:00 A.M. While the detectives questioned Roshanna, they also interrogated Tammi. In separate interviews, both girls adamantly denied knowledge of the Hardy murder. Also, each girl's version of the previous night's events matched with the other's.

Nevertheless, the detectives did not believe them. They threatened to charge each of them as an accessory to capital murder. After questioning both teenagers without benefit of parents or guardians for almost seven hours, the detectives released them.

The busy fifteen-year-old girls headed to a salon to get their hair done. There, according to court records, they talked to each other. Tammi told Roshanna that she would go to jail before she would lie and make up a story about a shooting she knew nothing about. Roshanna, on the other hand, said that she would lie rather than go to jail for something she didn't do.

A few hours later, authorities again picked them up and transported them back to police headquarters. After several more hours of questioning, Roshanna changed her story. The authorities released her without charging her. Tammi refused to change her original denials of knowledge about the murder. She was sent to a juvenile detention center where she remained incarcerated for months.

Before the evening of the murder, neither girl knew Ford or Johnson. Roshanna had only met Ford at a club two days before the incident. At that same club, she also met two other individuals. Neither knew Ford or Johnson.

At this point Roshanna had successfully avoided incarceration by implicating Ardragus Ford and Toforest Johnson in a murder that she did not actually witness. However, she faced some formidable and unforeseen obstacles. She would be forced to provide details of the murder, including who did the actual shooting, its exact location on the hotel grounds, where the cars were parked and the time and description of how it all happened.

Such details are normally not difficult for one who has actually witnessed a murder. Roshanna could not provide this information. Yet she possessed keenly developed street smarts and survival instincts, even though she was just fifteen. She denied actually seeing the murder; instead, she told the authorities that Johnson admitted to her that earlier that night he had shot Deputy Hardy when he walked in on a drug sale in the hotel parking lot. Thus, Roshanna maintained her credibility, since Ford and Johnson did not pick her up until after 2:00 A.M.

The detectives would have none of it. Although Roshanna insisted over and over again that she was not present when Hardy was murdered, the detectives continued to press her for details. Roshanna changed her story again and claimed to have witnessed the murder. With each new question and each succeeding interview she gave new details and erroneous information about more and more crucial facts. For example, she said Deputy Hardy wore a blue uniform (as do most police officers). However, Hardy, a sheriff's deputy, wore a brown uniform. She said Deputy Hardy wore his hat that night; actually he had left it in the hotel. She stated that he had his gun drawn, when in fact it was holstered. She even placed the shooting at the front of the building, which looked completely different from the side of the building where the shooting actually took place. She had no explanation for why she did not recognize Deputy Hardy, even though he was a friend of her family.

Roshanna told the detectives that Toforest Johnson shot Deputy Hardy and had blood all over him when he got back to the automobile. Yet no blood was found in Ford's car and the police officers who searched Johnson that night saw no blood on his clothes. When asked to describe the "failed drug deal" in more detail, Roshanna's story was that Ford and Johnson met two other young males in the parking lot at the trunk of one of their cars. She claimed that the trunk lid was raised when she saw Johnson shoot Deputy Hardy. However, none of the eyewitnesses described a scene anything like this. Furthermore, they only saw one car drive away and it did not resemble Ford's.

Roshanna's description of the other two young males was vague and general at best. Photographs of Quintez Wilson and Omar Berry, the two men she had met earlier that week at the same club she met Ford, happened to be lying on one of the officers' desks at the sheriff's office. Roshanna identified them as the other two males at the scene. At a subsequent interview, she identified Berry as the shooter rather than Johnson. At different moments during the fifteen or more interviews she gave detectives, she identified each of the four individuals as the shooter. Like Ford and Johnson, Omar Berry and Quintez Wilson had solid alibis that impressed no one.

On a Monday in July, just days after the murder, I received a call from Sergeant Dennis Blanton, head of the Jefferson County Narcotics Division. He had learned that Ardragus Ford's mother had retained me to represent him. According to Detective Blanton, law enforcement believed Ford simply had information about the incident. He asked me to agree to allow Ford to be interviewed by investigators, not as a suspect but as someone who could provide them with helpful information.

I received this urgent call from Detective Blanton just as we were beginning jury selection for another capital murder trial. I could not be present with Ardragus Ford if they interviewed him the following day. Based on my many previously positive dealings with Detective Blanton, I allowed Ford to be questioned without my presence, never dreaming that he would become a suspect.

The following day, while I continued to question potential jurors in my other case, Ford's mother guided him up the wheelchair ramp to the sheriff's office, one block away from the courthouse. After recessing for the day, I called to find out about Ford's interview. I was shocked to learn that almost nine hours later investigators were still questioning Ford. I couldn't believe it. I knew the lengthy interview did not bode well for Ford.

I rushed over to the sheriff's office, where I found a hustle and bustle of detectives in the large open area where many of their desks were positioned. I did not see my client. I sat down with one of the lead detectives, who told me the detectives knew Ardragus Ford was lying and he had a choice to make: he could choose to be a witness or a defendant. They wanted to give me a chance to convince him that he would prefer to be a witness.

Just then I noticed District Attorney David Barber huddling with some detectives in a far corner of the room. Ford sat in his wheelchair in one of the small closed-off interview rooms. I asked to speak to David. In an atmosphere thick with intensity, we talked.

"What's going on with Ardragus?" I began. "I understand that he only has knowledge of what happened but wasn't involved."

"He's definitely not the shooter, not from what we have found," David responded cautiously, "but he knows much more than he has told us about it. He was there. We know that. He's lying when he denies being there."

My chest tightened even more upon learning that they thought Ford was actually at the scene, if not an accomplice, but something wasn't adding up. Why eight or nine hours of questioning?

"The detectives have told me that Ford can be a witness or a defendant," I prodded, hunting for an opening. "I want him to be a witness rather than face the death penalty for capital murder."

David looked at me and said, "Well, we would rather have him as a witness since we don't believe he did the shooting."

"Then tell me what you think he knows and what I can do to help."

"Go in there and see if you can talk some sense into him. Either you can leave with him as a witness or we are going to take him over to the Jefferson County Jail. It's up to him."

I studied David carefully and then pressed my position. "David, if you expect me to go in there and get him to admit these things, then you are going to have to offer him immunity right here and now."

David thought about it for a very long moment and then reluctantly agreed. I insisted that he produce his immunity assurances in writing, which he did.

In Alabama, immunity agreements are legally binding only if a judge approves them. However, I knew David Barber's word to be good. I would deal with the legal aspects of it later.

Armed with Barber's handwritten immunity agreement, I walked into the interrogation room to speak with my wheelchair-bound client. Ardragus Ford was not happy, but he looked much better than I would have after eight or nine hours of questioning by investigators who believed I was part of the murder of a fellow officer and friend. I could feel Ardragus' anger, perhaps partly directed toward me for leaving him alone to be questioned by two, three and sometimes four detectives at once. At times, Ford told me, a detective screamed accusations of lying and threats of the electric chair, while others gently tried to coax him into admitting he knew more than he was telling them. The eight hours of threats and screams would have produced a false confession from most people, especially with no lawyer as protector.

With stubborn determination, Ardragus maintained his innocence during the entire taped interrogation process and again to me when we talked alone in the little office. I showed him the handwritten immunity agreement signed by District Attorney Barber. Ardragus looked up at me and asked, "So they want me to lie?"

I assured him that no one, especially me, wanted or would allow him to lie.

"Look, Mr. Jaffe," Ardragus slowly began, "Toforest and I are close, but not that close. I see where they won't charge me if I say he did it. If that were the truth, I would say it in a heartbeat. I would not lie for him and put my family through all these changes, including money to pay you to represent me. But I am not lying for anybody, including the cops."

When I emerged from the interrogation room, I told the detectives that my client could not help them. They promptly took him to the Jefferson County Jail and charged him with capital murder.

Ford now faced the electric chair. Even with that knowledge, he refused to say what he knew the investigators wanted—that he had watched Toforest Johnson fire two deadly shots into Deputy Hardy's face. A law enforcement officer was dead and reason can sometimes be thrown out the window when that happens. This young man, although certainly no stranger to the drug-infested streets, possessed more moral character than most stalwarts of society. I have cross-examined many people who have lied to avoid a theft case. This young man faced the electric chair and refused to lie.

Soon I learned that the authorities had also arrested Toforest Johnson, Omar Berry and Quintez Wilson. Surely one or more of them would turn on the others, especially since one pair did not even know the other.

The investigators charged four people with Deputy Hardy's murder. Only one person fired two shots from the same weapon; however, all four potentially faced the death penalty. Surely, at least one of the four would "flip" (give the shooter up in exchange for leniency or even immunity)—or so the authorities hoped. This presumption was logically sound.

I was as shocked as anyone that Ford chose to live in a jail cell while confined to a wheelchair, rather than enjoy the unsupervised freedom and comfort of his mother's home. The more I got to know Ford and the closeness of his family, the louder the sound of his reply when I had presented the option that he would not be charged resonated in my mind: *"Toforest and I are close, but not that close."*

Moreover, Ford had never even heard of Omar Berry or Quintez Wilson. When he was offered immunity, he did not know that these two other individuals were also going to be charged. Perhaps Ford would not have hesitated to finger them to avoid getting charged if he could have done so *truthfully*.

The next step would be the preliminary hearing. Finally, we would get to hear all the evidence and have an opportunity to cross-examine Roshanna. Judge R. O. Hughes set the preliminary hearing about six weeks after the police arrested the four men.

The publicity surrounding Deputy Hardy's murder generated so much ferocity that the judge had to move the preliminary hearing site to the ground floor courtroom, which was two and a half times the size of his regular courtroom. More than 750 law enforcement officers had attended the deputy's funeral and many also came to the hearing.

District Judge Hughes was in his early to mid-sixties, his evenly-cut full head of white hair accentuating his kind eyes and his tall, solid frame. He had only been on the bench for a few years. In his four decades as a lawyer, he had distinguished himself within the local bar association through his professionalism, particularly in the diligent way he handled his cases and the gentlemanly respect and courtesy he offered even to his adversaries.

The preliminary hearing lasted the entire afternoon. At first Roshanna seemed to tell a convincing story, but soon it became clear to us that her version was riddled with so many internal inconsistencies, contradictions and lies that any objective person would have a difficult, if not impossible, time believing it. It seemed clear to us that she had never visited the hotel but rather had resorted to her vivid imagination to fill in the answers to practically any question that was presented to her by either side.

During her testimony, Roshanna admitted that she and her mother had hired an attorney to obtain the ten-thousand-dollar reward. She also admitted that only after being threatened with an accessory to capital murder charge did she say she knew anything about the murder. On the other hand, her friend Tammi remained in the Jefferson County Family Court Jail, charged with hindering prosecution when she refused to change her story and implicate the four accused young men.

At the conclusion of the preliminary hearing, Judge Hughes seemed to have serious doubts about the validity of the State's case. Bail is rarely set in capital cases, especially when the victim is a law enforcement officer. But the judge listened to Roshanna misidentify the police uniform, fail to recognize Deputy Hardy, whom she knew quite well, initially state that the killing occurred at the wrong location, testify incorrectly about the hat and the gun and botch numerous other material facts. He set bail for each of the four young men.

Soon after the hearing, Ford's family bailed him out. I felt deep relief that the wheelchair-bound young man would not wait in jail for at least a year before his trial. Little did I know, though, how dramatically the circumstances would change between the preliminary hearing and the trial.

Quintez Wilson and Omar Berry also made bond. Only Toforest Johnson, whose family had little means, remained incarcerated in the Jefferson County Jail. That jail stay would influence his ultimate fate profoundly.

Meanwhile, we had much investigating to do and many motions to file to prepare for trial while the law enforcement community and local media constantly projected an open-and-shut case that would lead to the death penalty for all of the accused.

As a result of the discovery motions we filed, the prosecution began turning over numerous documents, but nothing could have prepared us for the shocking information contained within them. We discovered that Roshanna had actually given several contradictory statements, even prior to the preliminary hearing. By the time the trial began, she gave more than fifteen different recorded statements with wildly varying details. In fact, until forensics completed its ballistics report, Roshanna maintained that Wilson and Johnson fired three shots from two different guns. The ballistics and autopsy reports made it clear that a single gun had fired two shots.

With each successive recorded statement, her version of the facts conformed to the evidence that the authorities' continuing investigation generated. For example, after the preliminary hearing, Roshanna changed Hardy's uniform color from blue to brown. She changed the location of the shooting from the front of the building to the side where the murder actually had occurred. She changed her mind about whether he was wearing his hat. She first said she knew the time of the shooting, because she heard the time on the radio; then she stated that the radio was never on. She changed three shots to two shots, but she always maintained that there were two different shooters.

The investigation progressed and, as the months passed, none of the four boys cut a deal. It is almost unheard of when multiple people are charged with a death penalty offense (or any serious offense, for that matter) for someone not to break down and turn State's evidence in exchange for leniency or immunity. Working on these types of cases for many years, I was amazed, since even though Ford and Johnson knew one another, neither knew Wilson and Berry. Nor did Wilson and Berry know Ford or Johnson. As for the prosecutors, they must have been flabbergasted.

With Ford's permission, I wrote letters to the district attorneys requesting that a polygraph exam be administered to Ford. I deviated from my normal protocol, which was to hire my own polygrapher to administer the test first. If my client passed the test, I felt comfortable enough to allow the authorities to test him. If he did not pass the test the authorities conducted, I still would have one polygraph he had passed. The results are not admissible anyway, unless an agreement is made between the defense and the State. I believed that with all of Roshanna's lies, many of which were under oath, I could possibly use a successful polygraph test result to try to reason with the prosecutors handling the cases.

As a result of my letters, for reasons not apparent at the time, the prosecutors chose to administer polygraphs to Omar Berry and Quintez Wilson first. Not surprisingly, Berry and Wilson passed with flying colors.

About this time, another piece of evidence surfaced: the security video camera from a nearby bank had scanned the hotel parking lot. It revealed that Roshanna had lied about the location of Ford's car. She had claimed his car was backed into a particular space where she would have had a clear view of the killing through the windshield. The video revealed that parking space and those around it were filled with parked cars at the time of the shooting. None was Ford's. Now the prosecution faced two new crucial pieces of contradictory information: Berry and Wilson had passed polygraphs and Roshanna had lied about the position of Ford's car. Again questions were raised as to how she could have actually witnessed the murder.

The investigators confronted Roshanna with their new information prior to administering the polygraph to Ford. Incredibly, she gave a new statement in which she claimed she had lied about Berry and Wilson. She had only met them once in a club several days before the killing. When she saw their pictures on the desk of one of the homicide investigators, she just decided to say they were involved, too. Then she admitted that she also had lied about the location of Ford's car. She changed her entire story and made both Ford and Johnson the shooters, despite the fact that Deputy Hardy had been shot twice with a single gun.

The physical evidence showed that after the first shot entered his mouth, Deputy Hardy retreated approximately thirty feet up the parking lot, as revealed by a path of blood and some of his teeth. He was then shot in the head at point-blank range, execution style. The shooter had chased him down to fire the second shot.

However, Ardragus Ford was confined to a wheelchair.

At least six hotel guests heard the two shots before looking out their hotel windows to the parking lot below, which gave them a clear view of the fairly well-lit lot. If Ford had actually left his car to shoot Deputy Hardy, the residents would have seen Johnson wheeling Ford back to Ford's automobile, getting him out of his wheelchair, placing him in the driver's seat, placing the wheelchair in the car and then going around to the passenger's side, opening that door and getting in. In addition, the witnesses had described a car that was not Ford's.

Armed with Roshanna's newest version of the facts, the prosecution dismissed all charges against Berry and Wilson but offered no apology. Neither flipped. Both had alibis. Both had previously faced the electric chair and now were free. Interestingly, the State used a different polygraph examiner to administer the test to Ford. According to this polygrapher, either Ford answered deceptively or his answers were inconclusive on several questions as to his involvement in or knowledge of the Hardy murder.

When we received these results, we were in complete disbelief. We retained Pete Pound, the premier polygrapher in Alabama and head of the Alabama Polygraph Association, a strong law enforcement proponent. Pete had trained many of the law enforcement polygraphers across the state, including the one who administered the test to Ford. We asked Pete to review the charts, graphs and control questions of the polygraph test administered to Ford and then to draft his own questions and administer a completely new test.

Pete found that the control questions utilized to polygraph Ford rendered the test invalid and the polygrapher had misinterpreted the results anyway. When he administered his polygraph to Ford, Pete unequivocally concluded that in his thirty years' experience, he had never seen a test reflect a stronger showing than this one. He was absolutely convinced that Ford was telling the truth.

Judge Alfred Bahakel scheduled the Ford and Johnson cases for trial. He, like most of the criminal circuit trial judges, usually set the lower numbered case first in multi-defendant trials. Although Ford's was the lower number and, therefore, expected to go first, Judge Bahakel set Johnson's date first. We believed the reason was that the prosecution wanted that order. The State's evidence against Johnson was even weaker than its case against Ford. We anticipated that the prosecution would not even call Roshanna in their effort to convict Johnson. If the prosecution could obtain a conviction against Johnson and then try Ford just a few weeks later, convicting Ford would be much easier in light of the adverse publicity that would be generated.

We filed an aggressive motion objecting to the prosecution's tactics. After our persistent protestations, the judge relented and set Ford's case first. The prosecution would have to use Roshanna for our trial and we would be ready.

Judge Bahakel set Ford's trial for November of the following year. However, in October our investigators told us that Roshanna had admitted to several people on the street that she had succumbed to pressure and concocted all of her stories about actually witnessing the Hardy murder. For that reason, she said, she kept changing her stories, including her original (admitted) lies about Wilson and Berry, now dropped as defendants. Allegedly, she said she felt terrible about falsely accusing Ford and Johnson and wanted to testify to the truth.

We filed a motion to dismiss the case for prosecutorial misconduct and Judge Bahakel ordered a hearing. At the hearing, Roshanna testified under oath that she had in fact been lying the whole time. The motion failed.

The jury selection process proved difficult and intense. Deputy Hardy, a twenty-three-year veteran, was a well-known, well-liked and well-respected law enforcement officer and member of the community. Almost everyone had heard of the case. Many had read about it, saw it on television, heard discussions at meetings or at church or had talked about it with their friends and family members. Even with Roshanna's fifteen different statements and the hundreds of lies contained within them, we were facing a mountain of public outcries for justice and guilt-riddled pretrial publicity.

By the middle of the week, we had selected a jury. We waited anxiously to hear the prosecution's opening statement. We had no idea what Roshanna would say on the stand and we could not get the court to order the prosecution to tell us. The prosecutors simply said they did not know and it's possible they didn't. Who would she say did the shooting? How many shots would she say were fired? How many guns were used? Under the United States Supreme Court decisions in *Brady v. Maryland* and numerous federal and Alabama cases, we were supposed to know this information before trial. The court simply ordered that we had to rely on the information already provided to us.

In its opening statement, the prosecution revealed nothing other than that Hardy was brutally murdered and Ford was guilty. Long on platitudes but short on details, the prosecution took no chances by committing to any other specifics regarding the actual shooting. We believed that they too were unsure what their star witness would say once she took the stand.

In stark contrast to the prosecution's ten to fifteen-minute opening statement, we spent a solid hour detailing the innumerable inconsistencies, fabrications and imaginative lies which would spew from Roshanna, the street-savvy girl who seemed to hold no regard for the truth. We braced the jurors to hear about monetary motivations, fear-inspired lies and reckless inconsistencies. We predicted that the jurors would hear not only the numerous different versions Roshanna had already given, but also an entirely new collection of lies when she testified at trial. We contrasted Roshanna with her friend, Tammi, who found the courage to languish in jail as a consequence of telling the truth. We beseeched the jurors not to be fooled by Roshanna or the way the prosecution continued to allow her charade. We pointed out the prosecutors' dismissal of Omar Berry and Quintez Wilson and their picking and choosing which of Roshanna's lies they wanted the jury to believe. We let the jury know that at one time, Berry and Wilson were slated to be sitting in Ford's place, facing Alabama's electric chair, until Roshanna was forced to admit that she had lied about them. How could the jury remotely believe anything that she would say now?

Judge Bahakel called upon the prosecution to produce its first witness. When it did, we were stunned in disbelief: "Your Honor, we call as our first witness Ms. Carla Bowen."

We had investigated this case from top to bottom, yet we had never heard of this witness. I was so shocked I could not speak. I looked at Derek Drennan and he looked at me. "Who the hell is she?" I asked Drennan. His befuddled eyes let me know he felt as shocked as I did.

A rather tall and slim female in her late twenties walked into the room. Most striking was the fearful timidity her face displayed. I jumped out of my seat and asked if we could approach the bench. The court reporter joined us.

"Your Honor, as you well know, this is a capital case. You have ordered that the prosecution provide us with open file discovery. Therefore, we are supposed to know the identity of every State's witness. Neither Mr. Drennan nor I have ever heard of this witness. We ask that the court conduct an immediate hearing pursuant to Alabama Rule of Evidence 104(a) to determine whether the State has violated *Brady v. Maryland* and this court's order requiring full and open disclosure and we ask that we be allowed to examine this witness and the prosecutors on this crucial issue."[1]

"What says the State?" Judge Bahakel directed his comments to the prosecutors.

The prosecution took the position that they had only learned of her existence within the last few hours.

I countered, "Even if that is the case, the moment that the prosecution learned of this woman, whether it was an hour or a week or a year ago, they owed us a duty to disclose that information to us before trial. Bringing in this mystery woman as their very first witness, without any warning to us whatsoever, clearly violates the Sixth, Eighth and Fourteenth Amendments to the United States Constitution and Article 6, Section 1 of the Alabama Constitution as well as your direct orders. We ask to be allowed to examine Ms. Bowen outside the presence of a jury and we also request that the court order the prosecution to turn over any written or oral statements she has made in connection to this case."

The prosecution's next comments puzzled both my co-counsel and me: There were no written or recorded statements, they claimed, since the authorities had just located Ms. Bowen.

The judge dismissed the jury for the day and allowed us to examine Carla Bowen. Immediately, I sensed her terror. She was in some type of conflict which I could not quite identify. So I probed firmly but gently. Finally, I asked, "So, Ms. Bowen, is it your testimony to this court that the sheriff's investigators came unannounced to your home this morning and you felt you had no choice but to come with them here to court?"

"Yes," she responded meekly.

"And you are telling us that you have signed no statements nor given any recorded statements at all?"

Carla Bowen looked sheepish yet answered determinedly. "I didn't sign anything, but yes, they did record me when I got here to the courthouse." I felt a flushing sensation as the blood boiled through my face and toward my battered brain. Both dismayed and incredulous, I inquired, "And who was present during this recorded statement the prosecution just told us did not exist?"

Bowen replied that some police officers were present along with one of the prosecutors. When I asked her whom, she said it was not Mr. Wallace but the other prosecutor sitting next to him.

I was shocked.

"Your Honor, we demand a copy of that recorded statement or at least a copy of the tape, and we respectfully request a recess to review it before examining Ms. Bowen further. And we do intend to ask for a mistrial."

The judge ordered the prosecution to turn over a copy of the recorded statement and we recessed until the next morning.

That evening, we listened to Ms. Bowen's recorded statement and noted she testified accurately about who was present. However, Ms. Bowen's initial denials of knowing anything about the Hardy murder proved more revealing. She knew Ford, who had been over at her house one evening. He had a conversation with another young male while she stayed in her kitchen watching the crime drama *Matlock*. However, she said that she had heard nothing incriminatory coming from Ford about the Hardy murder.

The investigators had taken a familiar approach when they confronted her. They told her that she could be either a witness or a defendant. They had said the same thing to Ford and the young women with whom he partied. All but Roshanna were charged with a crime.

On tape, the investigators asked Carla Bowen how many children she had. "Three," she replied. They asked her if she was a single mother and, therefore, raised them alone. "Yes," she answered. The investigators asked her what she would do if she found herself incarcerated and unable to care for them. Would the Department of Human Resources be forced to take custody and control of the children? They said they would hate for Carla Bowen to risk losing her children when all she had to do was tell them the "truth" about what she knew about Ardragus Ford's involvement. There was no immediate reply from Carla.

Suddenly, during the audio recording, the cobwebs miraculously cleared from Carla Bowen's memory and she recalled overhearing Ford admit that he had knowledge and involvement in the deputy sheriff's murder. Familiar to us on the defense team but unfathomable to her, she now found herself in the same dark, frightened cave that Tammi and Roshanna inhabited. Like Roshanna, she could not withstand the pressure.

The trial recommenced. The jury sat riveted, listening to Ms. Bowen's direct testimony, but our cross-examination exposed a terrified woman desperate to keep her children. The jury must have sensed a significant degree of desperation from the prosecutors' desk over the way they had produced a "surprise" witness whom no one knew of during the sixteen-month investigation preceding the trial.

We felt that our examination of Carla Bowen left her sheepishly distraught, yet she maintained her finger-pointing at Ardragus Ford while admitting her terror over being suddenly thrust into her no-win dilemma. Judge Bahakel denied our motion for a mistrial based on prosecutorial misconduct. The *Birmingham News* mentioned the irony of Bowen watching *Matlock* when she overhead Ford's alleged confession and likened her entrance into the courtroom to a *Perry Mason* episode. The *Birmingham News* also accurately quoted me exclaiming that this amounted to a "trial by ambush" of the highest sort.

Soon the time came for the jury to hear the testimony of Roshanna. By the time she took the stand, tension had tightened in the courtroom to the point where the air seemed too thick to breathe.

In her testimony, Roshanna could not explain how Ford could have jumped out of his wheelchair and chased Deputy Hardy for thirty feet up an incline. The jurors heard testimony and saw phone records that conflicted with Roshanna's testimony and mounds of lies. They heard about the threats she received, the reward money she sought and the absurd versions that kept twisting around one another until all plausible truth was suffocated by her exhausting lies.

During closing arguments I reminded the jurors that four experienced detectives had spent an entire day interrogating Ford, who maintained his innocence under enormous pressure. The alibi witnesses he reported to the police had all testified and verified the fact that he was indeed at the bar on that July night from 9:00 P.M. until almost 2:00 A.M.

Finally, I shared my fears and concerns with the jury. Because this was a brutal police killing, someone might be tempted to discard the presumption of innocence and the burden of proof, contrary to the oath each juror took and the instructions of the court. I ended by softly saying that a guilty verdict in this case on behalf of a law enforcement officer like Deputy Hardy would be "an insult to his memory and a blow to justice." Deputy Hardy would not want a wrongful conviction with the real killer still at large.

Ten of the twelve jurors voted for acquittal. For reasons still unclear, two jurors held out for conviction. After two and a half days of deliberations, Judge Bahakel declared a mistrial, since the jury was hung with a less than unanimous verdict. We were very disappointed. Ardragus' trial would have to be reset.

With only a month or so separating his trial from Ford's and mountains of publicity about Ford's trial filling the short gap between the trials, it was now Toforest Johnson's turn to face a jury of his peers.

When the prosecutor made his opening statement in Johnson's trial, he never mentioned one word about Roshanna. The prosecutors in Johnson's trial rested their case almost entirely on a single witness, a supposedly neutral middle-aged woman who claimed she overhead Johnson admit to killing Deputy Hardy on the phone at the Jefferson County Jail. Johnson's lawyers contended that if she heard anything, she heard Johnson describing the allegations against him and how preposterous they were. However, the version she reportedly heard was not accurate, even more support that he was never there. It was significant that the prosecution produced no recording of this conversation, in spite of the fact that the Jefferson County Jail clearly notifies each inmate that all calls from the jail are recorded.

Did Johnson ignore the signs above the phones warning inmates that their conversations were being recorded? Or was he simply relaying his understanding of the allegations as he understood them, as his defense team argued? We believed that what this lady testified that Johnson had said was not how the crime occurred.

Could the prosecution really have it both ways? Could they present two different versions of the same crime in an attempt to convict two different people of it using different witnesses?

Incredibly, eleven of the twelve jurors voted to convict Toforest Johnson, resulting in a hung jury.

Johnson's case would also have a second trial.

Another person who would be forced to endure the legal system at least two more times was Deputy Hardy's loving widow. In the middle of Ford's trial, she told the *Birmingham News* she only wanted the truth to come out and wasn't sure that was happening.

When the court reset both of the Hardy murder cases for trial, the prosecution successfully convinced Judge Bahakel to deviate from his normal course and schedule Johnson's case first, with Ford's trial to follow a few weeks later. The judge would not change his mind, despite our loud protests.

The second Johnson trial began in August. Again the prosecution did not call Roshanna to the stand. Prosecutors argued that Johnson shot and killed Deputy Hardy. After the prosecution rested its case, Johnson's defense team changed its tactic in a maneuver that was truly a high-risk gamble. They called Roshanna to the witness stand! Although lacking in credibility, she was the only person known to either side that could place Johnson at the crime scene, even if she lied to do it.

Although her testimony and that of the supposed neutral lady could not be reconciled, the jury still found Johnson guilty and sentenced him to death.

It was now time for Ford's second trial. After his mistrial, our investigators had spoken to several jurors. Among other information, we learned that one of the jurors refusing to convict Ford still believed Roshanna.

I decided to ask my close friend and colleague, Emory Anthony, a highly skilled trial lawyer, to join the defense team. I felt he would add a fresh viewpoint to the re-trial of this death penalty case.

Ford's second trial began and again it took several days to select a jury with a makeup similar to the previous one. Unabashedly, the prosecution reverted to their claim that Ford was the shooter, not Johnson, even though Johnson was now facing the electric chair. We provided Emory Anthony with every inconsistent statement that Roshanna had ever made and his cross-examination of her proved to be absolutely brilliant. Every time she told a lie or inconsistency, he pointed it out and marked it on an easel containing white poster-sized paper. The lies became so apparent that Anthony began prompting her with, "And that was a…" pausing for Roshanna herself to fill in, "Lie."

Finally, the prosecutors offered to stipulate that she had already told over three hundred lies, which stopped Emory's unrelentingly tedious but necessary marking of the easel and counting of the lies.

The jury took only an hour to deliberate. Its verdict, finally a true one: "Not guilty."

Almost three years after Deputy Hardy's murder, Ford was finally free from the false charges. The authorities also dropped the hindering prosecution charges against Roshanna's friend Tammi.

Meanwhile, Toforest Johnson remains on death row. His case now rests in the capable hands of the Southern Center for Human Rights (SCHR), which we asked to handle his appeal.

That Johnson is even in this awful predicament leads to one central question: Where did the truth go? What had happened to the truth during all of these twists and turns, changing stories, jailed witnesses, inconsistent theories, codefendants once charged and then dismissed? How important is it to get it right in any case, especially a death penalty case? Did the truth get swallowed up by desperation to solve the senseless murder of a fine and respected officer? Did the criminal justice system devour it? Who was representing the truth? What happened to the search for proof?

24
....
PRESUMED INNOCENT
MEETS FATALLY ATTRACTED

One soft, sunny spring afternoon, I parked my car and made my
way to Birmingham's Sixteenth Street Baptist Church, where a
bomb blew four innocent African-American girls to bits so many years
ago. I was to address the ultimate civil right: the right to live. I walked
slowly as I thought about what I would say to this gathering of past
and present civil rights leaders, activists, concerned citizens and the
friends and family members of death row inmates. Although lawyers
relish speaking, I felt especially awed to be doing so at the lectern from
which Martin Luther King, Jr. once spoke.

The organizers had asked five people to speak of the injustices
inherent in the death penalty. I was the third speaker and the only lawyer.
I talked about my years defending the victims of a barbaric, arbitrary
system that favored the rich over the poor. I described the insidious
racial discrimination inherent in the system and the hypocrisy of the
Alabama law in particular, which allows a judge to override a jury's
recommendation of life and impose a death sentence.[1]

When the rally ended and informal mingling began, a deter-
mined-looking blonde woman in her mid-thirties approached me. "I'm
Brenda Massingill," she introduced herself to me. "Have you heard of
the Randal Padgett case?"

"No, I haven't," I replied with some curiosity.

"Randal is a friend of mine. I am trying to help him. He is charged with capital murder."

"What do they say he did?" I inquired.

Pausing for an instant, she looked directly into my eyes and said, "They say he stabbed his wife forty-six times and then raped her, but he's innocent. I know he's innocent."

As she spoke, I conjured up a bloody crime scene, a gory corpse and a likely death sentence. At the same time I was struck by her passionate belief in her friend's innocence.

"Mr. Jaffe," Brenda continued, "I don't like what's going on with the investigation. I'm afraid for Randal."

"Is Randal represented?"

"His family hired some lawyers to represent him, but I don't know what they are doing to defend him. Will you meet with him, you know, kind of give us a second opinion?"

"Well, who are his lawyers?" I pressed.

"Mark McDaniel and Bill Burgess, but Randal doesn't know what they are doing and I'm scared for him," she implored.

I had never met Randal's lawyers, but I knew Mark McDaniel to be the most well-known and successful criminal lawyer in the area. Bill Burgess shared a similar reputation. I told Brenda that Randal had excellent representation and I saw no reason to get involved. Firmly but politely, I declined to meet with Randal or discuss the case further. I wished Randal the best. I let Brenda know that if things didn't work out for Randal, she should feel free to contact me after the trial was concluded.

I left the rally never expecting to hear from Brenda Massingill again. I gave the Padgett case no further thought, concentrating instead on my caseload, which was the size of a small mountain.

Over the next four years I tried a number of capital murder cases. Each time, jurors answered with "not guilty" or the cases resulted in hung juries or a lesser offense but no death sentences. Not yet.

Then one Friday afternoon, my longtime legal assistant Meredith

Gray buzzed my intercom to inform me a woman named Carol Tabor wanted to speak with me about hiring me to represent her brother, Randal Padgett, who was on death row. The Supreme Court of Alabama had just issued an opinion ordering a new trial for him.

I was stunned. I thought about my brief five-minute conversation with Brenda Massingill almost four years earlier. I picked up the phone. Carol Tabor, Randal's sister, recounted the details of Randal's conviction and death sentence and the family's desire to retain new counsel for him. The family had checked me out carefully. She was curious to know if I'd be willing to have a meeting with her and two of her brothers.

"Mr. Jaffe," she concluded, "We are anxious to make a decision and if possible, we would like to talk about hiring you."

We agreed to meet in my office the following Sunday morning.

On Sunday, we sat in a small circle in my office: my young associate Derek Drennan, Carol Tabor and Randal's two brothers. Derek and I listened attentively as each of Randal's siblings discussed the background and the facts, the inquiry that their private investigators had conducted and the trial proceedings. One hour passed…then two…then three. Each of Randal's siblings displayed a different temperament, but I detected a great deal of distrust and anger emanating from all of them. I also sensed the palpable feeling of betrayal and disappointment that usually accompanies unmet expectations.

Carol took firm charge of the meeting and talked of Randal. He had been happily married to Cathy for about sixteen years. They had two sweet children he dearly loved. Then he began an on-and-off four-year affair with Judy Bagwell, a coworker whom he also supervised. Each time Randal moved out and threatened to divorce Cathy, he just could not go through with it. He always moved back, but at the time of the murder he was living in a trailer, because he and Cathy were again discussing a divorce.

The night Cathy's body was found brutally raped and murdered in her bed, Randal Padgett and his girlfriend Judy lay together in bed in Panama City, Florida. When the hotel owner knocked on the door of their room, which did not contain a phone, the half-asleep Randal edged open the door.

"Mr. Padgett," the man calmly stated. "There's a man holding on the phone in the office. He says he's your brother and needs to talk to you right away. It's urgent."

Randal rushed to the office. Within five minutes Randal returned to his hotel room, walked into the bathroom and threw up. Judy was apparently sound asleep. In total disbelief, amid tears and shock, Randal touched her shoulder and said, "You have to get up. We have to leave right away. Cathy's been murdered."

Judy woke up groggy from a seemingly sound sleep. "Why? Who would want to murder Cathy?" Surprise and concern sharpened Judy's exhausted-sounding voice.

"I don't know. I guess we will find out when we get back. I'm too shook up to drive. You've got to drive."

Within fifteen minutes, Judy began the six-hour return drive with Randal in the passenger's seat in a silent state of shock, still not believing his wife and the mother of his children no longer lived. They made the long trek back to Alabama on pitch-black, two-lane roads through the sleepy rural towns of Northwest Florida. It proved too daunting for Judy. Inside the first hour, Judy swerved dangerously on and off the road's unequal shoulders. After more close calls, Randal insisted that she pull over to the roadside. Although devastated, he drove the remaining five or so hours. Judy quickly fell asleep and awoke only when they pulled up at the sheriff's office. Although the significance of Judy's inability to drive escaped Randal at the time, he noted it curiously and ultimately it would haunt him.

Still, his mind raced with questions. What had happened and why? Did the police have any suspects? How did such a tragic event occur? His thoughts kept veering back to his children.

At the sheriff's office, after the exchange of a few formalities, sheriff's investigators placed Randal and Judy in separate rooms and began questioning them. It had been almost twenty-four hours since Randal had slept.

In a domestic homicide, the authorities almost always consider the spouse a prime suspect. By the time Randal and Judy arrived at the sheriff's department, investigators had learned that Randal lived in a trailer due to his separation from Cathy and that they were contemplating divorce. Family members informed investigators that Randal and Judy had left for Florida the morning after Cathy's murder, which the coroner estimated to have occurred around 1:00 A.M. on Friday. The detectives had also learned of a prior confrontation between Judy and Cathy.

Did either Randal or Judy have an alibi? Would they claim to be each other's alibi? The investigators saw an obvious motive. Yet Randal Padgett enjoyed a stellar reputation in the community and family members could not conceive for a moment that Randal could be involved in Cathy's murder in any way. Nevertheless, Cathy's house showed no forced entry, no items were stolen or removed and someone had brutally raped and murdered Cathy Padgett. The authorities had no leads to other suspects.

Judy Bagwell claimed she retired early on Thursday, August 16, the night of the murder, in anticipation of leaving on a pre-planned scuba diving trip early the next morning. Beyond that, she offered no alibi.

Randal Padgett recounted the last time he saw his wife and stated that both his children slept with him at his trailer. He, too, claimed to retire early. With only two bedrooms in his trailer, his eight-year-old daughter slept in the bed with him. The paper-thin trailer partitions would not have silenced the engine noise from his truck had he left to kill Cathy and then return. Neither trailer nor truck contained a hint of bloodstains. Had Randal showered after killing Cathy, the noise would have awoken both of his children as would the return of his truck.

The investigators claimed they needed Randal's help and he readily agreed to meet them the next morning at the Padgett home. The authorities released both Randal and Judy. They would not see each other again until the trial.

The following morning at 8:00 A.M., investigators met Randal at the Padgett home. The detectives videotaped him as he walked them through the home, answering every question they asked.

If Randal Padgett had murdered his wife, he stripped himself of every opportunity to deflect suspicion onto someone else. No, he did not for a moment think Judy capable of such a heinous act. No, an intruder could not have made the "old" scuffmarks on the front door panel. No, nothing seemed out of place in the house, other than blood-soaked sheets and blankets, torn and ripped clothing and undergarments and various odds and ends in Cathy's bedroom. No, Randal had not engaged in sexual relations for months with Cathy, so the sperm in her vaginal canal could not be his.

He readily consented to DNA testing and a polygraph.

Within a couple of days, Randal submitted to blood tests and gave hair and saliva samples to facilitate the testing. He also took a polygraph test that the authorities claimed to be "inconclusive." When asked about whom he thought might possibly have been motivated to kill Cathy Padgett, Randal offered, "I don't know anyone in the world who would want to hurt Cathy. She was as good as gold."

Randal focused on helping the police find the killer. The thought of retaining legal counsel never crossed his mind until the day the DNA test results reached the Marshall County Sheriff's Department. Randal's DNA matched that found at the scene of the murder. On that day, a swarm of police officers and detectives surrounded Cathy's parents' house, where Randal had been visiting, and arrested him for capital murder.

Randal knew he desperately needed the best legal representation in the area. However, with no prior criminal history and an unblemished background, Randal did not know any criminal lawyers. But Carol Tabor, Randal's sister, knew Mark McDaniel, who agreed to represent Randal Padgett for capital murder.

Mark McDaniel's southern drawl had successfully persuaded juries across north Alabama on more than a few occasions. Neatly dressed, always smiling, thin and affable, this Huntsville lawyer often quoted the Bible. Confident, articulate and charming, McDaniel had built quite a reputation in the community and legal circles.

McDaniel immediately associated Bill Burgess, a very bright and experienced attorney who shared space in his law office.

When McDaniel met Randal for the first time, he made Randal feel at ease. McDaniel assured Randal that he had successfully handled many other challenging cases. They just needed to find a way to dispute the DNA evidence, because nothing else linked Randal to the crime scene. McDaniel's constant assurances meant a lot to Randal, who could think of nothing else but his children and putting this horrid nightmare behind him. He looked forward to eventually rebuilding his shattered life. McDaniel and Randal corresponded frequently; McDaniel's letters contained quotes of Biblical passages and Randal felt safe and secure, confident that a jury would discover the truth and deliver a verdict of acquittal.

When Randal had learned the DNA test results implicated him, his mind swirled in confusion and questions bombarded him. Could the test results be faulty or perhaps could Judy have done it? Randal could find no answers that made sense to him. Yet whenever he mentioned investigating Judy Bagwell, McDaniel told him that calling Judy as a witness would be exceptionally dangerous. If pressured by the prosecutors, Judy (represented by Randy Beard) might strike a bargain for immunity in exchange for testifying against Randal and that could force Judy to implicate Randal.

For over two years, Randal, who was out on bail, tried to keep his life together, but the thought of the looming trial never left him. All of his acquaintances and everyone he met had heard or read of his case. He tried his best to live a normal life for his children's sake, but he found little solace outside of his immediate family and one or two close friends.

When the trial began on June 16, Randal's confidence in the process slowly began to shrink. He knew his case would probably rest on challenging the DNA evidence and a host of character witnesses attesting to his impeccable character (except for his well-known affair with Judy Bagwell).

The prosecution's case was powerful and armed with horrific and gory crime scene photos and slides, law enforcement's handling of the evidence and a DNA expert from the Maryland laboratory. This expert testified that the odds of the DNA not being Randal computed to one in millions. When the State rested its formidable case, Randal's chances seemed bleak. The prosecution's case was practically flawless but for one rather prophetic detail: when the Alabama State crime lab repeated a blood typing test of Randal's blood, the second test revealed a different blood type.

None of the experts from either the Alabama crime lab or the Maryland DNA lab could explain the discrepancy, which defied scientific reasoning. The same blood should reveal the same blood type each time the lab tested it. District Attorney Ronald Thompson failed to disclose this second test until just before the trial began. Bill Burgess and Mark McDaniel, both experienced and talented lawyers, vigorously objected. They argued, without success, to the trial judge that the late disclosure would not give them a chance to confront it adequately.

During the defense presentation, McDaniel and Burgess called a DNA expert they had retained from Florida. The expert convincingly testified on direct examination as to the possible imperfections in the science of DNA testing. Unfortunately, on cross-examination, the savvy and insightful assistant prosecutor Tim Jolley showed the defense expert Randal's DNA autorads (images of the testing) and asked him to inspect them. Then Jolley held up the autorads of the semen found in Cathy's vagina. While holding them up side-by-side, Jolley then asked the expert to compare the two. The defense expert conceded the two appeared to be close enough that the jury could conclude the Maryland lab's testing was accurate.

At that point, any hope Randal had harbored of an acquittal evaporated into the air like the mist off nearby Lake Guntersville, burned away by the blistering sun of the prosecution's case.

Randal Padgett next testified on his own behalf, but the jury did not appear overly interested. He seemed emotionless and distant, almost a bit vacant. The jury did not understand that Randal's withdrawn veneer belied the fear and pain that held his heart hostage. The testimony of the twenty or so character witnesses that followed—a quite impressive number for any defendant—echoed with a hollow emptiness.

It took the jury hardly two hours to pronounce Randal guilty of capital murder. After the sentencing hearing, that same jury recommended by a vote of nine to three he spend the rest of his life in prison, as opposed to recommending death. But Judge William Jetton overrode the jury's recommendation and sentenced Randal to death due to the brutal and heinous manner in which Cathy Padgett had met her end. Whoever killed Cathy brutally stabbed her forty-six times and both the judge and the jury had no doubt it was Randal.

McDaniel and Burgess appealed Randal's conviction and death sentence and wisely sought the help of the Equal Justice Initiative (EJI), the same organization that came to the aid of Bo Cochran. The Alabama Court of Criminal Appeals reversed the case because of the State's failure to provide the second blood test report showing the inexplicably inconsistent blood typing result. The court correctly reasoned that once the State discovered exculpatory (favorable) evidence, they must disclose it as soon as practicable. In this case, the court held that they had not.

"Well, if Randal would never even think of killing Cathy and if you believe that Judy would do anything do get Randal, I guess we'll have to begin to see if we can find any evidence to support that theory," I said to Randal Padgett's three siblings in my conference room.

I watched their faces and for a moment it seemed that each face softened—but only for a moment.

Stone-faced, the creases deepening in his richly tanned forehead, Randal's oldest brother stared at me, almost glaring.

Randal's family explained that the authorities had arrested him only after a Maryland forensics lab determined that the sperm found in Cathy's vaginal canal contained Randal's DNA. I asked, "What evidence do you know of that Judy planted Randal's sperm?"

His siblings believed something that at first sounded outrageous: Judy killed Cathy without Randal's knowledge and somehow planted Randal's semen in Cathy. Randal's lawyers did not pursue their theory. I could certainly understand the reluctance of Randal's lawyers to pursue this rather bizarre theory of defense, especially without any proof. But Carol emphasized that Judy was smart and cunning.

"We don't know how she did it," Carol tried to explain, "but she had to have done it. I know my brother; he is kind and gentle. He is incapable of hurting anyone. He loves his children more than anything. He never would have let them find their mother's mutilated body in her bedroom."

I dug deeper. "Then how do you think that Judy could have done it?"

"We don't know. That's what we need to find out. But there was this incident…" Cathy began.

I perked up. "What incident?"

"About a year and a half before the murder, Judy hid in the backseat of Cathy's car wearing a raincoat, a wig and gloves. Judy knew that Cathy went to church every Wednesday evening."

I saw the first signs of support for a motive surfacing. "Go on."

"As soon as Cathy opened the door, Judy ordered her to sit down so they could talk. Judy told Cathy that she loved Randal and Randal loved her. Judy begged Cathy to divorce Randal. Cathy said she had no intention of divorcing Randal. She loved him and would keep fighting for him. Cathy also told Judy to stay away from her children. Just then a church deacon walking to his car must have heard the commotion. He approached the car to make sure that everything was okay. Then Judy left."

"Is there a police report concerning this incident?" I assumed none existed.

To my astonishment, Thomas replied, "There is. A copy is in this box of documents, which also includes the transcript of the first trial and the appellate briefs."

I thumbed through the banker's box, which was packed with court papers and documents, official police reports and a folder with letters written to Randal from one of his former lawyers. I noticed that almost all of their letters contained numerous religious quotes and references.

I looked up. "What was the theory of defense that his lawyers chose?"

Kendal Padgett replied, "They argued that there was not enough evidence and that Randal had a good character and no history of violence in his background."

"Did Randal's lawyers try to show that Judy did it?"

"No," Carol replied. "They said that would be dangerous."

McDaniel and Burgess were right. It would be dangerous. I would not have done it either without a solid foundation. But for this next trial, a "Hail Mary pass" might be the only way, if we could find credible evidence to support the Padgetts' belief.

"Did Judy testify?"

"No. Both sides were afraid to call her as a witness."

We then set up a meeting with Randal in Guntersville, where he awaited his retrial in the Marshall County Jail. My team needed to read the documents in the box and attempt to speak to Randal's former lawyers before meeting Randal. It was hard to believe that years of a person's life could be distilled down to a box of paper, but as I read, a vivid picture began to emerge.

By all accounts, Randal and Cathy, proud parents of a son and daughter, seemed a model couple. Friends and family enjoyed their company and appreciated the respectful way Randal always treated Cathy. A man of few words, Randal loved to hunt and fish. But more than anything else, he adored his family, built on the foundation of the religious beliefs he and Cathy shared.

Randal's affair with Judy started as an office flirtation. They both worked at a textile plant where Randal was a supervisor. Normally friendly but quiet, Randal managed to keep to himself for the most part. But at the end of the night shift, he sometimes kidded around with the staff. On one occasion, when the subject of skinny-dipping came up, Judy dared him to follow her home, where she had a pool. He did and once at her house Randal quickly found out Judy wasn't joking: she stripped off her clothes and dove into the water. Randal quickly followed suit and a fiery affair began that never seemed to cool.

Randal told people that there was something strange and hypnotic about Judy that he could never really explain and that every time he tried to give her up, he kept coming back, knowing deep down that it was just not right. For some inexplicable reason, he could not stay away from her, no matter how much he tried.

The entire Padgett family enjoyed the highest reputation in their hometown and the surrounding towns. These small towns scattered across the South have unique characters. Generally, the people are hard-working, honest folks. A deep, genuine faith is part of everyday life. It is a place where you know your neighbors from the cradle to the grave. The community expressed shock over the affair and seemed to be too embarrassed to talk about it openly, out of respect for the Padgett family. Everyone knew about it, yet Randal was sucked into some sordid abyss of sensuality and Judy seemed to sense when Randal weakened.

The trial transcript also included in the box revealed another matter that would result in a life-or-death decision for us to make. It involved Judge Jetton, who had overridden the jury decision for life and sentenced Randal to death. Not only did Judge Jetton sentence Randal to death, but he also stated on the record when doing so that he had his own reasons for believing that Randal killed Cathy and therefore deserved death. After reading this remarkable portion of the record, we knew that if the jury found Randal guilty again, Judge Jetton would again sentence him to death, regardless of what the jury recommended. We also knew that under those circumstances we could file a motion to recuse (remove) Judge Jetton and he would have to grant our motion and step off the case.

While the concept of filing this motion seemed obvious, my gut told me something else. When I completed my reading of the Padgett transcript, I became absolutely convinced that Judge Jetton embodied every quality one could ever desire from a great judge. He knew the law and did not interfere unnecessarily in the trial, as some judges tend to do. The record revealed that he treated each lawyer with respect and listened patiently as they made their arguments and objections. Most of all, he aimed to be fair.

The fact that he would again sentence Randal to death did not influence me, as I felt any other judge presiding over this gruesome case in a small town would do the same. We decided that we would not file any motions to remove Judge Jetton. We would simply endeavor to win Randal's case. We would have to take measured and calculated risks at the trial. We learned from the first trial transcript what had not worked before.

After we finished going through the box of documents that Randal's family provided and the trial transcript, we formulated an investigative plan and made arrangements to make the first of many trips to Guntersville to view the crime scene and meet our client, Randal Padgett.

From Birmingham to the Marshal County jail is about a ninety-minute drive on a two-lane road. The road quickly turns into the windy, mountainous terrain of North Alabama.

At our first occasion to visit Randal, when we arrived at the Marshall County Jail we sat in a small conference room for lawyers. In more than a few Alabama jail visitor's rooms, lawyers stand or sit on thin mattresses or milk crates; at least this one contained chairs. Within minutes, our client walked into the room: a slow moving, gloomy, expressionless Randal Padgett. We stood up and shook Randal's hand-cuffed hand. His legs were shackled, too. He made little eye contact with us and took a seat in one of the chairs we had positioned a couple of feet from us.

The room we sat in was hardly big enough for three chairs. Randal, his face worn and eyes tired, gave us a weary semi-smile. On death row for five years, his pale skin blended with the cold and win-dowless room. The vivid orange of his jumpsuit was the brightest color in the room. He looked at us suspiciously as he waited for one of us to begin speaking.

25

GAINING A CONDEMNED MAN'S TRUST

"Randal, I'm Richard Jaffe and this is Derek Drennan," I began. "I'm glad we're finally able to meet you, although we know these are not the best of times."

"You got that right," Padgett deadpanned. He hesitated. "You know I'm innocent—now how are you going to get me off for something I didn't do?"

"I don't think we can tell you that today, after only being on the case for three weeks," Derek said. "But if there is a way, we'll do it."

"Well, is there a way?" Padgett's deep southern drawl rolled slowly off his lips.

"We believe there is, but I'm sure you understand it's going to take a lot of work and it won't be easy," I said. "And maybe not today, but at some point, you're going to have to trust us. But that may take some time."

"That's what my last lawyers said, too. I trusted them. And here I am," Randal's voice was almost a whisper. "I'm not sure I trust anybody. I may never trust anyone again."

"What about your family?" I asked. "What about them?"

"Well, I guess I trust them some, but then they got me my last lawyers…"

I took a silent breath and observed his diverted eyes staring downward toward his knees. I said nothing.

He continued, "I guess I'm going to have to trust you some, but it won't be easy."

"Randal, we're not asking for you to believe in us today, only to give us a chance to earn your trust. You know, we're a team. We take our mission seriously. We know that we hold your life in our hands. And the last thing we want is for you to be our first client to end up on death row."

"I've already been on death row and I don't want to go back," he quietly retorted with a twinge of sadness and anger.

"Then we're on the same team," Derek Drennan said, trying to assure him.

I asked Randal if he thought Judy had committed the murder. He told us that at first he didn't think so, but now he had his doubts. We promised to investigate the case from the bottom up and that no matter what, we would follow the evidence wherever it took us.

After a little less than an hour, we left Randal at the jail, having no idea how we would ever successfully defend him. The meeting had gone as well as it could have, but gaining his trust would be even more challenging than we had anticipated.

A successful outcome at a new trial depends primarily on a thoughtful, thorough and tenacious reinvestigation and evaluation of all evidence. We retraced how, once Randal Padgett's DNA test came back positive, the authorities looked no further. They had no other suspects, anyway. For all intents and purposes, the DNA test results had solved the case. Their investigation then moved on to the next phase: finding any and all corroboration that would seal Randal's fate. Any leads the investigators followed were those that supported the conclusion of his already-determined guilt.

For twenty years, Rick Blake, our in-house investigator, had trained police officers and detectives in the art and science of conducting homicide investigations. Blake had doggedly investigated the Bo Cochran case for us as well as many others. Perhaps Blake's strongest asset was his ability to get just about anybody to talk to him. For this case, we would rely upon that quality. Before we could develop our initial investigative plan, we needed to face some daunting realities. How would we convince a jury to find Randal not guilty, when every one of them would know that a previous jury had already determined beyond a reasonable doubt that he killed and raped his wife? Judge Jetton had overruled the first jury and sentenced Randal to death. New jurors would know that, too. We worried the judge would surely do it again if given the chance.

Since four years separated the first trial from the second, we did not think we could successfully seek a change of venue. We researched criminal lawyers in the area and kept hearing about Mike Mastin. I called Mike, who knew all about the case. We associated him as our local counsel and he proved very helpful, both inside and outside the courtroom.

As our investigation continued, Blake tirelessly and relentlessly investigated every aspect. The more information he uncovered, the more everything pointed away from Randal having anything to do with Cathy's murder. So we began to look more closely at the theory that Judy was the murderer, asking ourselves if Judy perpetrated this crime, how could she have planted Randal's semen in Cathy's vaginal canal? How would we prove that? Blake endeavored to interview every person he could find who had ever known Judy. Blake began at the beauty shops, where women tend to talk; he figured that Judy must have frequented one or more of them over the years.

Meanwhile, we built our defense, watching and waiting to see what Blake would hand us once he finished his investigation. We retained noted and respected polygraph examiner Pete Pound, who had helped me before. Six years earlier, a Marshall County examiner had found Randal's polygraph results "inconclusive." However, Pound concluded that, contrary to the report, Randal had passed it. Pound then conducted his own extensive exam and Randal passed "with flying colors."

Yet, without an agreement among the opposing parties, no court will allow polygraph results as evidence. Randal's success on two polygraphs simply added more pressure to the quagmire that most lawyers dread: representing a truly innocent client facing a sentence of death. In the pit of my stomach resided my worst fear: an innocent client of mine being found guilty and sentenced to death.

In September, Randal Padgett's second trial began. We faced the formidable challenge of identifying a group of jurors who would not factor into their deliberations their knowledge that, four years earlier, a jury in the same county had convicted Randal.

Possibly even more dangerous than Randal's previous conviction and death sentence was his brazen affair with Judy Bagwell. That threatened to derail any possibility of a favorable outcome. Several potential jurors acknowledged during jury selection that they could not presume Padgett innocent of murder knowing that he had committed adultery. A few even stated that certain Biblical scriptures required the death penalty for adultery.

It took almost a week to select and impanel a jury. From the deeply conservative pool, we ended up with a jury we felt we could trust. As in any case, the most difficult decisions come at the end of the selection process. If even one very powerful personality slips onto the panel and ultimately wants to vote to convict, that person could be the persuasive force that turns the entire case. Regardless, we followed our intuition and took the calculated gamble of keeping two who appeared to be leaders. They espoused moderate views on the death penalty; we felt both would make fair jurors. Still, we believed that a conviction would inevitably lead to a death sentence for Randal.

With the jury in the box, both sides delivered opening statements on September 18. Next, the State called a series of law enforcement officers to testify. The officers described the bloody, disarrayed crime scene in Cathy Padgett's bedroom and the condition of her body. The first officers to arrive at the scene saw no evidence of forced entry. Whoever killed Cathy had gained entry into the home without breaking into it. Blood splatters and drops littered the hallway leading to the bedroom.

Oddly, but significantly, officers found Cathy's petite corpse in an unusual position. Rather than lying on the bed with her head on the pillow, she lay parallel to the headboard. Her left leg hung over one side of the bed and her right leg was propped up on a night table. Her legs were widely spread. A visibly large, roundish blood stain, about eighteen inches in circumference, soaked the middle of the bed. It seemed the perpetrator(s) had physically moved her body after pints of blood poured out from her many wounds, then propped her legs in a position to make it appear as if the killer raped her.

I questioned the pathologist in detail regarding his findings. "Did you personally go to the crime scene?"

"Yes, I did," he responded from the witness stand.

"What time did you arrive at the Padgett home?"

"I arrived at the Padgett home at approximately 4:54 P.M."

"Would you describe the condition of the body?" I requested.

"The body was covered in blood from head to toe. There were numerous lacerations, contusions and wounds on her body. I noticed a large blood stain in the middle of the bed."

"Would it be fair to say that she had lost a great deal of blood as a result of numerous stab wounds?"

"Yes, that would be fair," he conceded.

"Did you have the occasion later to examine the vaginal area of Cathy Padgett?"

"Yes, I did."

"Did you notice any evidence of trauma anywhere in the vaginal area?"

"No, I did not."

"You were looking for it, were you not?" I asked.

"I was."

"So, if I understand your testimony, your examination revealed no cuts or contusions in the vaginal area."

The pathologist nodded. "That is true."

"No tears or lacerations."

"None."

"No bruising."

"That is true."

"So, in other words," I said, "after a careful and thorough examination you found no evidence whatsoever of forcible penetration."

"Correct."

I pressed on. "And if there were, you would expect to see some evidence of trauma."

"Yes, that's true."

"But there was none," I confirmed.

"Correct."

"And yet you found semen located in her vaginal canal."

"Yes."

"Doctor, do you have an opinion as to whether, if there was a rape, it occurred before or after Cathy Padgett died?"

"Yes, I do."

"What is your opinion?"

"If Ms. Padgett were raped, it would have had to have been after she had met her demise."

"In other words, doctor, if Cathy was raped, the perpetrator would have had to have raped a corpse?"

"That is correct," he agreed.

The pathologist's testimony, along with the propped position of the body, made it even more implausible that Randal Padgett or anyone else actually engaged in sexual intercourse with Cathy, whether or not she consented. Nothing in Randal's background suggested him to be capable of such an act. The undisputed testimony demonstrated that he had always treated his wife with respect.

"Doctor, I want to discuss with you for a moment the wounds you discovered and testified to on direct examination. How many wounds did you find on the deceased body of Cathy Padgett?"

"We counted forty-six wounds," he responded, "consistent with being inflicted by a sharp instrument, such as a knife."

"In fact, doctor, you have examined hundreds of knife wounds in the past, haven't you?"

"Yes, many hundreds."

"These wounds were mostly consistent with knife wounds?"

"Yes," he nodded.

"And, doctor," I asked, "do you have any reason not to conclude that they were all made by the same knife?"

"No, it seems they are all consistent as being inflicted by the same sharp instrument."

"Doctor, you told the jury that many of the wounds you examined were what you termed 'defensive wounds'."

"Correct."

"How many of the forty-six wounds were defensive wounds?"

"Most of them."

"What is a defensive wound?"

"A defensive wound," the pathologist explained, "is normally a superficial cut or laceration on the extremities, usually inflicted on someone who is using the arms or legs to prevent being wounded."

That was significant. "So, the great majority of these wounds occurred when Cathy Padgett attempted to defend herself against her assailant?"

"That appears to be the case."

"Cathy Padgett literally fought for her life, until overcome by her assailant through the inflicting of lethal wounds."

The pathologist quickly responded: "That is my opinion."

"Doctor, how many clearly identifiable fatal or death-producing wounds did you find?"

"I found three: two in her upper chest and one in her abdomen."

"Doctor, this struggle must have lasted for quite a while—at least long enough for someone to stab her forty-six times."

"Yes, I would say that is accurate."

"And the great majority of the defensive wounds you found were on Cathy's hands, the inside of her fingers and the inside of her arms," I said.

"Yes."

"Doctor, are you aware that my client, Randal Padgett, is six feet, 230 pounds?"

"I will take your word for it."

"Of the three fatal wounds, did any of them penetrate Cathy's body beyond three and a quarter inches deep?" I asked.

"No, that was the deepest."

The State next called a forensic scientist to testify regarding blood testing. On cross-examination, I questioned him about the articles of clothing he examined. "Did you examine a pair of lady's underwear?"

"I did," the forensic scientist confirmed.

"Would you describe the condition of it?"

"The lady's underwear was soaked with blood I determined to be that of Cathy Padgett."

"But the underwear showed no signs of being torn or ripped off, correct?"

"I saw no signs of that."

"In fact, the underwear appeared as if it had been neatly cut off by scissors, did it not?"

"Yes, it did," the scientist replied. "There were no signs of jagged edges or stretch marks, so most likely a sharp instrument such as a pair of scissors was used."

"Did you examine a pair of scissors?"

"I did."

"And did the scissors have blood on them?"

"They did."

"Whose blood?"

"Blood consistent with Cathy Padgett's."

"Yet there was no sign that any resistance was offered to keep the pants from being cut off?"

"None."

"I understand that there was a bloody fingerprint caked on the abdomen of Cathy Padgett," I continued. "Is that true?"

"Yes, the first officers at the scene reported that."

"Did you personally see it?"

"Yes, I did."

"In such circumstances, bloody fingerprints on a body can be photographed and compared to the known prints of a possible assailant. Is that true?"

"Yes."

"Did you do that in this case?"

"No, I did not."

My eyebrows rose. This was simple police procedure, as far as I was concerned. "You didn't photograph it?"

"Mr. Jaffe, I was not able to, because one of the investigators had slightly moved the body before I arrived, resulting in a portion of the fingerprint collapsing."

After the crime scene forensic witnesses testified, the State called its DNA expert. Derek Drennan cross-examined the expert, who could not explain the existence of a DNA strand that matched neither Randal's DNA nor Cathy's. Nevertheless, we did not intend to challenge the DNA findings and certainly had no intention of calling our own DNA expert.

When the State rested its case, it seemed clear to us that Cathy's vaginal area contained Randal's DNA, but we felt we had established that someone neatly choreographed and staged the rape crime scene. In addition, we established that the rapist, if there were one, would have raped a corpse.

On the following day, we called witnesses to demonstrate that Randal had neither opportunity nor motive to kill his wife. We brought out that the theory upon which the State's case rested—that Randal brutally murdered Cathy and then had sex with her corpse to deflect suspicion—was flimsy. The State contended that Randal killed Cathy for financial motives. We felt that we could show the nonsense of these theories, but we still had to explain why Randal's DNA was lodged in Cathy's vaginal canal.

In the first trial, the defense decided not to play the video of Randal taking the detectives through the house, candidly answering every question they asked. In this trial, we played it in its entirety. No guilty person would be so helpful and cooperative. For example, had he told the authorities on videotape that he had had sexual intercourse with Cathy in the last seventy-two hours, who could disprove it? Therefore, the fact that his semen was in her would no longer be of importance. Still, he declined to lie about such a devastating fact. The jurors watched the videotape of a man shattered and shocked at his wife's murder and willing to help investigators in any way. On the video, he readily agreed to take a polygraph. He appeared eager to help find the real killer.

After we played the video, we called both of Randal's children, who remembered well that their father went to sleep early the night before the scuba diving trip and remained asleep after they woke up. His young daughter slept in the bed with him. Both testified they would have heard him come and go had he left the trailer at any time. Neither saw a scratch on him that morning nor noticed anything unusual about his attitude or demeanor. Neither saw any blood in the car or on any clothes nor heard the shower running during the night. Neither heard the truck start or the trailer doors open or close at any time.

Next, we called the attorney who was to handle the amicable divorce that the Padgetts had finally agreed to obtain. He assured the jury that, although not desiring the divorce, Cathy had agreed to it along with a property settlement. Contrary to the State's promises in opening statements, the financial arrangements would be neither burdensome to Randal nor unfair to Cathy. Most importantly, their one life insurance policy paid just ten thousand dollars, most of which would go to burial expenses. That was hardly enough for anyone to claim Randal possessed a financial motive.

We also called Jimmy Gullion, a truck driver who Blake found during his investigation. Gullion testified that about 12:30 A.M. the night of the murder, he saw two people in a white sedan with a missing hubcap driving from the remote road where the Padgett home stood. Gullion testified that one of them appeared to be wearing a wig. Gullion knew that secluded area well and found it highly unusual for anyone to be on the road at that time of night.

Another witness we called had seen Judy driving a white car with a missing hubcap a week before the murder.

At that point we were running out of witnesses. Nevertheless, the summit of the mountain loomed far away. We had hiked part of the way, but if the jury had to take a vote at this point, I held little hope they would acquit our client. The DNA evidence presented such an insurmountable climb.

Almost three weeks of trial had come and gone. The judge wanted to know how many more witnesses we intended to call in order to hold a charge conference and inform the jury of when he anticipated the end of the trial would be. We informed the court that our next witness would be Randal Padgett and then we would take a recess to decide whom, if anyone, we would call on his behalf. Judge Jetton agreed.

Walking slowly toward the witness box, Randal placed his hand on the Bible and swore to tell the truth. As I've stated before, I tend not to call my clients as witnesses, for a variety of reasons. If the accused lies or makes even minor missteps in his testimony, the lie is imprinted in the juror's minds as if branded. They neither forgive nor forget.

However, with the devastating DNA evidence and our theory of defense, we felt it necessary to put Randal on the witness stand. We'd taken on a burden that we had to carry. Just as he did in his first trial, he needed to look the jurors in the eyes and convincingly swear to them that he knew nothing of Cathy's murder, which had devastated his life even before he was arrested. He needed to express remorse for his adulterous affair and take the appropriate responsibility.

We were aware that, unfortunately, Randal's stoic, expressionless demeanor might project a lack of feeling to twelve people who didn't know this to be his normal personality. Before he took the stand, we did all we could to prepare him to show the true emotions buried underneath his cool façade, to express his inner feelings. He listened well and presented himself as a quite acceptable witness on direct examination.

During his cross-examination, knots in my stomach threatened to twist me into the agony of dejection. On several occasions, after being asked a rather poignant question, probably due to nervousness and strain, Randal slowly reached for his cup of water and drank as if it contained an elixir of truth serum. Each time that occurred, I cringed but consciously pretended that nothing disturbed me.

"Mr. Jaffe," Judge Jetton asked upon the conclusion of Randal's cross-examination, "do you wish to redirect?"

"No, Your Honor," I calmly replied with mustered confidence. "We do not."

"The court will be in recess for fifteen minutes. I would like to see the lawyers in my chambers."

As we sat in Judge Jetton's chambers, the lawyers stared blankly at each other, exhausted and unsure as to what would happen next. While Randal had made no serious mistakes when testifying, Derek Drennan, Michael Mastin and I all felt that if the jurors voted at that moment, they would convict him.

The judge looked at me and inquired, "Mr. Jaffe, I am only trying to get an idea of where we are for scheduling purposes. Do you have any idea of how many other witnesses you intend to call, if any?"

I hesitated and looked directly at Derek. He had consistently maintained that we had no choice but to gamble it all by calling Judy Bagwell. Mike Mastin agreed. But the decision rested with me and we all knew that her testimony could be dangerous. Derek stared at me; I knew we needed go for broke.

"Your Honor, for our next witness we intend to call Judy Bagwell."

A silence enveloped the judge's chambers. I did not look at the judge; I looked directly into the face of Ronald Thompson, the district attorney. Experienced and successful, DA Thompson rarely lost a case. In fact, the scuttlebutt at the courthouse was that he had never lost a murder trial. However, his normally tan and handsome face paled and his jaws clenched tightly when I uttered what he never expected to hear.

"Judge," I continued, "we can have her here in ten minutes."

We immediately called her attorney, Randy Beard, whose office was across the street from the courthouse and where we understood Judy was waiting to see if either side called her to testify.

After the recess concluded, the courtroom filled with spectators. Word travels fast in small venues. The already large audience had grown to a standing-room-only crowd that overflowed the space.

Judge Jetton called the courtroom to order and looked at me. "Mr. Jaffe, call your next witness."

"We call Judy Bagwell."

I had no idea what to expect, since the only person on our defense team who had ever spoken to Judy was Rick Blake. At first she had refused to speak to or meet with him. The ever-resourceful Blake shifted his tactics and befriended her sister. His investigation gave us reason to believe that Judy still loved Randal and knew he had nothing to do with Cathy's murder. In addition, Blake understood that Judy had turned down several offers of immunity from prosecution if she gave the authorities any evidence to help convict Randal. Even an inadvertent admission by Randal to her on the drive back to Marshall County from Florida would suffice, investigators had told her. She refused to implicate him.

Still, Judy remained unpredictable. If she testified to what we expected, the tone of the entire case would alter dramatically. If she surprised us unpleasantly, Randal would soon occupy a death row cell again, making time until his various appeals ran out and then preparing to be executed.

The bailiff quickly walked out the back door of the large, marble-floored courtroom of oak benches and long glass windows; he returned behind a tall, thin Judy Bagwell. With my heart pounding almost uncontrollably, I took some slow, deep, innocuous inhalations and watched her approach the witness stand. Her short hair and muscular frame more closely resembled a man's physique than a woman's. I could easily envision a person of this stature and build surprising a sleeping Cathy Padgett in her bed, repeatedly stabbing her and then inflicting the fatal wounds in her chest and abdomen. Had it been Randal wielding the knife, his 230-pound bulk and strength would have killed Cathy in one or two stab wounds, not forty-six. Also, if he wanted to kill Cathy, a knife from his hand would have penetrated well beyond the mere three and a quarter inches the pathologist described.

Sitting eerily erect with a tall, stiff spine, Judy waited for my first question. "Would you tell the ladies and gentlemen of the jury your name, please, ma'am?"

"Judy Bagwell."

Each juror sat propped up in his or her seat. The courtroom was pin-drop quiet.

"Before today, have you ever met or spoken to me?"

"No."

"Do you know Randal Padgett?"

"Yes, I do."

"How do you know him?"

"I met Randal at work. He was my supervisor."

I slowly and carefully guided Judy through the history of when and how she met Randal and the circumstances under which their relationship changed. I measured each word and especially my tone. I spoke with deliberate softness, almost with kindness, knowing that I walked a tightrope below which lay a minefield.

I asked Judy to recount the church incident when she hid in Cathy's car, showing her the police report. She confirmed its accuracy. Then I queried, "Ms. Bagwell, do you love Randal Padgett?"

"Yes, I do."

"Do you still love him?"

"Yes, I do."

"Have you ever been to the Padgett home before?"

"Yes, I have."

"On how many occasions?"

"About five or six."

"Have you been inside the home?" I pressed.

"Yes, I have."

"Do you know where the various rooms are located inside the house?"

"Yes, I do," she continued her affirmative answers.

"Do you know where the children's room is located?"

"Yes, I do."

"In fact, you recently remodeled your home, did you not?"

She nodded. "I did."

"And did you replicate the children's room in your home, so that it looks exactly like the children's room at Cathy's house, even the exact furnishings and color scheme?"

"Yes, that is true."

"And what possessed you to do that?"

"Well, I just wanted them to be comfortable when they would visit Randal and me."

"But Randal didn't live there," I pointed out.

"Yes, but he and I planned to get married after he divorced Cathy."

I clasped my hands and prepared to delve deeper. "Now, at the time of the murder of Cathy Padgett, where was Randal living?"

"Randal lived in a trailer about twenty to twenty-five miles from Cathy's home."

"And was it your understanding he was in the process of a divorce?"

"Yes, that is what Randal told me."

"But you never saw any divorce papers or had any clear proof."

"No, but I believed him."

"This was the third time Randal actually physically separated from Cathy, was it not?"

"Yes, I think it was."

"And the other two times, though he thought he would be able to go through with the divorce, each of those times he moved back in with Cathy."

"Yes, that is true."

While my questioning proceeded, I knew that each question carried the possibility of eliciting some devastating answer that could propel Randal back to death row. I studied Judy's facial expressions and each tiny movement of her body meticulously. It was if we were playing cat and mouse, but not for a moment did I think I was the cat. Judy never changed her vocal pitch. Her facial expressions remained almost constant as she sat straight and erect. I gained a bit more confidence as I continued on.

"And you had no way of knowing for sure if this time he would move back again, did you?" I asked.

"No, I could only hope he would go through with it this time."

"In fact, you hoped this more than anything in the world, didn't you?"

"Yes, I loved Randal that much and he loved me."

"How much did you love Randal Padgett?" I pressed.

"Enough so that I would go to sleep many nights and pray to God that something would happen to Cathy so that she would die, so I could be with Randal."

I heard gasps from the courtroom spectators. The pounding of my own heart almost drowned out their sounds.

I paused longer. "Ms. Bagwell, you told the jury that you were familiar with the various rooms of the Padgett home. Can one gain entrance to it from the utility room attached to the kitchen door?"

"There is a k..." Judy began but swallowed her words. With my eye on the jurors, I noticed that when Judy started to say *key* some of them noticed. They probably remembered that investigators found a key hanging in the utility room. Marshall County District Attorney Investigator Billy Strickland had previously testified that he learned the key stayed there in case the children returned from school when their parents weren't home. Randal had also previously testified that Judy knew about the key. She regained her composure and hurried on. "We would sometimes go in the kitchen door entrance."

I believed in Randal's innocence and I believed Judy knew he was innocent, too.

Quickly I changed subjects and asked perhaps the most loaded of all questions: "Ms. Bagwell, if that was truly Randal Padgett's DNA found in Cathy Padgett, how do you think it got there?"

I waited for Ron Thompson to object. For a reason I will never know, he did not. My assumption can only be that Ron did not object, because he believed Randal guilty.

Judy did not hesitate in answering. "If that was Randal's DNA in Cathy, it must have come from me."

The gasps of the spectators could probably not match the expressions on everyone's faces. I tried, hopefully successfully, to keep my expression unchanged.

After that incredible answer, I had very few additional questions. I did ask if Judy had driven the car that a witness testified to seeing her driving the week before the murder and consistent with the one seen by Gullion, the truck driver. She denied ever driving, owning or being driven in such a car. Also, she could not explain a cash withdrawal of $5000 from her checking account not too long before the murder.

When I took my seat, I did not look at anyone on the defense team or my client. That one question and answer said it all. I looked straight ahead at Judy and anxiously waited for Ron Thompson's cross-examination.

In Thompson's cross of Judy he tried unsuccessfully to shake her testimony. Soon Thompson asked the court for a recess, with leave to continue the cross-examination of Judy the next morning. The court granted it.

Then the tension intensified. Derek Drennan asked Judge Jetton if he and Ron Thompson could approach the bench before the court recessed the proceedings. While Derek and Thompson approached the bench, I leaned over to speak to my client. The jury remained in the box. Derek requested that Judge Jetton issue a directive to both sides preventing them from having contact with Judy Bagwell, lest she feel undue influence or pressure.

Thompson was *livid*. "Judge," he stated for the record, "if I were not an officer of the court and a gentleman, I would knock [the] shit out of him."

Unsure exactly how to react but mindful to keep his cool, Derek laughed. Judge Jetton issued the order and recessed court for the day.

The next morning, Thompson declined to cross-examine Judy Bagwell further and the court dismissed her as a witness. Next we called a coworker and friend of Judy's. She told the jury she visited Judy at her home two days after the murder to find out if Judy felt better. She recounted that she noticed numerous scratch marks on both of Judy's arms and Judy complained her arms were sore. When she questioned Judy about them, Judy said that while she was moving the bicycles she had bought for Randal's children for Christmas to another room, one of them toppled over, causing the marks. Judy's coworker further expressed perplexity that Judy had taken off work for two weeks following the murder.

Meanwhile, Rick Blake had hidden our final witness in the bathroom one floor below the courtroom, as we feared that if the authorities discovered her, they might attempt to intimidate her. Through his beauty shop stops, Blake had discovered three women to whom Judy confided that she used to save the sperm of her ex-husband and mix it in a blender when she made milk shakes. Two of the women hid from Blake and avoided subpoenas. Blake was taking no chances with the one he successfully served with a subpoena.

We knew the invaluable nature of this woman's potential testimony. We could show that Judy Bagwell knew how to save and store semen. She had done it on previous occasions and had bragged about it. With the woman's testimony, we could then argue in our closing that no trauma to Cathy's vaginal areas would have resulted from inserting a syringe of stored sperm into Cathy's vagina.

Thompson argued vehemently in vain for Judge Jetton to disallow this witness from testifying. The judge allowed her and the woman testified with authority and credibility. The dramatic nature of the testimony from this very believable acquaintance of Judy electrified the courtroom even more.

Neither side called additional witnesses. We prepared to sum up the case. For the prosecution, Assistant DA Tim Jolley delivered the closing argument. Brilliantly organized and articulate, Jolly left out no significant detail. I had never heard any attorney master the facts in such an organized manner and deliver a summation with such powerful eloquence.

I delivered the closing on behalf of Randal Padgett. Since the DNA results supported our entire defense theory, I borrowed the odds concept from the State's case. The sperm found in Cathy led only to Randal; the odds against it being anyone else were astronomical. I argued that the same odds applied to the perpetrator being anyone else other than Judy. Each piece of testimony, from the defensive wounds and the staged rape to the lack of trauma in Cathy's vagina and the scratches on Judy's arms, pointed straight to Judy. She had even testified that she prayed for Cathy's death, had replicated the children's room and, on a previous occasion, had hidden in Cathy's car while wearing gloves, a wig and a raincoat. Judy's obsession and lack of understanding of

DNA supplied the motive and opportunity. Unlike Randal, she had no alibi, not even a record of phone calls.

I reminded the jurors of Jimmy Gullion's pointed testimony about the person who appeared to be wearing a wig in the car he saw on the night of the murder. The jurors now knew how unusual it would be for any car to be in that remote area at that time of night. Although witnesses had seen Judy in a similar car shortly before the murder, she had denied any association with such a car.

I softened my voice and looked directly at the jury. "It all points to Judy," I said, "and now it is time for healing. We can't get Cathy back, but a jury verdict of not guilty will send Randal back to his children and the healing process for all could finally begin."

Ron Thompson delivered the last closing argument. Thompson had grown close to Cathy's family, one of the finest and most respected in the community. He developed a powerful analogy and delivered it eloquently. He told the jury that Randal Padgett's actions made the State's case irrefutable and argued that Randal, by raping Cathy, had fired the deadly bullets of his DNA directly into her vagina.

After Judge Jetton instructed the jury, it retired to deliberate. In Alabama, it is rare for a jury to take more than a day to return a verdict, unless it is hung. After two and a half days, this jury still deliberated. I drove back and forth between the hotel where I was staying and the courthouse. When at the hotel, I stared at the placid water of Lake Guntersville and tried to curb my terrified and turbulent thoughts. While at the courthouse, I tried to soak up the energy from the praying Padgett supporters, who refused to leave the courtroom except to go to the bathroom and eat.

On the third day, the packed courtroom seemed even more somber and tense. By then, my fears had overtaken me. Judge Jetton summoned the lawyers to meet him in his chambers with the court reporter. I felt he was going to declare a mistrial.

Brenda Massingill asked me what the judge wanted to discuss. I told her he probably intended to call a mistrial. "Richard," she riveted her eyes directly to mine, "don't let it happen. Randal will be found innocent. I know it. Last night I had a vision from God. Randal will be found innocent. They have to continue to deliberate."

Inside his chambers, Judge Jetton did not waver about a mistrial. The more I protested, the stronger his voice. "Gentlemen," he sternly stated, "I do not believe in forcing jurors to bend their wills. It is not my way and it is not right. I won't do it. I have decided."

We marched into the court, with me at the back of the line with Judge Jetton. I turned and looked him directly in the eye. "Please, Judge," I begged. "Just ask them one more time if they think they can reach a verdict."

Solemnly the judge took the bench, looked over at the jury and addressed it: "Ladies and gentlemen of the jury," he began, "you have worked long and hard and I commend each of you for your efforts. But after two and a half days, I feel I have no choice but to…"

The judge glanced my way and our eyes locked for an instant. He turned back to the jury. "Ladies and gentlemen, is there any one of you who feels that more deliberation would be fruitful?"

To my absolute incredulity and relief, two jurors answered affirmatively. Judge Jetton asked them to return to the jury room to resume their deliberations.

The crowd of supporters resumed their prayers, many holding hands, others tearful but hopeful. Fewer than forty-five minutes later, with no one having moved an inch in the courtroom, especially me, the jury foreperson knocked on the door. They had reached a verdict.

After what seemed like hours but was only a few minutes, Judge Jetton walked into the courtroom and looked at the jury box. "Ladies and gentlemen, I understand you have reached a verdict."

The juror we had suspected to be the foreperson rose slowly. "Yes, Your Honor, we have."

"The bailiff will hand me the verdict." He read it, looked at the jury and then at me.

He then said to the foreperson, "I will ask the bailiff to hand your verdict to you so you can read it."

"We, the jury, find the defendant, Randal Padgett, not guilty."

Silence in the courtroom. Astonishingly sweet, exquisite silence. After that, screams and gasps. I looked at Randal and saw his tearful eyes and the corners of his mouth edging toward a smile.

I collapsed my head on the table. It was over.

Judge Jetton first thanked and then discharged the jury. Then he told Randal he was free to go.

Randal, the rest of the defense team and I walked between the rows of spectators out to the waiting cameras. No one else in the courtroom, not even the judge, had moved. I felt as if I was striding down an aisle of bliss.

Fifteen minutes later, as I was walking out to my car, two of the jurors came over to me: a woman in her forties whom we thought hated us and an older, gray-haired female juror. They stopped and smiled warmly at me. "Mr. Jaffe," one of the women said, "we noticed Judy trying to take her words back about the key and we heard it loud and clear."

Purposely, I never mentioned the key in my closing argument. I had only hoped one or more jurors would pick up on it during jury deliberations.

"The first vote was ten to two for guilty," she explained. "But I got on the table in the jury room myself and spread my legs and propped my right foot up. Only a woman could know you can't have sex in that position."

I was speechless.

"You tell Randal to stay away from Judy Bagwell and spend time with his children where he belongs."

"Yes, ma'am," I managed to speak. "He has had no contact with her at all."

Then the two women walked away.

26

LETTERS FROM DEATH ROW

Nearly every week I receive letters from individuals in various prisons in Alabama or even in federal prisons in other states. Most are serving lengthy sentences for serious crimes such as murder. Some are on death row. Regrettably, due to overwhelming time and court commitments to my clients, I cannot answer most of these letters. Some I refer to the Southern Center for Human Rights (SCHR), the Equal Justice Initiative (EJI) or the American Civil Liberties Union (ACLU), which are organizations set up to help these desperate individuals. Embarrassingly, Alabama is the only state in the country that provides no funds for death row inmates to obtain lawyers to appeal their cases to the federal courts.

But there was something about the letters that death row inmate Gary Drinkard wrote that caught my attention. In each brief letter he declared, *"I am an innocent man."* Gary set out some credible evidence and wrote that when someone murdered Dalton Pace, he himself was at home, thirty-five miles from the crime scene, and he had witnesses to support his alibi.

A jury in Decatur, Alabama, took but forty-five minutes to convict Gary for the capital murder of Dalton Pace, a junkyard dealer, at Pace's home, which was also the location of his business. It took less time than that for that same jury to recommend his death sentence. Gary had convinced EJI attorneys Bryan Stevenson and Randy Susskind (the same attorneys who successfully appealed the cases of Bo Cochran, Randal Padgett and numerous others) to handle his appeal.

If the Alabama Supreme Court overturned his case and granted him a new trial, Gary wrote, he wanted me to represent him. In his letters, Gary did not portray himself as a perfect citizen. In fact, he stated that the main reason he thought an appellate court would grant him a new trial resulted from the trial court permitting the prosecution to admit evidence of Gary's previous history of thefts, thus prejudicing the jury in the murder for which he was being tried.

About a year and a half after Gary first began writing to me, the Alabama Supreme Court reversed Gary's conviction and death sentence and ordered the trial court to hold a new trial but this time without the poisoning evidence of Gary's irrelevant past.[1] Gary urged me to request that the trial judge appoint me. I had a decision to make. I had never handled a case in Decatur, which is about two hours from Birmingham. Also, I did not know Gary's trial judge, Steven Haddock. Some judges outside of Birmingham hesitate to appoint Birmingham lawyers to handle cases in their jurisdictions.

I wrote Gary back and told him that I would contact my close friend, Decatur criminal defense lawyer John Mays, one of Alabama's most experienced and successful death penalty attorneys. If John could get us both appointed, I would represent Gary as his lead lawyer.

When John Mays approached him, Judge Haddock balked at appointing me. But John's persistence ultimately prevailed and Judge Haddock agreed to appoint me, along with John, on one condition: nothing about my trial schedule and my practice in Birmingham was to delay any of the proceedings or the trial. I agreed and then, surprisingly, John convinced Judge Haddock to appoint my then associate (now partner) Derek Drennan as well.

For Gary's first trial, Judge Haddock had also appointed three attorneys, but not one of them concentrated his practice in the criminal defense area and certainly not in the death penalty. One evening a few weeks later, nationally acclaimed death penalty lawyer Steve Bright called me at my home. Steve, who has introduced me as an Atticus Finch from *To Kill a Mockingbird* before his criminal law class, is a law professor at Harvard and Yale and was the director of the Southern Center for Human Rights (SCHR), located in Atlanta.

"Richard, how are you?" Steve inquired with his characteristic enthusiasm. "It's great to hear your voice!"

"Great, Steve, and how are you?"

"I'm fine, Richard. I was delighted to hear that you are representing Gary Drinkard."

"I am, Steve. I can't believe I've agreed to take on such a difficult death penalty retrial."

"Well, I'm glad you did," he said. "By the way, I just hired a talented new lawyer, Chris Adams, to our staff. He went to Georgetown Law School and has wanted to work at the center for a long time. Finally we had an opening. Now, he's never tried a death penalty case, but he's been very successful as a trial lawyer for the public defender's office in Charleston. He could get some great experience working with you on this case if you would be comfortable with that. It won't cost the State anything and we can work up the mitigation."

Now that was an offer I could not refuse, not that I could ever refuse Steve Bright anything; I had been working closely with Steve over the years and his counsel, advice and friendship had been very valuable.

"Steve, I would be delighted to work with Chris. When can I meet him?"

"Richard, that's great. I'll have Chris call you tomorrow."

When I hung up the phone, I felt even more excited. Our team would gain the energetic, gifted and insightful mitigation investigators of SCHR. A thorough mitigation investigation could cost well into six figures and no judge in Alabama would approve anywhere near that amount.

Mitigation investigators recreate the entire life history of the client. They gather everything from birth certificates to school and hospital records and every other public or private record or document that pertains to the client and even those of key family members. The fruits of that investigation form the basis of the evidence we present at the sentencing hearing held after the jury returns a capital murder conviction.

Soon we got our chance to meet Chris Adams, who drove from Atlanta to meet with John Mays, Derek Drennan and me in Birmingham. Chris, who was thirty-four, stood a little over six feet tall, was lean and in good physical shape. He wore his light brown hair in a long ponytail (although Steve Bright would convince him to cut it off a few days before the trial). He had perceptive brown eyes and a disarming smile.

With the trial team now formed, we left to meet Gary at the Morgan County Jail, where he had been transferred from death row to await his new trial. As we sat in the small room, I wondered what Gary would look like, how his voice would sound, what feeling I would get when looking into his eyes and whether, after the meeting, I would still think him to be innocent.

In walked an approximately forty-five-year-old, six-foot-three-inch tall man rather on the thin side, clean-shaven, a bit nervous but smiling and very excited to meet us. The conversation flowed and nothing I felt or heard changed my view that he was truly an innocent man falsely accused and facing death. Yet about halfway through the several-hour meeting we ran in to one major glitch: Gary had instructed his previous lawyers not to bother with any mitigation investigation. In fact, he forbade it.

He explained, "I will tell you guys honestly, I am innocent of this crime. But if I am convicted, I don't want to live, especially for the rest of my life, in prison. Prison with no hope, to me, is really not living. I did not do this and for me it is all or nothing. If they convict me after a fight to the death, let them kill me. Besides, the appeals courts are more likely to overturn a death sentence if the State screws up like it did last time."

"Gary," I said as I looked squarely at him, letting him know I meant it, "you know how much effort it took to get this experienced trial team in place. It would really be a shame if we had to quit before we start, because you won't let us fulfill our professional responsibilities. Whether you agree or not, ethically we must try to save your life by presenting mitigating evidence if a jury convicts you. Gary, the choice is yours, but we have no choice."

Gary didn't flinch. It was obvious to me he had played more than a few poker games in his past. But the stakes in this pot were higher than in any card game. I wasn't bluffing and he certainly knew it. With hardly any hesitation, Gary agreed to our demand but took the opportunity to negotiate some limits on the type of evidence he would allow us to present. He assented to sign a letter memorializing our agreement, in which I wrote:

> Speaking of mitigation, I understood your initial position to be that you would not allow us to present mitigation. As we discussed, this is something that the lawyers on your defense team have serious problems with. We certainly agree with most of your reasons and yet we cannot adequately defend you without being fully prepared to present and, in fact, presenting a powerful mitigation case, as well as a powerful guilt phase defense case.
>
> Therefore, this letter is to confirm our agreement as we discussed on Tuesday that we intend to develop our mitigation defenses, just as we would in any other case. Hopefully, we will not have to present a mitigation case, but we will be prepared to do so and will do so if that unfortunate situation arises. I have also agreed to work with you as best we can on the sensitive issues that you mentioned. We are and will continue to be sensitive to the issues about your mother and understand that you love her very much and do not want to do anything to embarrass her. We will certainly remain open to these very sensitive and significant concerns of yours and look forward to addressing them as they come up.

With Gary agreeing to cooperate with us in developing a mitigation case, we actively began forming an investigative plan. If Gary Drinkard was innocent, what evidence had the prosecution presented in his trial that had compelled the jury to convict him so quickly? What defenses had Gary's defense team presented?

The pathologist estimated the time of death of Dalton Pace, a very large and powerful man, to have been on a Thursday night between 8:00 and 9:00 P.M.

Disliking banks, Pace was known by many to carry large amounts of cash in a pocket of his pants. Based upon the condition of the room, police determined that some sort of struggle had occurred before someone shot Pace three times, once in the chest and twice in his back on the left side. When the police examined Pace's lifeless body, he was wearing blue coveralls. The killer(s) did not take his wallet, which contained one thousand dollars cash.

Pace's fingernails appeared to contain skin underneath them, raising the possibility that he had scratched someone during an altercation. The skin could possibly have been subjected to DNA testing. There was also a half-full glass of whiskey in the kitchen and an empty whiskey bottle. The authorities lifted prints and compared them to Gary's with negative results. For whatever reasons, the authorities did not attempt to compare the prints obtained to any other possible suspects. The authorities left the whiskey bottle at the residence, which burned down mysteriously three months after Gary's arrest.

A neighbor described a car that had a missing taillight lens parked at Pace's home on the evening of the murder at around 9:00. The description did not match Gary Drinkard's car. There were also tire tracks photographed in the yard of Pace's house and these could not be matched with Gary's car either.

Within a few days of the murder, a case began to build against Gary Drinkard. His half-sister, Beverly Robinson, contacted the police and informed them that she had information about the Pace murder. Robinson told the police they needed to talk to her boyfriend Rex Segars to corroborate her story. Segars could not afford to be arrested for anything: he was currently on parole for robbery and he faced returning to serve a lengthy prison sentence if linked to any criminal activity.

Just as significantly, both Segars and Robinson were suspects in a series of burglaries and drug offenses. If Segars were convicted of any of these offenses in Alabama he would face a life sentence due to his habitual offender status. Our investigation revealed that the police had discovered marijuana plants, syringes and cocaine in the trailer in which Segars and Robinson lived. Both of them had desperate motivations to cooperate with the police and took full advantage of the opportunity to avoid going to prison. Much of this information did not come out in the initial trial.

We strongly felt Beverly went to the police because she believed that she and Rex were about to be arrested. However, the police arrested Beverly on a theft charge anyway. At some point either before or after her arrest, Beverly implicated Gary in the Pace murder, but her bare assertion had little value unless it could be corroborated.

To obtain the needed corroboration for Beverly's allegations, lead detective Gary Walker wired her and sent her to Gary's residence at 6:30 A.M. to see if she could get Gary to admit he murdered Dalton Pace. Detective Walker and other officers sat in a van hidden nearby and with the earpiece he wore, Walker could hear the conversation in real time while a machine recorded it. For reasons unknown at that time, the tape recording itself sounded distorted and garbled. In fact, it seemed most garbled during the key portions in which Beverly attempted to discuss the murder with Gary.

The meeting concluded and Beverly reunited with the officers. Gary got into his car and began to drive away. Suddenly, patrol cars swarmed in from all directions and surrounded him. An officer put handcuffs on Gary's outstretched hands through the car window. Then the officers pulled him through it and onto the pavement, scratching his left side against a post and bloodying his knees on the pavement.

Gary's first trial did not last a week. The prosecution's case rested on Rex Segars and Beverley Robinson. The prosecutors produced no murder weapon, eyewitness, car tag or corroboration to support Segars and Robinson. They did play the tape-recorded conversation between Beverly and Gary. Detective Walker testified that although the tape was distorted, he was able to hear Gary admit to the murder. He told the jury he heard Gary say, "The old man grabbed me and I went for my gun."

After the prosecution rested its case, the defense introduced medical records showing that on the day of the murder, Gary had driven to a doctor's office in Huntsville and obtained powerful medication for his back, but they did not subpoena the treating doctor as a witness.

The defense called two alibi witnesses. Gary's stepdaughter testified that she and her girlfriend were at Gary's house that night when an elderly lady came over to birth her dog. This was a memorable and exciting occasion for the stepdaughter, who remembered well both the birthing and that Gary could hardly walk. She recalled that he was heavily medicated and sitting in an easy chair during the birthing.

Willodene Brock, a lady in her eighties, testified that she vividly remembered birthing the dogs while Gary Drinkard, apparently in pain, sat in a chair that night. Although Brock kept a calendar, the prosecution did a good job of confusing her. Still, she insisted it was on the Thursday night of the big dance at the veterans' lodge. She had a date that night with Thomas Carter, a gentleman even older than she was. The defense did not call him to buttress her testimony.

Willodene Brock also remembered that the stepdaughter had a friend with her that night at the dog birthing. The defense did not call the friend to testify either.

I have always maintained that juries expect near perfection from defense witnesses. This jury proved no exception and they chose not to accept the alibi witnesses and medical records offered into evidence by the defense. Instead, the jury chose to accept Detective Walker's testimony that Gary had confessed to the murder. However, when listening to the taped conversation, one could hear no such confession, only distortion in key spots.

It took hardly an hour for the jury to convict Gary of capital murder. With no mitigation presented, Gary soon found himself on Alabama's death row waiting on the appeals process, which stood between him and an execution date.

Thanks to the usual extraordinary efforts of Bryan Stevenson's team at EJI, Gary did receive a new trial. But Gary Drinkard's lungs continued to inhale the stale air of the Morgan County Jail in Decatur while we conducted our investigation into every possible detail of this murder in anticipation of Gary's new trial.

John Mays' in-house investigator, Gary Fox, was a former Alabama Bureau of Investigation (ABI) agent. He took a law enforcement officer's approach to the crime investigation. SCHR mitigation investigator Kate

Weisburd, along with other talented SCHR mitigation investigators, began to recreate the life history of Gary Drinkard. SCHR lawyer Chris Adams led the mitigation investigation and also worked on every aspect of the trial investigation. John Mays, who authored an Alabama manual on defending capital cases, filed over fifty pretrial motions. Derek Drennan and I met, debated and argued every strategic angle that occurred to us.

During the three weeks before the trial began, the pressure and investigation intensified. As much as our investigators tried, they could not make contact with Gary's stepdaughter, who had moved to Florida. Kate and other investigators from SCHR camped out near the stepdaughter's new home. If we could not talk to his stepdaughter, we would dig to find out all we could about her life since the first trial.

Chris Adams rushed into my office a week before the trial. Although I was on a phone call, Chris shoved a transcript into my hands. I began reading it as I ended my call. The prosecution had sent the distorted tape to the FBI to enhance its quality, but there was still no admission by Gary Drinkard of anything. The more we studied the transcript the better we felt.

Only a few days before the trial, Gary's stepdaughter reappeared. We received her new statement that the police had obtained only weeks prior. The new statement maintained that she could not remember which night her dog birthed. In fact, on the Thursday night of the murder, she claimed she was not at Gary's home at all. The crucial center of Gary's alibi had just exploded in our faces. We would have to go to trial not only without his stepdaughter as an alibi witness, but also with her as the prosecution's star witness. Even though we would not have his stepdaughter as a defense witness, we still had his stepdaughter's friend—or so we thought.

Judge Haddock refused our motions for a jury questionnaire and to question each prospective juror individually about his or her views on the death penalty as well as any pretrial publicity generated from the crime and the first trial. However, he did allow in-depth questioning of the prospective jurors in panels of fourteen. It took almost a week to complete the jury selection.

John and I worked closely together for days, making sure his opening statement mirrored our theory of defense and what we expected the cross-examinations would reveal. The jury seemed to us to be open-minded when John concluded his opening. We felt this was a favorable omen, since most of the jurors probably knew something about the crime and that another jury had given Gary the death penalty.

Right out of the box the prosecutors called Gary's stepdaughter as their first witness. She testified that she did not see Gary the day of the murder. She went further and said that the day before Gary was arrested for the murder, she was at his residence and he was wearing a tank top. When he reached up to the cupboard to get a water glass, she noticed scratches under his right arm.

She then testified that Gary admitted he murdered Pace. One thing I knew for sure: Gary was no stranger to the legal system and would have never admitted anything to anyone if he had committed a crime, especially one that carries the death penalty.

My cross-examination of Gary's stepdaughter went well at first. She admitted that she was facing pending criminal charges for drug possession and theft in Florida. Although she denied that the prose-cution promised to help her with the Florida authorities, we felt that defied logic and common sense. I asked her to describe the location of the scratches she claimed to have seen almost ten days after the murder and the day before Gary was arrested. As the words tumbled out of my mouth, I tried to grab them and pull them back, but it was like grasping the wind. I began to sweat, beads that fell like warm raindrops.

Unfortunately, the police had shown her photographs taken of Gary the day of his arrest (ten days after the murder). She described the scratches as they appeared in the photos: long red scratch lines down his arm and side. It was only 11:25 A.M. In my acute distress I could think of no way to recover. Mercifully, Judge Haddock granted my plea to recess for an early lunch break.

Our team sat together at a local restaurant and talked about various matters, but I only noticed the moving lips. It was as if I were looking at someone talking while underwater. I ate nothing and thought only of how I might rescue myself and Gary.

At the end of lunch I still felt Gary's stepdaughter's testimony about the scratches was false. Empowered, I felt eager to overcome my mistake and even benefit from it.

When court reconvened and my cross-examination continued, I asked her to describe the scratches more specifically. "What exactly did they look like?

"I could see the long, red, thin scratch lines from his underarms halfway to his waist."

"Red scratches?"

"Yes."

"And you saw no scabbing at all, did you?"

"No."

The only scratches I believed she had seen were in a photograph of Gary taken after the arresting officers pulled him out of the window of his car and dragged his exposed arm and side on the pavement. He had fresh scratches on him from the struggle with the arresting police officers. Had she seen marks on Gary ten days after the murder, any scratches would either not be there or be scabbed from the healing process.

With new life for Gary (and for me), I continued my cross-examination of Gary's stepdaughter, having slid back into the rhythm and groove invaluable to this type of cross-examination. Next I asked her if she had stolen from her employer who owned the hotel where she had worked. The owners had not only trusted her as an employee, but also befriended her and allowed her to say in their home for a while. At that point, the prosecutor leapt up to object.

Judge Haddock halted the proceedings. From his bench, he stared down at me and slowly motioned for me to approach his bench with his index finger. With no hesitation, I confidently walked up to him. We were nose to nose, practically touching.

Glaring and smiling simultaneously, Judge Haddock looked intently at me and said rather pointedly, "You better be able to back this up." The judge was reminding me that it is unethical for a lawyer to imply with a question information in the form of impeachment without factual support to back up the question. Courtesy of mitigation investigator Kate Weisburd and company, we did have that support.

Frequently, when such a sensitive matter occurs, a judge will dismiss the jury to address it. Judge Haddock did not.

I politely asked the judge to give me a moment. I walked to Derek Drennan to retrieve five sworn affidavits of people from Florida in regard to Gary's stepdaughter, including two from the hotel couple. I delivered them to Judge Haddock. It took him at least ten minutes to read them while the jurors remained at rapt attention as if watching a scene in a movie.

When the judge finished inspecting them, he looked up and then down to me and dryly stated, "You may proceed."

After putting several police officers and evidence technicians on the stand, the prosecutor called the "snitch" witnesses: Gary's half-sister, Beverly Robinson, and her boyfriend, Rex Segars. Both had claimed that Gary confessed to them in separate conversations.

On the stand, Beverly Robinson seemed tensely wound and talked like a machine gun firing. We often objected to her efforts to inject unsolicited, irrelevant and prejudicial information about Gary. The judge repeatedly warned her to refrain, to little avail.

On cross-examination she became even more aggressive and openly hostile. She admitted that when she met with Gary and wore a wire, she brought with her a newspaper containing an account of the Pace murder. She had it with her as they sat and talked at the kitchen table. Over the State's objection, we introduced a copy of that newspaper into evidence.

After one stern warning during my cross-examination of her, she blurted out that this was her first experience with the criminal justice system and that she had never been in any trouble before. That was the opening for which we had hoped. Without skipping a beat, I turned toward Derek. We had obtained a certified copy of Beverly's prior conviction for issuing worthless checks and driving under the influence (DUI). Drennan had them in his hand when I faced him to retrieve them. The records also contained a mug shot of a younger her.

Normally a lawyer cannot impeach the credibility or character of a witness by citing a misdemeanor conviction such as a DUI, but it can be used to show that a person has given false or inaccurate information under oath in a trial. Beverly had lied under oath by attributing her hyped-up jitters to never being in trouble before and an unfamiliarity with the court system.

I handed Beverly the official record of her conviction and her photo. Her face froze. After squirming a minute in the witness chair, she stated, "This isn't me." Eventually I got her to verify all of the other identifying information of her in the records. She finally owned up to DUI, but explained weakly, "It happened so long ago I forgot about it."

Prior to the trial I had learned from some law enforcement sources in another jurisdiction that Beverly had a history of serious drug problems. In addition, she had served as an informant for them at the time when she had given the police Gary's name. I questioned Beverly about her drug involvements and motivations in this case.

When I was finished, a much-deflated Beverly slowly left the witness chair. But she retained some venom. When she was halfway to the door she stopped dead in her tracks. With a contorted face, she looked at Gary and shrieked, "I've always loved you!" Our entire defense team jumped to our feet objecting and moving for a mistrial. Taken off guard like the rest of us, the surprised judge, with barely restrained irritation, firmly ordered his bailiffs to take her out of the courtroom.

The prosecution then called Rex Segars, Beverly's boyfriend. On parole for armed robbery, Rex faced decades in prison if the authorities caused his parole to be revoked, and a life sentence if charged and convicted for any significant crime in Alabama. He told the jury that Gary admitted to him that he had robbed and then killed Pace.

But Rex could not keep his story straight. He repeatedly gave entirely different information from that contained in his statements to the police when he implicated Gary. As with Beverly, the authorities held possible charges for theft and drugs over his head. Throughout the entire cross-examination of Rex, he gave argumentative and combative answers. He could not hide his motivation to cooperate with the authorities to avoid going back to prison or being charged with other crimes here.

Our theory was that the evidence strongly suggested that perhaps Rex had used Beverly to get Pace to open the door to his house on the night of the murder, thus allowing Rex to gain entrance, not the physically impaired Gary Drinkard who had solid alibi witnesses. Neither Rex nor Beverly had an alibi for their whereabouts that evening.

Robert Fayard testified next, saying that at one time he bought a .45 from Gary, which was consistent with the murder weapon used to kill Pace. A firearms expert had earlier testified that the recovered bullets were fired from a .45. Fayard said that he found out the weapon was so defective it would "not hit the broadside of a barn."

Then the prosecution played its trump card, the one that played so well in Gary's first trial. The prosecution called Detective Gary Walker. The detective testified very credibly and professionally on direct examination. When the detective listened to the wired conversation between Beverly and Gary, he maintained that he heard Gary confess to murder. The detective also explained to the jury that he had sent the original tape to the FBI laboratory in order to take advantage of their sophisticated equipment for tape enhancement.

Next to be called to testify was the FBI expert who had enhanced the tape.

As the FBI tape-enhancing expert testified, he explained the many efforts and numerous techniques employed to remove background noise and clarify the conversation. The prosecution then played the tape for the jury and the judge ordered a recess before cross-examination.

I approached the lead prosecutor and asked if I could talk with the tape-enhancing expert. The prosecutor agreed to my request. I then asked the expert, "When Detective Walker listened to the conversation with his earphones in real time, did he hear the exact conversation between Beverly and Gary that the tape captured?"

"Yes, exactly. Detective Walker could not have heard anything that we cannot hear now on the tape. It wasn't the tape that was distorted; it was the transmission that was distorted. He did not hear anything we cannot now hear on the recording."

On cross-examination we again played the tape and nowhere did Gary admit to murdering Pace. That was my cross-examination of the FBI tape-enhancing expert.

Detective Walker testified a second time. In spite of the tape enhancement expert's testimony, he still insisted he heard Gary confess.

We played the tape several times more during our cross-examination, but no one in the courtroom heard any such admission. Instead, it became clear that Beverly had brought over a newspaper reporting the details of the murder and was simply discussing the account in the newspaper with Gary.

There was nothing on that tape that was not reported in the newspaper. But some key moments of the conversation were distorted. We strongly believed that Beverly, who wore the wire between her legs, had rubbed her legs together when she did not want certain parts of the conversation to be heard.

The prosecution rested its case and we began calling witnesses. John Mays called the Huntsville doctor who had treated Gary on the day of the murder. He told the jury that Gary's back debilitated him to the point that he could hardly walk and the pain medication would have significantly impaired his ability to drive thirty-five miles and then engage in any sort of physical struggle with a large man.

Next Chris Adams called Willodene Brock, the elderly lady who birthed Gary's stepdaughter's dogs. She testified she knew the birthing happened on that particular Thursday because she and her boyfriend had a date for the veterans' dance that night. They arrived late because of the birthing. We had obtained proof of the dance and introduced the flyer she had kept.

After she testified, John Mays called her boyfriend, Thomas Carter, a spry and energetic lover of dancing. He confirmed her testimony exactly.

Paul Mathews, the chief deputy district attorney, bore down hard on Carter in an attempt to trip him up the way he so skillfully did with Brock in the first trial. Carter testified that he and Gary watched the news together during the birthing. After repeated questions as to where Gary was sitting, Carter lost his patience and stated, "He could have been sitting on a box of nails for all I know, but he was in the living room with me the whole time."

The only witness left for us to call was the stepdaughter's friend. We had obtained an affidavit from her where she clearly recalled the dog birthing on the night of the murder and Gary sitting in his chair in obvious pain. However, the authorities found out we had flown her to Decatur from out west where she had moved. According to the step-daughter's friend, the prosecution had sent investigators to her parents' home in Decatur. She was convinced that if she testified for us they would charge her with perjury.

When we learned of her terror, John Mays called a Decatur lawyer to advise her and we alerted the court of our concerns. The judge held a hearing to address the issue. In the end, the friend decided against the risk and chose not to testify as an alibi witness for Gary. She would have made a very convincing witness.

We had no choice but to rest our case.

The time had come for closing arguments. The judge limited the time for each side to no more than forty-five minutes, in spite of this being a trial over someone's life. John Mays took the first fifteen and began by holding up Beverly Robinson's DUI mug shot and asking the jurors, "If someone showed you a picture of yourself, do you think you would know it was you in the picture?" The jurors nodded, acknowledging Beverly's lack of credibility.

When it was my turn, I had much to cover in a fleeting thirty minutes with Gary's life at stake. Utilizing overhead transparencies, I pointed out the many things that the investigators failed to do or establish. They did not order the fingerprints lifted off the whiskey glass to be compared to Beverly Robinson, Rex Segars or anyone else other than Gary Drinkard. They presented no evidence that the tire tracks found on the Pace property were consistent with Gary's vehicle.

The detectives took no notes when they first interviewed Beverly, who supposedly provided key information in regard to this highly publicized murder. I pointed out that no efforts were made to take statements from the alibi witnesses who supported Gary's innocence, yet they expended significant efforts as it related to Gary's step-daughter, who changed her testimony from the first trial.

I asked that the jurors compare the newspaper report of the crime with the taped conversation. The similarities would be obvious. Most importantly, we had established through Beverly and Detective Walker that Beverly had worn the wire taped between her legs. It was no coincidence, I argued, that at crucial points during the conversation it ended up garbled with static—the kind of static that would occur if Beverly rubbed her thighs together.

I reminded the jury that the defense had absolutely no burden to prove Gary Drinkard innocent of this crime. However, I maintained that the evidence itself pointed much more toward other individuals as the perpetrators and that alone presented a reasonable doubt sufficient to acquit him. In fact, were it not for Beverly Robinson and Rex Segars, Gary would have never been implicated in the first place.

"If you will lie about the little things, you will lie about the big ones. And if you will lie to and about your friends and family, you will lie for your freedom," I concluded.

The jury deliberated for over an hour before returning a verdict. It declared Gary Drinkard not guilty. (In later interviews with our investigators, most jurors said that it took hardly five minutes to decide he was innocent, but they did not want to appear hasty like the O. J. Simpson jury.)

Gary Drinkard's time on death row was now over. He had been cleared of a crime he did not commit and was set free. I cannot describe the feeling of elation as we, his defense team, his mother and two children accompanied him to the county jail to pick up his belongings. He had spent seven years and ten months incarcerated for a crime he did not commit. For more than five of those years he had awaited execution on Alabama's death row.

The next time I met Gary was in Washington, D.C. We were there to hear Steve Bright testify before the Senate Judiciary Committee on wrongful conviction and the Innocence Protection Act legislation. Steve highlighted Gary's case and introduced him to the committee.

Gary Drinkard had stared directly into the eyes of death and never blinked. His near-death experience has forever changed him. Like many of my clients, Gary had supported the death penalty until falsely accused of a death penalty offense.

But what happens to Gary and the other 137 exonerated human beings who languished on death row hoping for a miracle that would reverse their death sentences, once they receive freedom?[2] Soon after his release Gary worked odd jobs as a carpenter before he enrolled in college to become a respiratory therapist. However, with only six months left before obtaining his degree, Gary found that no hospital would hire him due to his past, which included his arrest for capital murder.

Gary continued with carpentry jobs for a while and resumed his close relationship with his two children. At the time of the retrial his daughter was thirteen years old. His son was then sixteen. Gary had written to each of them weekly while he was on death row and did a remarkable parenting job in his letters, assisting his ex-wife with whom they then lived.

Gary is now on the board of directors of a national organization dedicated to abolishing the death penalty, called Witness to Innocence. He travels frequently and speaks nationally and internationally on the horrors of facing the death penalty. The organization has participated in successful efforts to abolish the death penalty in both New Mexico and Illinois.

He now devotes his life to advocating against the death penalty. I still have the letters he wrote in which he proclaimed his innocence.

27

ERIC RUDOLPH AND ME

An anonymous 911 call warned the Atlanta Police Department that someone had placed a bomb in Centennial Olympic Park during the 1996 Olympic Games. Soon after, the bomb exploded and killed a female spectator, injuring over one hundred others. A man later died of a heart attack as he rushed to film the chaos that erupted after the explosion.

In the next year, two other explosions occurred in the area surrounding Atlanta. In January, two bombs went off at an abortion clinic in Sandy Springs, injuring seven. A month later, a bomb exploded at a nightclub named the Otherside Lounge, injuring a handful of people. This time, investigators found a second bomb before it detonated.

That year went by without any further incidents being reported. However, on January 29, 1998, a bomb exploded at the New Women All Women Health Care Clinic, an abortion provider on the south side of Birmingham, Alabama.

Because of threats made against the New Women All Women Health Care Clinic by pro-life protestors, it had received a highly enhanced security detail. On that fateful day, the guard was off-duty Birmingham police officer Robert "Sandy" Sanderson, who was filling in for another off-duty officer. When Sandy reached down to examine an unfamiliar plastic shrub near the clinic's front entrance, the bomb hidden underneath blew him to bits, killing him instantly. The blast could be heard for miles in every direction. The deadly shrapnel that was attached to the explosive device flew through the air and tore into nurse Emily Lyons, shattering her body, blinding her in one eye and permanently maiming her. Today, more than twenty surgeries later, she still lives in constant pain and unimaginable trauma.

    I knew Sandy Sanderson from my criminal defense work in the state courts. I found him to be different from many of the officers on the force. When Officer Sanderson appeared in court for various cases in which he was the arresting officer, he did not inject himself into the plea negotiations or try to control them. Rather, he left the disposition of the cases to the deputy district attorneys and kept a pleasant demeanor. For that and many other reasons, I respected him greatly.

    Immediately after the Birmingham explosion occurred, a young college student who was doing his laundry looked out of the window of his dorm, which was very near the clinic, and saw someone with a back-pack walking quickly along the sidewalk. The student jumped into his car and endeavored to follow the man. However, the student lost this man twice while pursuing him. The student parked at a nearby restaurant and called 911, then thought he saw the suspect out the window. The student and another individual, a young lawyer, hopped into separate cars and began to look for the man. Suddenly a truck drove past them and the lawyer wrote down the license tag and a description of the vehicle. The description and the tag led the authorities to Eric Rudolph's home town of Topton, North Carolina, where they found his truck abandoned. While Eric was driving home to his cabin outside Topton, he heard on the radio that his truck's tag had been identified and the authorities were looking for the owner in connection with the Birmingham bombing. He rushed to his cabin and hurriedly packed what he could, stopped briefly at a fast food restaurant and a local grocery store, then disappeared deep into the mountains.

    Once law enforcement identified Eric Rudolph as the primary suspect in the bombing of the Birmingham abortion clinic, Rudolph became one of the most mysterious and elusive fugitives in United States history, including Billy the Kid, Jesse James, Bonnie and Clyde, Butch Cassidy and all those whose tales and legends fascinated me and countless others during their childhoods. For one thing, a segment of the American population secretly (and not so secretly) rooted for Eric's actions, his cause and his continued mastery at evading arrest. No one truly knew if he was dead or alive, but some people saw him as a noble freedom fighter for the rights of unborn children. The question of his guilt or innocence and how he managed to elude the authorities for over five years became a riddle that would take someone like Sherlock Holmes to decipher.

The longer it took to capture Rudolph, the more his mystique grew. Perhaps Rudolph was a folk hero of the rugged, wild mountains, as some thought him to be. Before his capture, many questioned if Eric was still alive. Others believed that if so, he must have received help from sympathizers. Yet to this day, in spite of extensive, expensive and enormous efforts and investigation, the government has not located anyone (other than George Nordmann) who rendered Eric any aid over the five and one-half years he evaded capture.

Doug Jones was a friend of mine, serving at the time as the United States Attorney for the Northern District of Alabama. Doug's persuasive abilities proved instrumental in convincing the Department of Justice to choose Birmingham over Atlanta to prosecute Eric. The United States Attorney's office in Birmingham is located less than two miles from the clinic that was bombed. My office is a mile southeast of it.

When I heard about the clinic bombing, I asked myself if I would be comfortable representing the man charged by the government for this crime, whoever he was. I knew that my experience and successes in defending death penalty cases, including rare federal capital prosecutions, distinctly qualified me. I expected the courts would request me to take the appointment as lead defense counsel. In fact, that is exactly what happened.

When I became Eric's lawyer, my ability to represent him effectively depended in large part on getting to know him. The American Bar Association (ABA) standards and my oath as his advocate required that. However, I wanted to know this man's inner world, his motivations and influences. This desire only grew after I met him. Over the ensuing four-teen months, I spent numerous hours learning the details of the case and getting to know Eric as a person who loved his mother as much as any son could and who loved his brother as much as any sibling could. His brother must have loved Eric just as much, since he sawed off a portion of his arm, taped the proceedings and sent the video to the FBI to protest its actions.

In spite of the devastation Eric caused and the lives he shattered, I came away from my many jailhouse visits with an understanding that might surprise you: love lives in his heart. I know this as an inescapable truth, though this is understandably unfathomable to most, especially those whose lives he destroyed irreparably.

Eric held a very clear point of view: he believed the federal gov-ernment, by legally sanctioning abortion with the *Roe v. Wade* decision, had declared war on babies. Eric's love of children ran indelibly deep in his psyche. In his mind, legalized abortion amounted to an act of aggres-sion, a state of war declared by the government. To him, attacking an abor-tion clinic was no different from the government launching bombs and sending troops to Iraq in a preemptive strike against Saddam Hussein. Eric argued that bombing an abortion clinic had more justification than invading Iraq, because the clinic killed babies every day and to him that threatened national security; these unborn babies were not kept secure by the law of the land. Therefore, Eric believed, legalized abortion and its clinics provided a clear, present and ongoing danger to American society—making the bombing a justifiable act in defense of others.

Yet these positions and constructs only partially defined him. They certainly did not explain the Olympic bombing or the explosion at the Otherside lounge, an Atlanta gay bar.

To understand Eric, I looked into his major life influences as he developed. He was born the fifth of six children to Patty and Robert "Bob" Rudolph. Eric lived with his family in Florida, eventually settling just south of Miami in Homestead. In Eric's first ten years, America experienced profound social change concerning issues that would shape his psyche and his actions. The Vietnam War deeply divided the country. Most gays remained in the closet. The United States Supreme Court ruled on *Roe v. Wade*, legalizing abortion. Racial tensions still ran high. Some people replaced organized religion and the establishment with drugs, cults and individual or Eastern spiritual pursuits. The women's movement began to take off.

All of these social and political winds profoundly influenced Eric's parents. Patty and Bob Rudolph, in their thirties, were social activists during this period. Prior to her marriage, Patty had lived in a convent and became a devoted follower of social activist Dorothy Day. For his part, Bob played guitar, wrote songs, ran a prison ministry and participated in other causes. An airline mechanic, Bob loved carpentry almost as much as music. Both sought solace in religion; Eric later described his mother as a "seeker." Patty characterized herself as an idealist and a pacifist, one who sought involvement in various causes and particularly empathized with the needy. She and Bob participated in social demonstrations; together, they sought the "perfect church."

Patty, who seemed immensely complex and passionately opinionated, told me she was a "liberal, then a conservative, then a liberal again" during her adult life. She objected deeply to the racial injustices in Selma, Alabama, and around the country. She identified with the nonviolent teachings of Martin Luther King, Jr. Patty told me that she taught her children to question everything, "including the Holocaust." Eric seriously doubted it at one time; in high school he even wrote a paper questioning its existence.

Patty became involved with the Pentecostal religion; Bob eventually joined her. They regularly hosted prayer meetings at their home. Sometimes, Patty and others talked in tongues. She also distrusted all conventional medicine. She birthed Eric at home with the aid of a midwife. She told me that Eric never once went to a doctor until required to do so when he joined the military. Patty and I even discussed alternative medicine. When I told her I suffered from severe migraines, she instructed her alternative medicine practitioner to call me with his advice. For a Christmas present, she sent me *Original Self*, by Thomas Moore, an author I had read for years. She inscribed it, "Pat Rudolph, Mother of Eric Rudolph."

I found Patty, like Eric, to be a multifaceted, conflicted person. Like Eric, I recognized the "seeker" in Patty, a woman who grew very emotional and strong-minded when it came to political, religious and social issues. While Eric hid in the mountains, she wrote a book about Eric (never published) revealing the vicissitude of her views and her deep anger that Eric stood in the crosshairs of the FBI, the Bureau of Alcohol, Tobacco, Firearms and Explosives and authorities in Georgia, Alabama and North Carolina as a suspect in the bombings. I formed a close relationship with Pat, who steadfastly believed that Eric could not have committed the violent acts of which he stood accused.

Such strong, passionate and driven actions served as the roots of Eric's upbringing, sowing one sentiment above all others: *Sometimes, you just need to take action yourself to get things done.*

In death penalty work, we seek to uncover pivotal points when our clients' lives took a turn, they made decisions or something happened to them that changed their lives immensely and irrevocably. Certainly, when Patty and Bob befriended Tom Branham at a religious gathering while the Rudolph family lived in Homestead, it changed Eric's future life path irreversibly, especially when you consider that strong anti-establishment attitudes already percolated within Eric.

Tom harbored some highly controversial and radical views of government and religion. He eventually moved to the rural North Carolina hamlet of Topton, where he built a cabin in the mountains that Eric visited in the summers. Tom's extensive library contained many books espousing extremist and anti-government views, including a copy of one of Eric's favorite books, *Imperium Europa: The Book that Changed the World*, by Norman Lowell.

Then Eric's father, Bob, was diagnosed with cancer. Patty and Bob tried many alternative methods to heal him, even going to Mexico for an experimental treatment prohibited in the United States. During this time Eric stayed with Tom in Topton. Eric probably didn't know the extent of Bob's sickness; his dad's death was quite sudden and unexpected and Eric returned to Homestead for the funeral. I doubt that the vulnerable fourteen-year-old boy ever completely grieved the loss of his father.

After Bob died, Eric and his younger brother Dan moved to Topton permanently. Tom helped Eric and Dan build their own cabin on land Patty purchased next to Tom's. During this time, Eric and Dan slept on box springs in Tom's barn, with Tom serving as a surrogate father. They really roughed it for a while. Soon, Patty moved there as well. After the government charged Tom with illegal possession of explosives and weapons, Eric often visited him in jail. When the appeals court overturned Tom's conviction, Patty put up her house as surety for his bail as Tom waited for a retrial.

Eric found himself surrounded by not only Tom Branham's radical views, but also those of many others living around rural Tennessee and North Carolina. This included extremist Nord Davis, whom Tom utilized instead of a lawyer for the opening stages of his defense. (He later hired a licensed attorney.) Both Eric and Patty also interacted with George Nordmann, a devout Catholic with unconventional views who owned a health food store that Eric and Patty frequented. Nordmann and Eric had many conversations about alternative health remedies, religion and government. According to Eric, Nordmann denied the existence of the Holocaust, reawakening Eric to the subject of his high school paper. At the behest of Nordmann, Eric visited a religious extremist group under the direction of a western Tennessee doctor.

To attempt to truly understand any accused murderer facing the death penalty, we must intimately and thoroughly know the losses, sufferings and pain he or she endured over a lifetime. Eric experienced a number of impacting disappointments at pivotal points in his life. The death of his father and separation from his mother at age fourteen affected him deeply. His relocation to North Carolina not only robbed him of his youth baseball successes (he remained an outstanding athlete, which offers insight into why he maneuvered so well in the North Carolina mountains), but also landed him squarely in the lap of the radical Tom Branham.

Eric wouldn't talk much about that period of his life. Nor did he offer much about perhaps his deepest and most painful loss: the sudden death of his one-time fiancée, Joy, and her two young children. When he did discuss her, Eric's eyes softened noticeably and he lowered his head slightly. The sadness that surrounded us was palpable. Once Eric also perceived it, he quickly changed the subject.

Eric exhibited real talent when he mimicked others; he could impersonate nearly everyone with whom he interacted, including me. At times, his energetic, loud and expressive mimicking reflected anger or hostility as much as it did humor, giving me valuable added insight into one of the most complex characters I have ever known. From a psychological point of view, a person mimics others repeatedly or otherwise alters his speech when he is afraid of his own authentic voice being heard or he doesn't want people to get to know him intimately. One thing about the most complex people: they develop countless psychological devices, ruses and other diversions to prevent others from knowing them completely. Eric was no different.

However, when Eric spoke of Joy, I sensed profound loss and respect, a reverence unlike any of his other relationships we discussed. I have no doubt that Eric loved Joy deeply. They met while she attended college in Denver, but she spent as much time as she could at her father's home in Arkansas. Eric rode his motorcycle from North Carolina to Arkansas—a distance of more than six hundred miles—on at least three occasions to visit her. Eric never told me they were engaged, but other family members verified it. He did tell me that the last time he drove to her father's house, Joy gave him a sweater. Deeply religious, Joy wanted him to express his commitment to Christ in order for her to make a full commitment to him. Eric told me that when he would not say, "I am saved," Joy broke up with him. I firmly believe that his breakup with Joy was a pivotal point in Eric's life and greatly influenced him.

Five years later, to Eric's disbelief and dismay, Joy married an older man whom Eric believed had both a gambling problem and mental health issues. One day, Joy and her two beautiful children, ages one and two, sat close together in her car. She turned on the engine, killing herself and her youngsters by carbon monoxide poisoning. She left a suicide note.

When Eric learned of this tragedy, his heart broke. As with the untimely death of his father, I doubt he permitted himself to grieve this profound loss entirely. During my extensive experience representing individuals accused of violent crimes, especially those eligible for the death penalty, I have found that most have experienced severe life disappointments and profound losses. Many never learn basic, essential grieving skills, but instead build up defense mechanisms to deal with these losses. Many never experience support from family or friends. They internalize their pain, but they don't heal their wounds. Underneath, they not only feel emotionally empty and lost, but also experience anger and rage. They are like volcanoes. All it takes is something to trigger them—a broken relationship, a family death, an intense social situation—to create an eruption that defies any description of rational behavior. Nationally prominent psychologist Mark Cunningham has analogized a person to a bridge. Each disappointment, disadvantage and loss piles up on the bridge until it finally collapses.

To the surprise of several family members, Eric enlisted in the Army. Eric never told me what prompted him to enlist, but I believe that his breakup with Joy contributed greatly. Why else would this loner, who resented authority from a young age and was raised to question authority, volunteer for employment with Uncle Sam?

Soon enough, though, a triggering event occurred. On a routine training mission, a helicopter crashed, killing several of Eric's friends. When I tried to speak with Eric about the tragedy, hurt pooled in his eyes and face. Eric blamed the Army's incompetence for these deaths. He did not discuss it much, just like his father's death and just like the tragic loss of Joy.

Our investigation of Eric's eighteen months in the military revealed unexplained contradictions. No consistent profile emerged. Some of his former Army buddies said Eric showed no signs of racial bias or other extremist views, including attitudes regarding abortion. Others painted a picture of serious racial prejudice and resentment toward authority. One man had kept a couple of letters Eric sent him, one of them signed "Adolf." Eric told me he wrote that in jest.

If the government believed Eric received explosives training in the Army, he steadfastly denied this. Our investigation supported Eric's position. During his short stint, he only achieved the rank of E2 or private; any exposure to explosives at that level would not have been sufficient to teach him to design and build the devices utilized in the four bombings for which he was charged. However, someone using a pseudonym had ordered a book on bomb building. The book was sent to Eric's last known address, a fact that Eric would not explain.

Only eighteen months after his enlistment, Eric wanted out of the Army. He had been written up for bringing an unregistered female into his barracks. Eventually, the Army sent him to counseling. During those required sessions, Eric made it clear that he wanted a discharge. After the Army ignored his efforts and requests, Eric self-reported marijuana use, resulting in a positive test. Eric received the misconduct discharge he sought, although it was officially given under "honorable" circumstances.

During the first minutes of most of my visits, Eric appeared aloof and withdrawn. Human contact still startled him after so many years away from it. It took some time for him to warm up. After he did, he craved contact and often he spoke as if he had not talked to anyone in years—because he hadn't. When Eric talked of his survival experiences, the words chugged out of his mouth like a runaway locomotive. Once on a roll, he could not stop and did not want us to leave.

The more I met with Eric, the more he seemed to trust me. Yet, I remained mindful that all of our experiences influence and change us in varying ways and degrees. How would I change if I lived in isolation for over five years, knowing that hundreds of government agents continually hunted me and that at any time I could perish from starvation or sickness or injure myself without anyone to render me aid?

As much as we discussed the evidence and our investigation and strategies, we talked even more about his life as a fugitive and his sole focus on survival every minute of every night and day. Eric's disclosures did not occur immediately. As we grew closer, he began to share many of his adventures and escapades, along with some, though certainly not all, of his innermost thoughts. Once, he spoke of an instance when he truly thought that death would overtake him on a particularly frozen, foodless night. Then, something profound occurred which forever transformed him and convinced him that God existed. When I pressed him for specifics, he said, "Some things are so personal that I can't discuss them with anybody."

While Eric spoke, I felt just how much potential we have as human beings to focus entirely upon any challenge that life presents. Eric certainly created his own circumstances and challenges. He also relished his ability to outwit those who sought to capture him, a characteristic you will find in any of history's most notorious fugitives. He evaded infrared helicopter sights, countless agents, skilled and seasoned survivalists and the general population seeking the million dollar reward. At times, huge numbers joined one of the largest manhunts in United States history. When Eric discussed his momentous challenges and successes—feats that almost no one else could accomplish, including the most rugged Army Rangers, Marine Special Forces or Navy SEALs—his face lit up. It seemed as if he had suddenly transported himself back to one of his two chief campsites hidden deep in the mountainous woods.

The Jefferson County Jail feeds its inmates at 5:00 P.M. and makes lawyers leave. But Eric's guards, most of whom liked him, almost always let me stay much later. One day when the guard brought Eric his tray and an extra tray, I started to pack my briefcase. But Eric asked me to stay while he ate his dinner. He offered me the extra tray, which I declined.

We talked until nearly 8:00 P.M. Eric launched into a vivid explanation of the location of each camp he constructed while he was in hiding, how neatly he arranged each sock and bit of clothing and the protection and preparation of his food. I marveled at his extraordinary attention to every detail, all of them essential to his survival. Eric set up three different camps: a summer camp, a winter camp and an FBI camp. The last served as a diversion that he hoped agents would find (and eventually they did), but he never used it. He transported food and supplies from the winter camp to the summer camp and vice versa when necessary.

He built his summer camp high in the mountains, virtually overlooking the FBI field headquarters. It was like a mouse perched above the trap set for its capture. This gave an undetected Eric the advantage of watching his pursuers. He could also walk from his lookout to town to pilfer food from trash bins and books from the library.

I believe that Eric thrived by merging with nature and, in the process, defying the odds of being captured. In his previous, rather mundane life, after earning his general equivalency diploma he worked with his brother Dan on various carpentry jobs, read incessantly, watched a lot of television (often while high on marijuana) and rented movies. Eric's life largely lacked direction and purpose.

Once he had fled Birmingham and disappeared into the mountains, every minute detail he addressed and every decision he made potentially determined whether he lived or died. In each movement, thought and action, he truly seized and mastered the moment, as no room for error existed. Eating the wrong plants or berries or drinking the wrong water could prove deadly. Failing to kill a turkey or other wild animal or sustaining the smallest tear in his shoes could result in his demise. For years, Eric had frequented gun shows and had stashed a cache of weapons in the North Carolina mountains long before he entered them as a fugitive.

Eric emphasized that his close encounters with starvation, death and capture convinced him that "God had a plan for me to live," or else he surely would have died on several occasions during his years in the wild. He told me, "When you get close to death, you get close to God. And I came real close to death. I had always thought there was a God, but I didn't know it. Now I know there is a God."

During that time, Eric's life contained no ambiguities, no ambivalence and no second chances, just a singular clarity borne by the will to survive. He spent forty-eight thousand hours focused on this mission.

Eric always insisted that no one ever helped him with food or gave him shelter. He occasionally broke into empty cabins and took any edible leftovers. With a million-dollar bounty hanging over his head, Eric trusted no one.

Except George Nordmann.

At one desperate point, when food and supplies had diminished at his summer camp, Eric walked over thirty miles through the most rugged terrain to seek Nordmann's assistance. Eric believed his old friend would help him and not turn him in. Eric set up a place to camp right above Nordmann's cabin, so that he could observe his friend's daily activities. For a few days, after Nordmann left for work, Eric gained entrance into his basement. There he cooked eggs, showered and ate from the food that Nordmann had stockpiled in the basement.

One morning, one of Nordmann's children entered the cabin while Eric was still inside. Undoubtedly she smelled Eric's cooking. Eric quickly left, then waited a few days to see if the authorities visited the cabin or the area. They did not. Satisfied and encouraged, he approached a startled Nordmann early one morning and asked him for help. He told Nordmann that the government had framed him and that he was innocent and starving. Eric requested enough food and supplies to last several years and gave Nordmann a list. Nordmann agreed to help him and Eric devised a plan to protect Nordmann in case the government found out.

The next morning, Eric saw Nordmann again. As he hurried from his cabin to his truck, Nordmann spoke in a low voice: "God said no to the supplies." He gave Eric a small amount of food, roughly a three-month supply. He admonished Eric to leave and not return, then sped away in his truck.

Nordmann had another truck sitting dilapidated in his yard. Eric hotwired it, filled it with additional stockpiled food and supplies from Nordmann's basement and drove off. He left Nordmann four hundred dollars in cash and an apology note. Nordmann kept the money but destroyed the note.

Eric did not get far, as the truck engine siezed up after only a few miles. He carefully hid and safeguarded the supplies and then

hiked the thirty miles back to his summer camp, worrying that the
supplies would perish unless he retrieved them soon. The night of his
arrival back at camp, Eric descended into town and broke into a used
car dealership he had previously cased. He knew the employees hung
the keys on a wall in the office. He broke the glass to the office, found
the keys to a pickup truck and sped off. En route back to the supplies,
he ran out of gas. Local patrol officers picked him up, took him to get
gas and returned him to the truck he had stolen!

Eric drove to where he had hidden the supplies, loaded them in
the bed of the truck and headed back to his camp. Still, he had to leave
the truck and traverse the last part of the journey by foot. Somehow,
he figured out a practically impossible way to haul huge sacks on foot
at night up the mountain. Using screen, wire and other materials, he
devised a method to preserve the food but also to bury it to stymie
the constant threat of pillaging from native black bears. Eric took great
pride in this amazing accomplishment.

Eric told me that he left a note in the pickup truck in the hope
that the FBI would make it public. His purpose was to let his mother
know he was still alive. But the FBI, to Eric's dismay, did not release his
note to the media.

During growing seasons, Eric climbed large bins containing
various grains, filled burlap sacks he took from town and hauled them
up the mountain. A close encounter came while Eric was climbing one
of the thirty-foot-tall grain bins. He spotted hunters below. They had
discovered his backpack and a fire he had made to cook the grains. This
was not the sort of food that hunters would normally expect campers
to roast. They rifled through his pack but then drove off. They never
reported the incident.

Eric did whatever it took to survive, even eating salamanders,
but only after removing the skin which could be poisonous. When he
could, he shot wild turkey and learned how to preserve the meat by
wrapping it and submerging it in the cool waters outside caves and
within crevices. The western North Carolina mountains offer some of
the finest underwater caverns and subterranean streams in the United
States and Eric knew how to utilize them.

Then came the near-miss that topped them all. One winter, Eric heard a car behind him while he was walking along a road at 3:00 A.M. Tired and weary, he slipped into a ditch but did not try hard to hide. The car belonged to a police officer, who thought the form he saw in the ditch "was a dead body until I talked to him."

As Eric told me, mimicking the officer's deep southern drawl, "The cop grabs a shotgun and asks, 'What you doin' in a ditch?'"

"I said, 'Not hidin'. Did not want to scare a granny.'"

The officer called for backup and handcuffed Eric, who gave a false name. The cop ran it on his computer, then asked the fully-bearded Eric, who was dressed in camouflage, the other states in which he had lived and if he was presently homeless. The backup officer checked Eric's backpack, which contained food and a few knick-knacks. "Any bombs in thar?" the cop asked.

"No bombs," Eric replied.

After giving Eric a field sobriety test, the officer and his backup put Eric in one of the patrol cars and searched his pack again. They kept looking at the road and conferring.

"Finally," Eric related to me, "they let me go and gave me half a pack of cigarettes."

When Eric related his astounding adventures and his narrow escapes from capture and death, at times I almost felt my breath taken away. I could sense Eric's excitement and I almost had to suspend my rational beliefs, since his escapades were so far beyond any world that I could imagine. Ironically, his stint in isolation as a survivalist, in a class of his own, had brought him a measure of fame and distinction that he had never achieved before he became an infamously destructive bomber. The highly opinionated, critical and intolerant Eric who had fled to those mountains no longer had any place in his psyche if he were to survive. Eric's proclivity toward the obsessive fixation that led to the bombings served him, if not saved him from certain death in the wild. By contrast, the organization, focus and structure of the Army still required him to confront the imperfections and hypocrisies of the world as he saw it.

Other than relating his adventures, Eric liked to discuss religion and philosophy more than any other topics. He loved talking about Nietzsche and could quote him as well. He certainly conversed his way through a plethora of subjects. We talked about anything and everything, including history, poetry and politics. Regarding the Holocaust, Eric told me he did not deny that the Holocaust existed, but he doubted that as many as six million Jews were killed. He felt that the actual number was much lower. When he spoke of anti-Semitism, he tried to contextualize it within economics, since "It is a fact that Jews control the banks, lending institutions and the media." Eric feared the coming of the New World Order, believing that the white race stood in danger of annihilation.

He also talked regularly with another member of my defense team, Hube Dodd. They were close to the same age and Eric offered his advice regarding Hube's social life. When Eric shared some of their conversations with me, I could tell that he genuinely cared for Hube's well-being. Eric also spoke about the Bible. He always had one with him and agents found one at his summer camp after his capture. Once, I suggested to Eric that his view of the Bible amounted to a personal interpretation and that others might interpret it differently. Clearly offended, he emphatically proclaimed, "It is not an interpretation. There is no other way to read the Bible. It says what it says." Eric truly saw a world divided by good and evil, wearing only the colors of darkest black or purest white.

While in the mountains, Eric always found a way to read. Brazen enough to pilfer not just from trash bins, he occasionally ate at the fast food restaurant within sight and walking distance of the FBI headquarters below his summer camp. After ordering a meal, he strolled into the adjacent local library and walked out with books hidden under his clothes. The books covered a range one might not ordinarily expect from a man whom the media (to his eternal disdain) constantly lumped into the right-wing extremist camp. His reading spanned history and philosophy, extending from Gandhi to the influence of Jewish music in Europe, from Shakespeare to books about the Third Reich. Eric loved Ayn Rand's *Atlas Shrugged* and *The Fountainhead* and particularly enjoyed talking about these books with Hube. While incarcerated in the Jefferson County jail, Eric read such books as *Prison to Praise* by Merlin Carothers, *The Ellsworth Letters* by Roy Ellsworth, Shakespeare's *As You Like It* and scores of others. He always read his Bible.

Eric's luck in evading capture for over five years abruptly ran out at 4:30 A.M. on a Saturday morning in the small, mountainous town of Murphy, North Carolina. Twenty-one year old rookie police officer Jeff Postell spotted what he thought was a prowler about to commit a burglary. Eric was hiding behind some milk crates near a trash bin. Postell did not recognize Eric, who gave his name as "Jerry Wilson." However, other officers thought they recognized him. Apparently weary yet clean-shaven, Eric answered "Eric Robert Rudolph" when asked who he really was. Eric was unarmed and offered no resistance to the arresting officers.

Since the question of which jurisdiction would try him first had already been resolved, Eric was flown to Birmingham for an arraignment early the following week.

Which begs the question: Who *was* Eric Rudolph, this man who subsisted in harsh conditions for so many years with more than one thousand people hunting him down at one point and no known human contact? I doubt that anyone, even members of his immediate family, really knows. Eric displays too many complexities and contradictions; too many shades and layers of words, thoughts and acts. Eric also possesses qualities that demonstrate both kindness and violence. There are many places in Eric's soul that no one, perhaps including Eric himself, has visited.

However, out of all the people with whom Eric Rudolph was in contact during the last ten years, I developed a real rapport with him. U.S. District Judge Lynwood Smith had appointed me as the lead defense counsel to represent Eric, who now faced the death penalty for allegedly bombing the abortion clinic in Birmingham. Eventually he was also charged in the Atlanta bombings.

The commotion stopped me cold. Police officers had blocked off the northwest side of Birmingham's federal courthouse to make room for more press than I had ever seen before. I could not see the street beyond the sea of hundreds of cameras, whose operators and accompanying reporters had traveled like lightning from all over the world. It looked like a conglomeration of symphonies gathered to perform in the street on this clear, sunny afternoon in Birmingham.

Only this was no symphony. It was the initial global sighting of the near-mythical lead character in a very dark tale, a man who had somehow eluded the finest human trackers in the land for more than five years.

Amidst the incredible clamor outside the courthouse, my focus lay with the task at hand: the arraignment of Eric Robert Rudolph. My client was somewhere beneath this mass of humanity, being whisked into the building via an underground entrance and flanked by security befitting a president.

Or America's Most Wanted Man.

A flood of reporters and cameramen descended upon me. I gave no comment at that time but promised that we would make a brief statement after the arraignment.

The rather wide concrete steps contained such a crowd of reporters that my co-counsels and I could not make our way through on our own. We had to be escorted by United States marshals through the courthouse doors, the hallway and the entrance to the courtroom. The courtroom itself overflowed with spectators; the only empty seats were those at the counsel tables.

After a fifteen-minute explanation of rights at the arraignment, my associates and I walked out to face the eager orchestra of reporters and cameras. I made a brief statement: "The government has been working on this case for over five years. We, on the other hand, have been on it less than a day. The only thing we ask is that everyone keep an open mind and not prejudge this case or our client, Eric Rudolph, who has an absolute right to and deserves to be presumed innocent."

I drove straight to my office, only to find reporters already there. I took a deep breath that I didn't really want to release. I had tried tough, well-publicized cases with clients facing the death penalty before, but this was completely different. When I finally exhaled, I made another short statement on the front porch of our 1906 Georgian office.

Afterward, I retreated inside to begin poring through thousands of pages of articles and e-mails about what most people knew simply as "the bombings" and the ensuing five-and-a-half-year federal manhunt for Eric Rudolph.

A death penalty case consists of two phases, so it essentially involves preparing for two separate but intertwined trials. The first is the guilt/innocence proceedings—the main trial. That is followed by the punishment phase. Both cases are heard and decided by the same jury. In the first phase, the jury must unanimously find the accused guilty beyond a reasonable doubt in order to reach the punishment phase. In the punishment phase, the jury then must choose between death and life without the possibility of parole (LWOP). As opposed to non-death penalty cases, LWOP means there is no parole, no matter how well the accused behaves behind bars. The jury also has to vote unanimously for death in federal death penalty cases. One vote for life results in a sentence of LWOP.

Because the punishment phase requires the jury to consider every aspect of the life and history of the defendant, it takes enormous time and money to prepare properly for it. In fact, the American Bar Association guidelines require counsel to investigate a client's entire life and that of his or her family, taking the investigation back through three generations.[1] The vast majority of lawyers lack the time and the training to undertake and coordinate this kind of investigation, which is almost always multi-state, sometimes international. Only a properly trained "mitigation investigator" has the qualifications and experience to perform this work adequately.

This is one reason why death penalty defense teams are much larger than normal criminal defenses. The presiding judge appoints at least two lawyers plus a fact investigator, a mitigation investigator and appropriate mental health experts to comprise the basic defense team. The prosecution also investigates both the crime and the defendant's life history. For these and other reasons, such as constitutionally mandated appeals, jury selection procedures and courtroom and outside security, the costs of pursuing the death penalty far exceed the costs to incarcerate someone for life. It's a grueling, enormously stressful and time-consuming process. Most death penalty cases are overturned due to the ineffective assistance of counsel during the investigation of a client's life history. In complex, high-profile cases, such as the federal government's prosecutions of Timothy McVeigh and Eric Rudolph, millions of dollars are spent before the cases are resolved.

Furthermore, virtually all sociology and criminology studies conclude that the threat of imposing the death penalty fails completely to deter violent crime. In fact, violence begets violence; most murders and violent crimes occur in jurisdictions and locations that carry the death penalty as a possible punishment.

Even before government agents captured Eric, millions of dollars had been spent looking for him. But when it sought the death penalty in two different jurisdictions—Birmingham and Atlanta—the government expended many millions more.

I focused on building a team that could take on the mountainous task of defending a man the government desired to execute nearly as much as it did McVeigh, who was a Gulf War veteran and homegrown terrorist who killed 168 people, many of them federal workers, by bombing the Alfred P. Murrah Federal Building in Oklahoma City.

I had the good fortune of knowing I could rely on the valuable cooperation of the federal defender's office in Atlanta to work with us in organizing, assimilating and reviewing the hundreds of thousands of documents. These included thousands of interviews the agents conducted during Eric's five and one-half years as a fugitive.

Stephanie Kearnes, the head Atlanta federal defender and her associates—chief federal defender Paul Kisch and assistant federal defenders Carl Leitz and Brian Mendelsohn—contributed immensely to our Birmingham team's ability to have a successful and quick start. These devoted and highly skilled attorneys collaborated with our team at least weekly and sometimes several times a week as we coordinated Eric's defense.

However, we also had to conduct our own investigation and interviews as well as recreate Eric's entire life history and learn all of the influences on his life.

I knew that I would need another accomplished death penalty lawyer to join our team in Birmingham. Should we end up in a trial, the proceedings would certainly take months. The government had assigned three experienced full-time trial lawyers to this case; because of that, I felt we needed to add two more lawyers with death penalty expertise to our team. My associates Hube Dodd and Derek Drennan were invaluable in preparing the case, but at the time neither had the trial experience for this mammoth undertaking.

I considered many experienced lawyers. I approached Atlanta attorney Jack Martin. I would have loved to work with Jack, whose skills and ethics I trusted deeply. However, Jack thought his former client, Richard Jewell, who was wrongfully accused in the Olympic bombing, would be brought into our case. I assured Jack we had no intention of doing that. Instead, we planned to use the wrongful allegations against Jewell and the government's earlier portrayal of him as the bomber to illustrate that the government gets things wrong sometimes. We would use as an example the search warrant for Jewell's property, which contained several erroneous conclusions, such as that the "materials" found contained bomb components consistent with the device employed in the Centennial Olympic Park bombing.

However, I could not convince Jack to join us at that point.

At the urging of David Bruck, one of the finest death penalty lawyers in the nation and one of the people who had recommended me to Judge Smith, I asked David's close friend Judy Clarke if she would consider serving as co-counsel, with me leading the way. Judy had second-chaired David in the Susan Smith case (a woman who drowned her small children by driving them into a lake) and brought about the plea deal in the Ted Kaczynski "Unabomber" case. She had also worked for a while on the case of Zacarias Moussaoui, the alleged twentieth intended hijacker in the September 11 attacks. I knew Judy distantly when she served as president of the National Association of Criminal Defense Lawyers (NACDL) and recognized her to be talented and skilled in death penalty litigation and federal law. I told Judge Smith I had spoken to Judy Clarke and he conducted his own research. When he got back to me, he conveyed that he wanted her on the case.

However, I encountered a great deal of resistance within my camp. I perceived that Judy had a strained relationship with the Atlanta Federal Defender's Office in charge of Eric's Atlanta defense team. Also, within the administration of the National Federal Defender Organization, others strongly and vocally tried to block her entry. It took months for Judy to get clearance to join the team. Were it not for Judge Smith's efforts, it never would have happened.

Judy and I discussed this resistance often. I also met with her in Birmingham, as I wanted to make sure that Judy would be willing to accept me as lead counsel, given her strong personality. Judy assured me that she would have no problem serving as second-in-command. She did say something that was both very concerning and revealing to me: She was from North Carolina and had always thought that this would be her case.

She eventually proved to be right.

While waiting for Judy to be appointed, my co-counsels Derek Drennan, Hube Dodd and Bill Bowen (who was appointed the day before me) worked tirelessly with the Atlanta team to learn every aspect of the case and Eric Rudolph as a person. Within six months of my appointment, Judy gained clearance to join the team along with Emory Anthony from Birmingham and Michael Burt from San Francisco. Now we had seven attorneys representing Eric in the Birmingham case. At that time we did not know if the Atlanta cases would be joined with the Birmingham case and all tried together. This meant we needed to know everything about the Atlanta cases as well.

Eric displayed many different moods during the many visits Hube Dodd and I made to him. At times, the stark reality of Eric's situation, his isolation in jail and the bleakness of his future—a future potentially to be spent alone, either on death row or in a maximum security institution as an inmate of the highest risk—caused him to vent in loud and angry rants with biting sarcasm and seething anger.

Hube Dodd and I both observed a pattern. Every time we met with Eric, he became fixated on a subject or idea. Eric and I discussed this several times. As he explained it, when he hid in the mountains, he became "one with nature" and his only human interaction occurred when he risked occasional trips to the local fast food restaurant, library or discount store.

Eric's relocation to the Jefferson County Jail caused him to remain isolated from other inmates because of the high-profile nature of his case. His human interaction was limited to the guards and his legal team. Now the tables were turned: instead of Eric watching pursuers from his various perches in the mountains, jailers watched him twenty-four hours a day on video cameras. Guards reported Eric talking to himself more and more as time trudged forward with the slow pace of this complex death penalty case.

When we spoke of his defense, Eric vehemently refused to allow us to blame the Birmingham bombing on anyone else, although a number of other interesting suspects existed. He strenuously objected to my calling anyone as a witness for the purpose of shifting blame to that person. Eric would not allow anyone else to be the fall guy or scapegoat. "I would rather lose my life than my dignity," he proclaimed.

On the other hand, he firmly stated, "If they call people who agree with my views to testify against me, I expect you to totally destroy them on the witness stand."

I welcomed Eric's input in building his defense. In spite of the heinous nature of the crimes for which he was charged, there were some things with which no one could argue: he was intelligent, media savvy, able to think strategically rather than reactively and had insight into his cases. When I asked him to write out a profile of the type of juror he preferred, he handwrote a fourteen-page paper that offered adept and thoughtful insights on religious, politically conservative white female jurors who might read romance novels, were probably unmarried and without great means, yet were old enough to feel maternal instincts for him. This profile resembled the many women who wrote to him every day, twenty or so with whom he regularly corresponded. He also keenly opined that his ideal juror might well resent it if he or she learned during the course of the trial of his past involvement with marijuana.

I reminded him that lawyers do not pick jurors but instead strike the ones they distrust the most. His ideal female juror made plenty of sense, as did the type of juror he most feared. He did not want financially advantaged, college-educated working women or authoritarian businessmen, especially if they were liberals. Regarding potential male jurors, he mentioned with a serious lightness that it would not hurt if a "Bubba" or two ended up on his jury.

During a number of our meetings, I stressed to Eric the importance of an honest relationship between attorney and client and how and why that contributes to effective legal representation. Eric understood how traveling too far down the wrong road, expending resources and money along the way, could adversely affect how we advised him and prepared his case. I made a point of not promising something I could not deliver and I endeavored to convey accurate information to him. However, Eric, like other astute clients, questioned whether a lawyer would put his or her heart as much into the defense of a client perceived to be guilty as opposed to one wrongfully charged. I tried to make it clear that a true advocate focuses on the client and the available defenses; otherwise, the lawyer is violating his or her oath as well as the Constitution.

"In a death penalty case, the government seeks to kill our client," I told him. "The prosecutors are more than capable of protecting their interests. The system fails when we fail to fight zealously for the people we represent, and we fail as well. I won't ever lie for you or to you, but I will fight with all my being to represent you as if you were family; there is simply no other way."

Eric looked skeptical. I continued, "The one thing you may want to keep in mind is that our interests are the same as yours. Although they are trying to kill you, not us, we want to succeed for you. How in the world would it ever help us if we lose your case or fail to give you the best representation we can?"

Defending people on trial for their lives most often presents extraordinary challenges. Knowing that our efforts and our skills could well determine if someone lives or dies creates constant stress and the person accused lives with looming death at all times. It must have been easier for Eric to survive in the mountains, where he controlled much of his destiny, than to linger in his jail cell, where he depended on his lawyers to save his life.

Eric liked to debate but not argue. He asked well-thought-out, intelligent questions and offered keen insights and observations. Often, he expressed appreciation for our efforts. His quirky sense of humor and dry wit added to the refreshing nature of our relationship. Eric listened attentively and remembered conversations from one meeting to another. He was not demanding and he did not complain.

Defending Eric brought me face to face with my core principles and reasons for defending people on trial for their lives. As I told the judge who appointed me, "Our system only functions when those accused of the worst and most heinous crimes receive the highest quality of representation." The health and stability of our adversarial system depends on it. If the apparently guilty do not get the benefit of the presumption of innocence, neither will wrongfully charged innocent people. Each citizen, no matter how horrid the charges, must receive the same rights the Constitution guarantees everyone else.

Eric Rudolph embodied one of the reasons why I do what I do. Representing the most unpopular and despised of our society is, in my opinion, the hallmark of a true criminal defense lawyer. John Adams did this when he defended the British soldiers who shot their weapons openly into the crowd during the Boston Massacre. When advocating for someone this unpopular we are also representing our profession, which is committed to safeguarding the rights of the least among us and the constitutional protections that everyone has, no matter what he is charged with or what his beliefs are.

I also met regularly with the Birmingham prosecution team, which consisted of Mike Whisonant, Joe McClain and Will Chambers. Each man was a skilled, trustworthy and ethical prosecutor, not to mention very experienced and smart. Although none of them had my expertise in death penalty cases, they had been on this case for almost six years and were certain to be formidable opponents. I had faced each prosecutor at various times over the years. While we certainly gave away no strategies to each other, I trusted them not to lie or mislead me and they trusted me similarly.

In January, after one of our meetings over discovery issues, I turned to walk out of Mike Whisonant's office. As I reached the door, Mike, almost nonchalantly, dropped his version of a bomb. "Richard, let me mention something to you. If you have any intention of entering into plea discussions, you better not wait until the last minute."

Stunned at this unexpected statement, I stopped in my tracks. "What are you saying, Mike? This is the first you have ever mentioned to me about a possible plea and I assure you I have never discussed that possibility with my client."

"My point is this, Richard: I am simply saying we know you. We trust you. We do not know any of the out-of-town lawyers. We're not going to be able to work anything out if you wait until the last minute in this case. That's all I am saying."

"Well, what about the Atlanta case? Will they be on board for this? Because, you know, all the cases would need to be disposed of if we are ever to work anything out."

Joe McClain, who was also in the room, spoke next. "Let's put it this way. We are in constant communication with the Atlanta team." Joe chose his words carefully. "We have discussed this with them. We understand what you are saying. I don't think in the end Atlanta will be a problem, but we'll just have to see."

Mike added, "Let me be clear. I'm not making you any offers. I don't have that authority. As you know, the attorney general has to sign off on any plea deals personally. I'm just saying don't wait until the last minute. I suggest you start discussing it with your client and see if there is any interest. And then we can go from there. Again, just don't wait until the last minute or it will never happen."

I walked out of that meeting realizing what I had always thought: the government saw problems with its case. It would just take one person with strong anti-abortion views to slip onto the jury and find reasonable doubt or vote for life without parole. The government would consider that a loss. It was just too big a risk for them to take. I also knew that the government had obtained very few federal death verdicts (as opposed to state death penalty prosecutions), even in much stronger cases than this and without the highly charged political and emotional abortion overtones.[2] The government did successfully secure the conviction and execution of Tim McVeigh, but he had killed 168 people in a single blast, many of them federal workers. It was not easy for the government to obtain a sentence of death, especially in cases without certain proof. The fact is that juries only choose death for a small percentage of those charged with federal death penalty offenses.[3]

We still were poring over thousands and thousands of pages of discovery. While our research was far from complete, we knew that the Birmingham case had problems establishing unquestionable proof and the Atlanta cases contained hardly any proof at all. Also, our investigator, Rick Blake, had informed us that cameras were supposedly at the clinic at the time of the bombing. I did not mention this very sensitive aspect of the investigation which we were still developing in the first of three meetings I had with the prosecutors to discuss the possibility of a plea.

As soon as possible, I discussed my conversation with the prosecutors with Eric. After explaining the entire meeting in great detail, especially the carefully-timed pronouncement at the end, I asked him, "If given a chance to enter a plea to all of the charges and receive a life sentence, would you consider it?"

Eric let my query sink in. He asked me some questions and then said, "I would consider it."

"Well," I said, wanting to know for sure, "let me put it this way: Do you want to live?"

This time Eric looked deeply into my eyes and said softly, "Yes, I want to live. I think there are ways I can still make a difference if I am in prison. I could write and continue to make my views known."

"Well, as you know, I have a great working relationship with the Atlanta team," I said. "They are well aware of my experience in trying these cases. After the trial here in Birmingham concludes, you will be transferred to Atlanta to deal with the charges there. The Atlanta team has told me that they want me to join them in representing you on the Atlanta cases then. So, either way, I expect to be with you."

Eric also acknowledged our dilemma in winning his case outright. He would have to receive not guilty verdicts in all of the federal cases he currently faced. Then, like accused (and later convicted) Oklahoma City co-conspirator Terry Nichols, he would have to face state death penalty charges in Atlanta and Birmingham and win acquittals on those, too. He saw what I saw: the odds stacked against him. However, if he denied the government a chance to kill him, that would amount (in his mind) to his victory and the government's loss.

I left the meeting encouraged that ultimately we could save Eric's life. This only began the journey to the final decision. I would have two other encouraging discussions with the prosecution in regard to a possible plea in the months to come. In the meantime, we still had much information to digest and investigation to pursue as well as subsequent negotiations. But the fact that I could and did rationally engage in this type of conversation with Eric, who could be quite volatile on occasion, resulted from the quality of the relationship which we had built together in just nine months. By then, Eric and I had broken some barriers. A mutual trust and respect now existed between us. That only happens when a lawyer keeps his word and spends enough time with his client so the client knows that the lawyer cares about not only the case but also about the client as a person.

Late one day, while meeting with Eric, I spotted Cedric Cole, a six-foot-eight, nearly three-hundred-pound African-American prison guard. Cedric was a former student of mine at Miles Law School, a school outside Birmingham with a predominantly minority population, where I had taught night law classes for eight years. As Cedric walked past the attorney meeting room, I knocked on the window and he stepped into our small cubicle. I asked him, "When are you going to let Eric hit the basketball court again? He needs some fresh air."

"How about right now?"

I looked at Eric, then Cedric. "Sure! We can finish this meeting tomorrow."

"You can finish your meeting on the court. I'll lock you two in."

Cedric escorted us to the court and locked us inside for the next hour and a half. It seemed like an eternity, but not because I was sharing a confined space with a man accused of multiple bomb-related murders. Even though I am more than fifteen years older than Eric, I also know how to play basketball. A natural athlete who was still in exceptional shape from hiking the North Carolina mountains and their rocky dirt paths, Eric was quite good and beat me in a game of one-on-one. He actually felt sorry for me. On that day we formed a bond that served us both well as I continued the journey of giving him the best defense and advice I possibly could.

However, problems were brewing within the defense team.

At first our team worked well together. But that changed soon after we prepared for a change of venue hearing and filed a motion to continue the case. Once Judge Smith continued the case, Judy and some others on the team decided she should take over as lead. Furthermore, I perceived that she wanted nobody from my faction to work on the case with her. Instead, she wanted to replace us with a whole new team.

Right to the end, my group and I refused to walk away unless Eric wanted us to do so. We made that clear. Although we did not know it at the time, Eric did not want us to go. I wouldn't leave his case even though I saw the impending conclusion. To paraphrase Eric, I would rather lose my professional life than my dignity.

Later, in one of his three letters to best-selling author Maryanne Vollers during her work on her powerfully insightful book, *Lone Wolf,* Eric detailed his understanding of the conflict among the factions of the Birmingham team. He wrote that Judge Smith asked *Eric* to help him decide which grouping of the team to choose. Eric related that, after much consideration, careful thought and consultation with an attorney appointed by the court to advise him, he chose me and our part of the team to remain as his lawyers. Paul Kish, his lead Atlanta attorney, also recommended that if the team could not stay together, that our faction of the team should remain as Eric's lawyers.

That was not to be. On August 9, Emory Anthony, Hube Dodd, Derek Drennan and I withdrew as Eric's attorneys. Eric had a right to a team that could work together. Had we not withdrawn, it could have taken months to resolve the issues. This would have taken the focus off Eric, creating a significant distraction from providing him the defense that anyone deserves, especially when facing the death penalty. Fortunately, both factions of Eric's legal team were capable of giving him quality representation. Sadly, we could not move forward together.

Unfortunately, I did not get another chance to communicate with Eric in any way. But I received an e-mail from Patty Rudolph speaking of her disappointment that I was off Eric's case and that she still considered me a "great guy."

I sent Patty an e-mail back telling her that, under the circumstances, it would be best to wait until the cases had concluded to have further contact and that it was "an honor and a privilege" getting to know both her and Eric.

No time in my professional career has been more painful or challenging. From the disagreement about the team, I learned a lot about the deeper motivations of people in general, other lawyers and myself. At that time, I had handled over fifty death penalty cases and tried nineteen to conclusion. None of my clients had landed on death row; only a few were serving life sentences. I had also helped to exonerate three innocent men in new trials after they had been wrongfully convicted and sentenced to death.

As we faded away from Eric and his defense, my staff and I began to rebuild my law practice. During the fourteen months we had represented Eric, we had referred all of our larger cases, present and future, to my good friend and skilled Decatur lawyer John Mays, whom I trusted with my life and the lives of my clients. John achieved terrific results with each of them.

At his sentencing in Atlanta, in an action that shocked those in the courtroom, Eric calmly and wholeheartedly apologized to the victims in the Olympic bombing. However, during his sentencing in Birmingham, he ranted that his actions against the New Women All Women Health Care Clinic didn't even amount to a crime at all. He considered those killed and maimed in that bombing to be "casualties of war."

Eric pleaded guilty and received four consecutive life without parole sentences. Judy and her multitalented and experienced team had accomplished their primary goal of saving Eric's life. At the end of the day, the case must always be about the client, not the lawyers. We work for our clients and they face death, not us. Eric's attorneys prevented him from being executed. Like everyone else housed at the Penitentiary Administrative Maximum Facility (ADX) in Florence, Colorado, he spends twenty-two and one-half hours of every day alone in his eighty-square-foot concrete cell.

After Rudolph entered his pleas, Maryanne Vollers asked to interview me for her book, *Lone Wolf.* I could not do that unless Eric gave his permission by waiving the attorney-client privilege. When he did, I knew that Eric still trusted and cared for me. Instinctually, I knew that it was because we had always made his interests the entire focus of our representation.

When Maryanne sent me an autographed copy of *Lone Wolf,* I gave it to my daughter as a present. On the inside cover I wrote:

"To my Big Girl: Happy Chanukah! Maybe one day you will read this book. The experience of being lead counsel for fourteen months, then having my character assaulted, is an example of believing in myself—because I never let my experience or the outcome of it keep me down. I knew there was something else on 'the other side,' even when I felt crushed and crucified. I love you! You are a winner, because you know you are. Your Dad."

In a way, Maryanne's choice of title captured the essence of Eric, who lived his entire life as a loner, contributing greatly to his ability to endure mentally his years surviving in the treacherous mountains and now isolated for the rest of his natural life in a cell. But I never believed that he acted alone in any bombing. If he had worked alone, the evidence was thin. The evidence against him in Atlanta was even thinner, a central reason the case was resolved in the same manner as Birmingham.

Yes, Eric is a wolf. Like any wolf in the wild, he acted to protect his perceived young, the unborn babies of the world, by destroying the "factories" that killed them en masse before they could be born. That's how he saw it.

In no way would I ever justify or condone Eric stepping into the role of his perception of God and using terrible violence to achieve what he believed to be a greater good. It goes against everything a society should believe in and it is antithetical to my own anti-violent sentiments. To me, Eric resembles the radical Middle East terrorists who kill themselves and others to please the God they envision. As I see it, the havoc within Eric's psyche brewed and fed the internal storm: a damaged and oversensitive, though once innocent, even noble, heart turned black with outrage at the "evil" abortion industry.

This storm strengthened with his desire to make a difference in a world in conflict with his Biblical readings and particular interpretations. At one defining, irretrievable point of human destruction, his powerfully grandiose personality compelled him to act. In doing so, he risked his own life, forfeited his future and destroyed the lives of countless innocents who may never again see the world as safe.

Perhaps Eric's thought processes and deadly actions highlight the most critical difference between the two of us. In every case, my fervent stance against the death penalty precludes an individual or the government from taking any life, for any reason. Only the God I believe in should do that, without human intervention.

28

A SLAP IN THE FACE OF JUSTICE

On a dismal, dark night in downtown Birmingham, Carlyle Hall—known better by the street name "New York"—and Tavis Boxton were talking as they walked down 7th Avenue North.

Either a station wagon or an SUV which was dark green, light green or blue, according to police reports, pulled up and stopped fifteen or twenty feet from them. The front-seat passenger rolled down his window and motioned for New York to come over to the vehicle. According to Boxton, New York looked over at him and said, "I hope these ain't the same guys I shanked a few hours ago."

Those were the last words that New York would ever utter.

He trotted over toward the vehicle. When New York neared the car, the passenger opened fire, fatally shooting him. Boxton dove to the ground. The vehicle then took off while the passenger continued to fire his weapon at another man, Jarrett Norwich, who was riding his bicycle. At least one bullet struck Norwich's bike and he jumped off and ran to a convenience store a couple of blocks away.

Within ten minutes, Birmingham police officers arrived and secured the scene. The police report listed two witnesses, Tavis Boxton and Jarrett Norwich. The area was so dimly lit the police officers utilized the headlights of four police cars to illuminate the crime scene.

A meticulous and careful evidence technician, Officer Darryl Thomas, took photographs and collected evidence. Many of those photographs captured images of police officers and onlookers, including Boxton, along with Norwich's abandoned bicycle and the lifeless body of New York, who had quickly bled to death on the pavement.

Several homicide detectives arrived at the scene and began to interview everyone who witnessed the shooting or had information about it. They did not allow anyone with any information to leave the scene. Detectives took both written and tape-recorded statements from everyone present both at the scene and later at the police station, until the early morning hours. They interviewed Boxton, Norwich and three other men: Dalton Happ, Quincey Snow and Marcus Beddows. Earlier on that same day, Happ, Snow and Beddows had witnessed a man chasing New York with a hatchet and screaming, "I'll kill you! I'll kill you!" This incident occurred only two or three blocks from the location of the murder. Happ intervened in the hatchet incident, which afforded New York an opportunity to escape his attacker.

Happ and Beddows positively identified another man, Raymond Arthur Nichols, as the hatchet man from a photographic lineup. No one mentioned, knew or had ever heard of someone named Che Salvador Swindle until five days after the murder, when a person named Dickinson Walters positively picked Che out of a photo lineup as being the gunman who had ruthlessly gunned down New York.

Although Walters knew New York, Boxton, Norwich, Happ, Snow, Beddows and Nichols, none of them saw Walters at the scene at any time that day. Walters' name did not appear anywhere on any official police report. So how did he become the central player in this bizarre drama? What made him identify Che as the shooter? Who was Dickinson Walters?

Like every other person in this scenario, Dickinson Walters was homeless at one time or another. A handsome, six-foot-two-inch, 185-pound man in his late thirties, Walters had been addicted to alcohol and drugs since he was fourteen years old. He was smooth talking and highly intelligent, a loud and persuasive player. He was so convincing that, after Walters testified at a pretrial hearing, Judge Tommy Nail, who was not easily fooled, found him very believable. When Walters was given an opportunity to wax eloquent and was not seriously challenged, he could con the most astute. That is exactly what happened with lead detective Anthony Williams.

Contained in Detective Williams' file was an undated, unsigned, hand-printed note on a piece of scratch paper supposedly written by a Birmingham police patrolman named Parks:

B/M DICKINSON WALTERS
WITNESS: 830-11TH ST
6-02 185
HANGS OUT: CHURCH OF RECONCILER
STATED THAT HE OBSERVED
2 W/M SUSPECTS AT 1525-8TH AVE. N.
THE SUSPECTS WERE IN A GREEN
STATION WAGON.
SUSPECT ON THE PASSENGER
SIDE HAD SHAVED HEAD.

The mysterious note did not explain why neither Officer Parks' nor Dickinson Walters' name appeared on the official police report or in Evidence Technician Officer Darryl Thomas' report. Thomas' report listed eleven law enforcement officers and an Alabama Power security guard. According to Thomas' sworn testimony, he wrote the name of every officer at the scene, even if there for a brief moment, in his report.

On May 20, Detective Anthony Williams met with and audiotaped Dickinson Walters. The taped statement of Walters revealed his hidden agenda and his true motivation. When transcribed, the statement contained over forty pages; fewer than ten pages concerned the murder of New York. Strikingly, while questioning Walters, the detectives suddenly shifted their approach by reminding him that, off-tape, he had provided details of numerous other crimes and who committed them. Once that questioning started, Walters talked almost nonstop. As I later told the jury, Walters was a "street peddler of information." For years he had garnered the habit of collecting such information and using it for his own purposes and benefit.

Walters claimed to be an eyewitness to the shooting of New York. Although he could not remember the name of the perpetrator, he claimed he recognized and knew him from several years ago when they had both stayed at a local homeless shelter. He helpfully offered to pick the purported shooter out of a lineup.

Although Walters claimed that the shootings occurred at dusk, around 6:30 P.M., rather than at 9:00 P.M. in the darkness, and also erroneously stated many other significant details, his identification posed a dangerous situation for Che, because whenever a purported eyewitness claims to know the person he has identified, jurors tend to believe him. The public is willing to accept the sworn testimony of one who identifies a stranger whom he saw only for a few seconds. In that situation we focus on the weaknesses in the person's opportunity to make an accurate identification. When the eyewitness supposedly knows the person he identifies, it then becomes a question of motive. Why would the eyewitness identify the defendant as opposed to all of the other people in the world?

There was some other puzzling information. Walters and Detective Williams visited the homeless shelter to look through the shelter's records, which contained files with pictures and intake sheets for every resident who had stayed there. Although Che Swindle had stayed there at one time while Walters was a resident, for some inexplicable reason Che's entire file was missing.

According to Detective Williams, he compiled a lineup of men who had previously been arrested and at the time stayed at the homeless shelter. From that lineup, Walters picked out Che Swindle as the murderer. Based upon Walters' positive identification, Detective Williams dropped his investigation of the hatchet man. On May 27, as soon as Che learned from his mother that the police wanted to talk with him, he found someone to take him directly to police headquarters. He voluntarily waived his right to an attorney and submitted to an hour-long interview conducted by the detectives.

Che had no idea why the detectives wanted to question him. He soon figured out it concerned a murder about which he knew nothing. He adamantly denied any knowledge or involvement at all. When the detectives asked him where he was on the date in question, Che told them he was at the residence of two coworkers located at least fifteen miles from downtown Birmingham. Che lived with his mother, who usually drove him to work. He did not drive. Because his mother had been involved in a wreck several days before the shooting, Che had been staying with two of his coworkers.

He had been at the coworkers' residence since they got off work that day and assured the detectives that his coworkers would support his alibi. He also told them that his cell phone records would verify the times he was on the phone that day and evening.

During the interview, Che begged the detectives to obtain his cell phone records and the tower records, to establish his location when the calls were made, and to give him a polygraph test. The detectives complied with one of the three requests. Eventually they obtained the phone records. They did not subpoena the tower records nor offer him or Walters a polygraph test. Upon the completion of this interview, the officers arrested Che. A few days later, the State of Alabama charged Che Swindle with capital murder. Suddenly Che found himself facing the death penalty.

Attorney Amber Ladner approached me outside of a hectic courtroom in Jefferson County. She asked me if I would consider requesting Jefferson County District Judge Shelly Watkins to appoint me to represent Che in a capital murder case. I had at least three major death penalty cases pending and several huge white-collar trials ahead of me. I had no room for another death penalty case.

Che Salvador Swindle and Amber Ladner were cousins. As Che later explained it, "Amber and I both grew up the hard way. The only difference is she took one road and I took another—the wrong road. Sure, I got hooked on drugs and lived homeless on the streets at times. But I wouldn't intentionally hurt anyone and I don't have it in me to kill anybody."

Well after the detectives charged Che with the murder, the phone records confirmed that throughout the evening of the incident Che had called several numbers. The last call ended at 8:59 P.M.—one minute before the shooting. One of the two coworkers verified Che's alibi. The other could not speak sufficient English to be interviewed without a translator. Eventually, we obtained the services of an interpreter and the other person also verified Che's alibi.

At the appropriate time we filed a motion to suppress the identification made by Dickinson Walters. Then, on July 31, we received our first opportunity to question him. Derek Drennan did the examination. Just before Derek began to question Walters, a flash went through my mind: Did the detectives pay Walters after he picked Che out of the lineup? I asked Derek to explore this.

"Mr. Walters, let's get this out of the way now. Did you receive any money for the information you provided the police?"

"No, sir," Walters responded without hesitation.

I did not believe him. Although Derek questioned Walters repeatedly about this, each time Walters denied it. At the conclusion of Walters' testimony, the prosecutor then called Detective Williams. I approached prosecutor Mike Anderton. "Mike, would you please ask Detective Williams if he paid Walters any money? I'm sure that Walters lied about that."

Mike responded, "He better not have gotten any money, as I have no record of that."

He agreed to my request and walked out of the courtroom. Less than a minute passed before the prosecutor returned. "I was wrong," he meekly stated. "Detective Williams paid him fifty dollars."

Under oath, the detective confirmed the payment to Walters. However, when asked to produce a receipt, he could not do so.

Department regulations, which we had obtained from another capital case, required both a supervisor's approval and receipt. Furthermore, they expressly prohibited payment from personal funds.

We contended that Walters not only lied about being paid, but also gave a completely different version of the events than he did during his earlier interview with Detective Williams. At this hearing Walters claimed he knew from the beginning that Che Swindle committed the murder. He also swore that he was a graduate from Rutledge College.

Armed with two different versions of the story and a lie under oath about the money, we knew we had only scratched the surface of Walters' lies. We had no idea how many more untruths we would uncover. Based on past experience, my biggest fear remained that Walters claimed to know Che and that he had lied so convincingly.

A little over a year after the shooting, Che Swindle's trial began. We felt that we were sitting next to an innocent client wrongfully charged with capital murder. Che was dressed in a white shirt and tan pants. About five feet six inches tall and slight in stature, he did not look like a cold-blooded murderer and the prosecutor knew that. For those reasons, during *voir dire*, he asked the prospective jurors in the selection process if they would convict someone who did not look like a murderer if the State proved his guilt beyond a reasonable doubt. All affirmed that they would.

Both sides agreed that this case came down to the credibility of one witness: Dickinson Walters. I asked the prospective jurors if they understood that unless they could believe Walters' account beyond a reasonable doubt, they would be obligated to acquit Che Swindle. All said they would hold the prosecution to that burden of proof. I spent extensive time questioning the prospective jurors about their understanding of how an indictment is actually obtained. This process revealed and highlighted the secret nature of the grand jury system, which often (as in this case) involves the presentation of entirely hearsay testimony which is not challenged due to the absence of counsel at the proceedings.

The most revealing answers came when I asked prospective jurors to articulate reasons why someone might knowingly falsely identify another person for a crime. We made use of their answers not only in jury selection but also as the main focus of our closing argument.

In my opening statement, I warned the jury that Dickinson Walters would make a very believable witness on direct examination. I assured them that as this case developed, they would come to see him completely differently. Our strong belief was that he was a habitual liar and a drug addict and had the motivation to perjure himself. I told the jurors that once all the evidence was in, it was our contention they would know they could never rely on anything Walters might say. In fact, they would see that he was not even at the scene on the night of the murder.

The trial began.

On direct examination, Dickinson Walters testified with confidence and clarity. However, he did not know that since the hearing when he had testified regarding his identification of Swindle, we had obtained records from the Birmingham Police Department, Rutledge College, the Salvation Army and the Firehouse shelter where Walters resided after the murder. We also obtained an affidavit from his wife, who had been fruitlessly trying to serve him with divorce papers. In addition, our investigator, John Bishop, a former Birmingham police officer and narcotics investigator, had obtained statements from everyone he could locate who had any information about this case or about Dickinson Walters.

From our investigation, we learned that Walters had never graduated from Rutledge College; he flunked out after two semesters. In fact, Walters never even finished high school. The shelter records stated that he was a veteran of the United States Marine Corps. Under oath he admitted that he had never served in any branch of the armed services. Instead, he attributed the inaccurate information to the employee who interviewed him. The Firehouse shelter records showed that on the day of the murder, Walters was still addicted to drugs, including cocaine, marijuana, crack and alcohol. When I concluded my cross-examination of Dickinson Walters, I felt that no rational person could believe him. I could tell that Judge Nail no longer believed him and I doubted any jurors did, either.

After the State rested, we then called just one witness: Walters' wife. When she met Walters she was a volunteer at the Salvation Army. This sympathetic, highly educated and polished woman made the perfect witness. Testifying with sadness rather than anger or malice, she told the jury that Walters conned her into believing him to be a volunteer, too. Only after they married did she learn he was a drug addict and resident, not a volunteer. She testified that even when confronted with an undeniable truth, Walters never admitted a lie.

The jury began its deliberation, but something inside me felt uneasy and unsure. After three hours I could feel a familiar knot in the pit of my stomach. Shortly after that, the jury foreperson began sending notes out to the judge attesting to deadlock. The clock ticked off the minutes as I stared at the time inching by. Four hours later, one juror still was holding out for a guilty verdict, in spite of eleven other votes for acquittal.

Judge Nail confirmed the fruitlessness of further deliberations. He declared a mistrial due to a hung jury and set the case for retrial.

A deep, dark state of dejection settled over me. I could make no sense of the rationale of the lone holdout. For a moment I wondered if it was the wheel of karma turning on me, at the expense of my client, since I had hung up a half dozen juries in past murder cases. Then I realized that this case, like all cases, was not about me, the lawyer.

A few days later, the jury foreperson called me at my office. The foreperson was a friend of a judge in another court who had encouraged him to contact me. A devoted member of one of Birmingham's largest Baptist churches, the foreperson was no softy. Quietly assertive and keenly intelligent, he told me with frustrated apologies he did everything he could to persuade the lone holdout to vote for acquittal. The foreperson explained reasonable doubt to the juror and, at one point, the holdout seemed to reconsider. But in the end, he declared he would never vote not guilty. The foreperson told me he wanted to attend the retrial as a spectator.

To prepare for the retrial, we ordered a transcript and tried to determine any adjustments I might want to make in the way I would cross-exam Walters. We also learned more lies that Walters told under oath in the first trial and obtained even more records to demonstrate.

We then subpoenaed records from Lawson State Community College, a local junior college. At the first trial, when confronted with the Rutledge College records showing he dropped out after one semester, Walters had simply and nimbly testified that his actual degree came from Lawson State. The Lawson State records reflected that he took a few classes there after obtaining a tuition loan from the college, before dropping out without even completing a semester, still owing the entire amount of money he had borrowed.

We made a number of other adjustments too. The undated, unsigned, handwritten note that Officer Parks supposedly had written stated that Walters had information that the perpetrator had a shaved head. The only other person who had ever mentioned anything about a shaved head was Tavis Boxton, the last person to see New York alive. Our theory of defense was that Boxton told Walters the day after the murder about seeing a shooter with a shaved head. Walters then parroted that information to officer Parks, accounting for the undated handwritten note. I did not ask Boxton about this matter during the first trial, because he had sounded hostile to us and I was fearful of his answer. We maintained that Walters was not at the scene that night.

Six months later, we began jury selection for Che's second trial. In my opening statement, I spent even more time than in the first trial outlining the lies Walters had already told under oath and the new ones we expected him to invent on cross-examination when trapped. I also asked jurors to pay particular attention to the various times when I expected Walters to evade my direct questions or refuse to answer them at all.

When the prosecution called Walters, he testified true to form on direct examination, lying naturally and without hesitation. However, on cross-examination the jurors were primed and they were buying none of it. They zeroed in on Walters like a hawk to prey and seemed exasperated at Walters' cavalier attitude, deceitful dances and blatant lies in the face of certified documents. The scornful looks and quiet snickers of some of the jurors indicated they could see through Walters' lies and also could not believe anyone would lie so effortlessly.

Judge Nail also seemed more than a bit put out by Walters as he continually admonished Walters to answer the questions he tried to avoid and refrain from offering unsolicited comments. At several points Judge Nail seemed to struggle with his irritation at Walters' irrelevant insertions. Toward the end of my cross-examination I asked Walters if he had spoken with Tavis Boxton the day after the murder. Walters denied not only speaking to him but also knowing him at all. In the first trial Walters had admitted knowing Boxton quite well.

Following Walters' testimony the prosecution called Tavis Boxton. During cross-examination, Boxton confirmed that he, in fact, had met with Walters the day after the murder and told him that he, Boxton, had seen a shooter with a shaved head. I felt the jurors did not miss the significance of that portion of his testimony. Boxton also said that Walters definitely was not at the scene on the night of the murder.

The State then rested its case.

We called only two witnesses. First we called Dalton Happ, who had witnessed and intervened in the hatchet incident that had occurred several hours before the murder. Happ indicated that the person chasing New York was angry, because New York had sold him fake drugs earlier that day. A pathologist had earlier testified in the prosecution's case that he had found fake drugs in the pants that New York was wearing when he was killed.

Happ looked at Che as he spoke. He told the jury he did not know Che. He swore that Che Swindle was definitely not the person waving a hatchet and chasing New York. Happ said he knew Walters and swore that Walters was not at the scene that night.

As our last witness, we called Walters' wife, who still had not been able to serve him with divorce papers. I did not recognize her, as she had lost forty pounds since she'd testified in the previous trial. Again, she spoke with class and without anger—just sadness. The wife testified to the numerous lies Walters had told her, including ones about his education, income and military service. She told the jury that even if and especially when Walters became caught in a lie, he would never admit it.

But this time, she told the jury that she was disappointed with herself, since she was trained to spot sociopaths and liars like Walters. After only two weeks of marriage, Walters began to disappear for weeks at a time. Only then did she learn of his well-hidden drug problems. As in the initial trial, she made a compelling witness.

Derek Drennan and I split the closing. Using visuals, Derek matched the phone and corresponding cell tower records to show that only someone using Che's phone could have made the calls in Bessemer at the time of the murder and therefore could not have been the killer. It seemed highly doubtful that anyone other than Che would have been calling his mother and checking on his phone minutes. The jurors did not seem to mind that Che had registered the phone in the name of George Bush.

By Drennan taking this part of the closing argument, I felt freed up to concentrate on the inadequate and faulty investigation and the wasteful prosecution during my closing argument. I reminded the jury that, in the opening, the prosecution told the jury that Dickinson Walters was only at the scene for a couple of minutes and then quickly left. In this way, the prosecutors attempted to explain why the police failed to list Walters' name on any police reports. But I reminded the jury that Walters swore in his testimony he was at the scene the entire time that the police were present—several hours. The prosecution could not explain the fact that Walters knew all involved, but all of them swore that they had never seen Walters at the scene. Each person with any information had given a recorded statement to the police that night. But not Walters.

At the end I did what only prosecutors and plaintiff's lawyers usually can do: I made a plea for good law enforcement and the safety of the community. I urged the jury to send a message to anyone who would listen by the quickness of its verdict. I argued that the streets of Birmingham were dark and dangerous. I said that I would never walk alone in the area of 7th Avenue and 16th Street at night.

"The only way we can clean up our streets is to insist that, when a crime occurs, it be thoroughly and adequately investigated. In this case, it was not. By taking Walters's word, the detectives stopped their investigation and left the real shooter on the streets. We deserve better. By shortcutting an investigation in any case, especially a capital murder one, the investigators leave the real killer at large. The grandmother of New York, that sweet lady who testified—if you were to ask her if she would ever want to see the wrong person convicted on this kind of evidence, what do you think she would say?"

I went on to tell the jury that the investigation did nothing more than create another innocent victim: Che Swindle. Anyone falsely accused of a criminal offense, especially a capital offense, becomes a victim. I asked the jury to send Che out of this courtroom the same way he walked in: presumed innocent.

This time, relatively confident of an acquittal (as confident as any lawyer can be whenever twelve strangers decide his client's fate), I went back to my office to meet with a new client. Derek stayed in court to wait for what we hoped would be a speedy verdict.

Less than two hours later, I received a text from Derek: "NG!" Che was a free man.

Cases like Che Swindle's are the ones that keep me up late at night. He was innocent and wrongfully charged. The case was not based on real evidence—no gun, no forensics and no credible testimony. But any case can be lost on the weakest of evidence, especially when a person who claims to be an eyewitness also claims to know the perpetrator.

In this real world it is very difficult to prosecute the real perpetrator after so many mistakes are made. The losers are not just the people charged, but also the victims of such a violent crime.

Che Salvador Swindle dodged a bullet. So did the criminal justice system. New York did not. Unfortunately, the real killer is still out there.

29
CULPABILITY AND MENTAL ILLNESS

At a young age, Benito Albarran followed his older brothers to the United States. They helped set up Benito and his wife in a Mexican restaurant business in Huntsville, Alabama. Benito's wife was in charge of the restaurant, because he had neither the emotional tools nor the intellectual ability to run it. He adored their little girl. He really is a sweet person, but his frustration with his limitations veered him into the realm of substance abuse. Even before that, he had lacked sufficient coping skills.

While at the restaurant, Benny erupted during an argument with his wife, who called 911. When asked if Benny had a gun, his wife gave answers leading the dispatcher to believe he did not. Neither Benny nor his wife spoke much English.

While his wife remained on the phone speaking to the dispatcher, Benny walked out into the parking lot carrying two guns and tried to get in his car. Unfortunately, Office Daniel Golden pulled up just then, not expecting to see an armed man. A shootout followed between Officer Golden and Benny. During the shootout, Officer Golden shot at Benny eight times before his gun jammed. Benny shot Officer Golden, who fell to the ground. Extremely intoxicated and full of cocaine, Benny then shot Officer Golden twice in the face, at point blank range, while he lay helpless on the ground.

Benny's deadly actions could not be excused, but was it necessary for Benny to be sentenced to death? Was death the only sufficient punishment for him?

I visited Mexico and met Benny's entire family and many members of their small community of rancheros. People there are humble. They strive to live off relatively infertile, mountainous land to grow crops. For these reasons, children often come to the United States and send money home. The mental illnesses that doctors diagnosed Benny with were genetic, as his maternal grandmother and his father were significantly mentally deranged. When I met his father, he had just come out of a mental institution for the second time.

I got to know Benny. I saw a transformation as he waited in jail for his trial. His defense team—Bruce Gardner, Derek Drennan and I—tried in vain to convince the district attorney's office to allow Benny to plead to a life without parole sentence.

For over thirty years I have defended scores of people charged with death penalty offenses at the trial level and no one ended up on death row. Almost every one of the federal jurisdictions and the thirty-four other states that authorize the death penalty require a unanimous vote of all twelve jurors for a death sentence.[1] If even one juror decides that life without parole is the appropriate sentence in those other jurisdictions, execution will not result. In Alabama, the prosecution only has to convince ten jurors to achieve a death verdict.[2] And in Alabama, judges can override the jury's decision of life or death.[3] Only two other states allow for an override by a judge: Delaware and Florida.

I can still see the vein in the right side of the female jury foreperson's neck quiver as she stoically read the death verdict when the Huntsville, Alabama, jury sentenced our client, Benito Albarran, to die by a ten-to-two vote. I can still hear the quiet but icy voice that sounded like a shriek inside the deepest part of me. I can still feel the anguish engulf me. I can still taste and smell the thirst for blood that permeated that courtroom throughout the almost three-week trial.

The Benito Albarran that the jury recommended be sentenced to death was not the same person I came to know during my two years of trial preparation. Benny showed more remorse than any other person I have ever represented. He wanted to be punished severely. He made no excuses and prayed every day for Golden's family and his own. Benny sought and found redemption over the year and a half that he waited for trial. His heart held nothing but sadness and regret for the Golden family, his family and himself. He did not need to be executed. He was not the "worst of the worst."[4]

The day after the death sentence I wrote in my journal: "As exhilarating as it is to hear a verdict that saves my client's life, no words penetrated my heart with such anguish as, 'We, the jury, sentence the defendant, Benito Albarran, to death.' Although nothing close to the pain of a victim's family who loses a loved one, the pain and guilt from losing a client like Benny stays there forever."

One winter morning more than two years after the Albarran trial, as I sat in my kitchen sipping coffee, Bruce Gardner called me. Bruce and I had worked a number of cases together, including Benito Albarran's. But he was not calling about Benny.

"Richard, I have two things to talk about with you, one good and one bad. First, the good: My daughter is getting married in May and I need your home address."

Excited for Bruce, I gave it to him.

"Okay, now the bad."

"Bruce, I know the bad," I interrupted. "You want to discuss Leroy White."

"You're right. How'd you know?"

"Because I got the order for execution a day or two ago and thought I might hear from you," I explained.

Leroy White had fewer than ten days to live. I received the execution order, because for a brief period I had represented Leroy on his direct appeal through the Alabama Supreme Court. My representation ended when lawyers from a Maryland law firm took over the appeal, similar in that respect to Bo Cochran's case.

I only met Leroy White a few times, well over ten years ago, but once was enough for me to conclude beyond all doubt that he also was not the "worst of the worst."

Bruce Gardner was the deputy district attorney who had prosecuted Leroy. His powerfully persuasive courtroom expertise had overshadowed Leroy's court-appointed attorney, who is very skilled now, but then was young and untrained in capital litigation. Bruce and I had talked about Leroy's case many times over the years since we first met. We both felt the day would come when Leroy's appeals would run out—and now they had.

Leroy and his estranged wife Ruby had been embroiled in a domestic dispute. Emotionally distraught, drunk and armed, Leroy drove to the home he and Ruby once had shared to see their daughter. When refused entrance, Leroy shot off the door lock and then fatally shot Ruby while she was holding their seventeen-month-old daughter. He also shot his sister-in-law four times, though she survived.

When Leroy walked into the prison's small attorney conference room, it seemed to fill up with sadness. Leroy was a thin twenty-nine-year-old man. His face displayed a kind, gentle look. The sadness seemed to pour out of his eyes. He carried his weight so that his body bent like an old tree, but Leroy was neither old nor sick. Like Benito Albarran, Leroy White exhibited true remorse for his actions. Although he did not want to die, I am certain he would gladly have traded places with Ruby, his deceased wife, if that would bring her back to life. He had committed a crime of passion in a drunken, crazed state. In Alabama and most other jurisdictions, crimes of passion are not death penalty offenses.[5]

Unlike Seamus Duffy and his team, the Maryland lawyers never called me to testify but instead took my deposition. To demonstrate the arbitrary nature of Leroy White's execution, it is significant to note that the jury recommended he serve life without parole rather than death. The trial judge dismissed that recommendation and sentenced him to death. I never heard anything about Leroy's case again until the courts denied his appeals and set an execution date.[6]

Sadly, the State often focuses on the hyper-technical procedural requirements and raises them at every juncture. They are confusing and easy to miss for even the most experienced death penalty appeal lawyer. Some courts have not hesitated to allow the State to execute someone because a lawyer missed a deadline, failed to raise a legal issue or failed to present it in a timely manner.[7] The public has always criticized the courts for allowing a guilty person to get off on "a technicality." Those who complain hardly ever cite an example, because it happens so rarely. I cannot think of a time when the public ever complained because a person was executed due to a technicality. I learned the lead Maryland lawyer for Leroy had been disbarred and the associate who took over his case had missed a crucial filing deadline, foreclosing any further appeals.

When Bruce called me that morning, he asked my thoughts on what he might do. As a relatively young but very aggressive prosecutor, at the time of the trial he had felt that Leroy White deserved the death penalty. Now his heart was heavy.

"Bruce," I suggested, "it won't do any good, but all you can do now is reach out to his current lawyers at EJI and go public with your perspective." To Bruce's credit, he did just that. He contacted the media and stated that the death penalty system was "absurd" and that Leroy White's execution was a perfect example of that.

Leroy felt and expressed deep remorse for the permanent human destruction he had perpetrated. Isn't remorse the first essential step toward redemption? Do we, as a society, truly believe that we should eliminate a life and deprive a person of the opportunity to seek redemption? How do we know that someone won't discover it in his heart with time? When, if ever, does any person give up the right to redeem himself? Who should decide?

Even if you believe the death penalty should be applied in some extraordinary cases, Leroy was certainly far from deserving it. The ultimate penalty was not enacted to punish him rather than Gary Ridgway, the notorious Green River Killer of Washington, America's worst serial killer. Ridgway was convicted of murdering forty-eight innocent women, though he later confessed to killing seventy-one. He is serving a life without parole sentence.[8]

In fashioning the plea deal that eliminated execution for Gary Ridgway, Deputy Prosecutor Jeffery Baird stated, "At the end of the trial, whatever the outcome, there would have been lingering doubts about the rest of these crimes. This agreement was the avenue to the truth. And, in the end, the search for the truth is why we have the criminal justice system…Gary Ridgway does not deserve to live. The mercy provided by today's resolution is directed not at Ridgway but toward the families who have suffered so much."

This prosecutor did not focus on the politics or the publicity he would garner by insisting on a trial. He knew the enormous costs involved and that Ridgway would never get out of prison with this plea. Instead, he focused on the victims. He knew that their interests would not be served by years of seeking Ridgway's death, which would continually aggravate the open wounds. He would not allow the victims to become tools of politics or an enhancement to someone's career.

He also knew that the thought of the death penalty never entered Ridgway's demented mind and therefore did not deter him from his death hunts.

Nor did it enter the mind of Leroy White, who killed in an act of passion. The prospect of a life without parole sentence is more of a deterrent to a person setting out to commit such crimes. Many on death row have asked to be executed rather than live in a cage.[9]

The sad truth is that a person who kills in a rage is not deterred by either the prospect or the extent of the punishment.

Even sadder, the United States Supreme Court has never said it is unconstitutional to execute an innocent person, as long as he receives a fair trial.[10] Recently, people from all over the world protested the execution of Georgia death row inmate Troy Davis, who was convicted of killing a police officer.[11] Seven of the nine uncorroborated eye witnesses to the crime have recanted their testimony. His execution raises the question of whether the death penalty is ever appropriate when there is real doubt of a person's guilt.

··

AFTERWORD
The Life We Choose

To a diehard criminal defense lawyer like me, the sweetest words in the English language are *not guilty*. They resonate with the confirmation that all of my hard work, investigation, preparation and presentation, plus my steadfast commitment to my client, contributed to the jury's decision. They also follow a very scary series of weeks, days, hours and then minutes spent waiting to hear a jury pronounce that verdict. Yet, in a death penalty case, hearing the word *life* means almost as much to me as life itself. Being part of a jury determination which frees a person from the throes of death cannot be described in words; it is an act of grace which lives in my heart forever.

The concerns and challenges are potent for the criminal defense attorney. It has been said that trials of any nature, not just criminal trials, are not for the "faint of heart." I can tell you that my heart has felt both faint and frail many times while awaiting a jury's verdict. Unlike other fears that dilute through experience and familiarity, the power of these does not diminish. I still feel scared before every trial as I consider losing a case and possibly watching an innocent person sentenced to prison or even death. The thought that my best effort wasn't good enough agonizes me for a great deal of time afterward. I feel a sense of inadequacy that I missed something in my case preparation, presentation, arguments or examinations, or perhaps the lack was somewhere deep inside me. My heart pounds and my stomach clenches along with my client's when we hear those terrible words: "We, the jury, find the defendant guilty." The feeling grows exponentially when it concerns someone's life or death.

For each hour of a trial, scores of hours were spent preparing for it. Most skilled trial lawyers put their hearts and souls into each case for each client, regardless of what the government alleged he did or who he is. Putting ourselves on the line makes us vulnerable, but vulnerability is one key to success. If the media is involved, which happens many times in high-profile cases, that arena suddenly includes anyone who turns on the television or picks up a newspaper. The deeper we dig to present a winning argument, the more honestly and openly we expose ourselves. The higher the stakes, the harder rejection strikes.

Some trial lawyers, such as myself, may be shy in real life but not in the courtroom. It is our theater as much as our home. We do not just visit there; we inhabit it and some of us feel more comfortable there than in many social situations.

Criminal defense lawyers are a misunderstood lot. The public often perceives a criminal defense lawyer as someone who ignores ethics for the sake of money or the "win." The truth is that, for the most part, criminal defense lawyers focus on ethics as much or more than any other lawyer does; we are all potential targets for dissatisfied clients, some of whom would not hesitate to lie to us if it would serve their purposes. And there are those in authority who tend to believe them. Most interpret the famous Shakespeare quote, "The first thing we do is kill all the lawyers" as slander on attorneys.[1] In fact, it is an acknowledgement that lawyers protect the government and preserve order within it. We are indeed "Liberty's Last Champions."

Despite my sensitivity to injustice, I did not expect to end up representing so many people facing the death penalty. It all began when I was placed in the middle of a capital murder case, because the Honorable William Cole decided to appoint me to represent James Willie "Bo" Cochran, whom he had just sentenced to death. More than thirty-five years later, I am honored to stand before the bar with victories and defeats. I wear battle scars and carry tales of courtroom experiences weighted with the most ominous of stakes: Does this person live or die?

Throughout my thirty-five years as a criminal trial lawyer, I have struggled with whether to take down our firm's shingle, or at least the part with my name on it, and just walk quietly away from all the conflicts, political shenanigans and constant battles that leave winners and losers in their wakes. In most cases, everyone ensnarled within our imperfect criminal justice system ends up a loser, even when a falsely accused "wins" his case or when the system gets it right and convicts the truly guilty. Getting it right most of the time represents the best of our hopes, but getting it right remains an impotent justice for those hurt, violated and destroyed as the result of almost any crime. When the system fails us, an irreparable betrayal pierces the heart and penetrates the soul of each person involved, sometimes the soul of the whole community and occasionally that of an entire nation.

Yet if I walk away, I would miss the thrills of combat, the intellectual challenges the law bestows on lawyers and the collaborative approach my law firm takes in litigation. I would yearn for being sought after and often needed, even for those times which thrust me into the limelight of television shows, newspaper interviews and blogs after winning a hopeless case for the helpless. I would wonder, if I had just hung around for a few more years, whether I would be defending someone and stopping the government from ruining another life or extinguishing it.

Most of all, I would dream about those truly innocent human beings whose lives or freedom I might have saved because of my efforts and my commitment to them and my profession.

At this point, many lawyers and judges seem to respect my abilities. Now, more than ever, I am mindful that I must depend on others more computer-savvy than I. The demands of trial preparation cause me to live in a perpetual state of warfare. When, as a young prosecutor in the Tuscaloosa district attorney's office, I complained to presiding Judge Claude Harris about the rigors of trial practice, he sternly cautioned, "If you can't stand the heat, get out of the kitchen."

I believe that to survive over time in the chambers of the criminal justice system, particularly defending people who may receive the death penalty, one must view it as a calling. Not just see it that way, but also feel it in one's heart. The responsibility of defending someone's life or freedom is sometimes more than I care to contemplate. But to me, that is what being a lawyer is all about. It is the reason I became one and the reason I remain one. I am proud of what I do and to be associated with so many lawyers who protect the freedoms and lives of our citizens. It is not a job easily left at the office. Sometimes I feel a slave to the law but I know that, deep inside, I am a servant of it.

Since I began to defend people accused of death penalty offenses I have met one or two people who seemed to have lost the capability of experiencing either remorse or redemption. However, I doubt that they or anyone else was born evil. Certainly no one could have picked them out of a nursery and predicted they would become killers. Yet sentencing them to a cage would be more punishment than death *and cheaper*. In fact, when jurors really understand that a person whom a jury sentences to life without parole will *never* get out of prison, most prefer to mete out a life without parole sentence instead of execution.

Something beyond my meager understanding, something I can feel gnawing at my heart, keeps me in the midst of the battles in this sad, confusing and far-from-ideal world of pathos and pain. Lives already destroyed beyond repair dangle within the machinery of our criminal justice system as it struggles to achieve its professed mission, while "justice" often hides in its shadows, never seeing the light of day.

Always in the thick of battle looms the trial warrior, misunderstood, perpetually preparing for the next conflict and unsure of the outcome, especially when the decisions flow from elected political officials or from the belly of a jury made up of twelve strangers.

Many who were formerly fervent supporters of the death penalty have changed their minds once fully exposed to all its angles and miscarriages of justice. Former Supreme Court Justices Blackmun and Stevens have expressed regret or second thoughts about voting for the reinstatement of the death penalty in *Gregg v. Georgia* in 1976.[2] Two of my former clients, Randal Padgett and Gary Drinkard, were both adamantly in favor of the death penalty until the State of Alabama wrongfully accused them of capital murder. However, it doesn't take personally facing the death penalty to change one's mind about it.

Reverend Carroll L. "Bud" Pickett is a Presbyterian Minister from Huntsville, Texas. In 1974, two of his parishioners died in the Carrasco Prison Siege. As a result, he became an advocate for capital punishment even though it went against the Presbyterian Church's doctrine. In 1980, he became the chaplain of the Huntsville, Texas prison and worked for fifteen years with prisoners who were facing impending death. There he met Carlos DeLuna, a death row inmate. Reverend Pickett became like a father to DeLuna, whom Pickett now believes was wrongfully executed. He found that his attitude on the death penalty had changed.

Since his retirement from the Texas Department of Corrections, Reverend Pickett has written and spoken out against executions. He authored the award-winning *Within These Walls: Memoirs of a Death House Chaplain*. The documentary film *At the Death House Door: No Man Should Die Alone* chronicles his time in the prison system. In it he states that capital punishment is "biblically wrong." Reverend Pickett believes that several of the ninety-five men who took the last ten steps of their lives with him were innocent and asserts that "Practically every one of the men I saw die had been restored. They'd changed."

As a result of the efforts of Ann Cooper, executive director of the Alabama Criminal Defense Lawyers Association (ACDLA), Reverend Pickett honored us by being the keynote speaker at the annual death penalty conference that John Mays, others and I have organized for the last ten years. There we were able to see Reverend Pickett's transformational documentary.

Reverend Joseph Lowery, a civil rights icon who marched with Dr. Martin Luther King, Jr., also presented a keynote address to our ACDLA death penalty conference. There he anointed us "chaplains of the common good" for our defense of those facing the death penalty. That might not mean much to some, but for those of us who receive criticism rather than praise for our efforts, it took on deep significance. For me it felt validating. Even now, whenever I run into Russ Stetler, a nationally acclaimed mitigation expert, we refer to each other as "chaplain." Mostly misunderstood and more often criticized for fighting for life, we take our solace in the small acknowledgements from someone like Reverend Lowery.

Prison counselor Sister Helen Prejean gave a keynote speech at our death penalty conference and captivated a room full of lawyers, law students and the public. Like Reverend Pickett, she did not begin by opposing the death penalty, which was something to which she had not given much thought. She evolved into her worldwide campaign to abolish it. Her insightful and famous book, *Dead Man Walking*, became a classic and a film, and her new book, *The Death of Innocents: An Eyewitness Account of Wrongful Executions*, has created enthusiasm for the worldwide debate in regard to the death penalty.

On the day of Sister Helen's talk, we lunched with former United States Attorney Redding Pitt, who is "of counsel" with my law firm. Redding disclosed to us a striking revelation that highlights the conflict many find when wrestling with the concept of capital punishment. It involved his leading the prosecution of Marvin Holley, the sixteenth person to face the federal death penalty.[3]

Derek Drennan, Tommy Nail and I represented Marvin. Then United States Attorney Doug Jones of the Birmingham Office recused himself, as he had been Marvin's original attorney. The government attorneys were United States Attorney Redding Pitt in Montgomery and Birmingham Assistant United States Attorneys Jim Weil and Bob McGregor. The government had accused Marvin of killing a federal informer who had snitched on him for hauling hemp from the Midwest and selling it as marijuana. The government portrayed Marvin as a drug kingpin. It took the government almost a month to complete its case. We felt the prosecution team had begun to worry about even convicting Marvin, much less obtaining the death penalty.

Pitt cut a deal with the prosecution's last witness, Marvin's co-defendant Charles Holland. However, Holland testified to a version that was completely inconsistent with what the government had tried to prove for over a month. After a week's deliberations, the jury convicted Marvin anyway. We then introduced an extraordinary amount of mitigating information at Marvin's sentencing hearing. Assistant United States Attorney McGregor had conveyed to the Department of Justice that the government could find no mitigating circumstances at all when, in fact, Marvin Holley was borderline mentally retarded, had failed the second grade, had slept in a room while his mother had sex with strangers, and was forced by his father to kill his dogs as there was no money to feed them in the winter.

After almost another week of deliberation, the jury could not reach unanimity and recommended that Marvin be sentenced to life without the possibility of parole.

At our lunch, Redding Pitt told Sister Helen that every day the jury deliberated he went to an Episcopal Church and prayed to God that the jury would not sentence Marvin to death.

In the early 2000s, the Center for Wrongful Convictions reported that in Illinois, twenty-six innocent people had been convicted of murder as a result of unfair trials.[4] That same year, the center released a report showing that jailhouse snitches had sent thirty-eight innocent Americans to death row.[5]

On January 11, 2003, pro-death penalty Governor George Ryan announced clemency for all inmates on death row in Illinois. My former death row exonerees Bo Cochran, Randal Padgett and Gary Drinkard were invited to attend the announcement. I will not soon forget the Reverend Jesse Jackson, who sat in front of me, turning around and giving me a high five when my clients were introduced and given a brief opportunity to speak about their experiences. I felt the same deep humility and gratitude when Gary Drinkard, his lawyers and I accompanied Steven Bright to the Senate Judiciary Committee. We went to witness Steve's testimony in regard to the Innocence Protection Act that Barry Scheck, Peter Neufield, Ronald Tabak and others had worked so long and hard to present before Congress.[6]

In 2006, after years of study, the American Bar Association (ABA) issued a report with regard to five jurisdictions, including the states of Alabama and Georgia.[7] It recommended a moratorium on carrying out executions until many of the systemic defects could be addressed, including the risk of wrongful convictions. I was fortunate to have served on the study committee for Alabama that included representatives from the entire criminal justice system, including Arthur Green, a well-respected district attorney from Bessemer, Alabama, who personally favored the death penalty if it could be applied fairly.

To me, the most telling sign of change occurred in 2005, when the editorial board of the *Birmingham News*, the largest newspaper in Alabama and politically conservative by anyone's standard, published a five-part series loudly recommending not just a moratorium but full abolition of the death penalty in Alabama. The series was a Pulitzer Prize finalist in 2006.[8]

Like the ABA, the *Birmingham News* had spent months methodically researching and considering its position. Some of the factors the newspaper noted to support its courageous position included the fact that so many convictions and death sentences are based upon faulty eyewitness testimony and jailhouse snitches. They cited the enormous pressures (including political ones) that have resulted in prosecutorial misconduct or flawed investigations, the overwhelming influence of race, an inability to adhere to the ABA standards to provide qualified and effective counsel and the extraordinary costs that are involved when prosecutors seek death sentences.

The United States of America is currently the only industrialized nation in the Western Hemisphere that still imposes the death penalty on its citizens.

With regard to costs, the National Coalition to Abolish the Death Penalty has pointed out that some of the hundreds of millions of dollars spent each year to obtain the death penalty could instead be diverted to support the victims of murder, who spend years ensnared in a system focused on executions.[9] It is well-documented that it is much more expensive to execute people than it is to house them for the remainder of their lives, regardless of age at the time of incarceration.[10]

Over the years, it has been discovered that a number of crime laboratories in major cities have been caught doctoring the results of their tests, creating fraudulent findings to support convictions in close cases.[11] This would be intolerable in any case but is inconceivable in a death penalty case.

The *Birmingham News* series also pointed out that Alabama is the only state that does not allocate funds to pay lawyers to represent death row inmates in the federal courts once their state court appeals run out. Until recently, court-appointed lawyers for those charged with a death penalty offense in Alabama could only be paid one thousand dollars for trial preparation. If done correctly, trial preparation may take as much as five hundred hours, which means that lawyers appointed to death penalty cases earn just a few dollars an hour. Such compensation discourages and prevents so many quality lawyers from defending those charged with death penalty offenses.

The *Birmingham News* acknowledged the inherent immorality when we kill those who have killed others. The newspaper discussed the fact that the death penalty does not deter others from committing crimes and that many death row inmates are mentally ill, mentally disabled or brain damaged.

In addition, it is debatable whether anyone ever experiences "closure" from an execution.[12] Unfortunately, many victims and their families have reported that the death penalty did not provide anything for them. Since it can take as long as two decades—which could involve over two dozen appeals—to execute someone, every time a legal brief is filed or a hearing is held it only serves to open further an excruciatingly agonizing wound. One may suggest shortening the appeals process, but it is because of and during the appellate process that wrongfully-accused people have been exonerated and are alive today. There is also a devastating impact on the innocent family members of someone sentenced to death, such as the daughter of my former client Benito Albarran.

On March 9, 2011, Illinois Governor Pat Quinn, who supports the death penalty, signed a law ending capital punishment in his state, saying it was impossible to fix a system that wrongly condemned twenty men who were later found to be innocent. Illinois became the sixteenth state and the fourth in four years to dispense with the death penalty, following New York, New Jersey and New Mexico.[13]

Governor Quinn reflected on the decision and Reuters quoted him as stating, "To have a consistent, perfect death penalty system… that's impossible in our state. I think it's the right and just thing to abolish the death penalty and punish those who commit heinous crimes—evil people—with life in prison without parole and no chance of release."

The next day, award-winning *Chicago Tribune* reporter Steve Mills wrote, "It wasn't the question of morality but the question of accuracy that led the State to abolish capita l punishment."[14] He continued, stating, "If there was one moment when the Illinois death penalty began to die…" it was when Governor George Ryan watched Anthony Porter's release and questioned how an innocent man could sit on death row for fifteen years. Porter came within forty-eight hours of execution and was only saved due to the investigative efforts of a group of Northwestern University journalism students and their professor.

The successful demonstration of the critical defects in the Illinois death penalty (which is no better or worse than that in many other jurisdictions) to the State legislature and then the governor can be attributed to a small number of lawyers, such as Bill Wolf, a member of the death penalty committee of the National Association of Criminal Defense Lawyers (NACDL), organizations such as the Illinois Coalition Against the Death Penalty and other committed abolitionist organizations and individuals.

For a few fortunate people like Anthony Porter of Illinois and my former client Bo Cochran, the fickle hand of fate played its best card. The hand dealt to Colorado death row inmate Joe Arridy did not contain such a lucky card.[15] With an IQ of thirty-nine, Arridy falsely confessed to the murder of a fifteen-year-old girl in 1936 after the police browbeat him. While waiting for his execution, Arridy played with toy trains and ate ice cream. Ultimately, the real killer, Frank Aguilar, confessed and was executed. He had never heard of nor met Arridy. In January 2011, Colorado Governor Bill Ritter, a former prosecutor, posthumously pardoned Arridy and formally apologized on behalf of the State for "the tragic conviction [based] on a false confession."

All of these atrocities and so many more raise the question: Is our system of criminal justice a search for truth, either in theory or in practice? The answer is a resounding "No." In fact, it is a search for *proof.* Not just any proof but that which is so strong as to amount to proof beyond a reasonable doubt. That standard serves as the most effective way for us to ensure that our citizens remain protected by the presumption that they are innocent and free from the unchecked power of the government.

Even armed with the presumption of innocence, 138 of our citizens (that we know of) have been wrongfully convicted and sentenced to death.[16]

We cannot speak of our system's search for proof without defining the purpose and scope of the roles of the prosecutor and the defense lawyer. It is the prosecutor who is supposed to search for truth. The prosecutor chooses whom to charge, when and sometimes where. By investigating and merely charging someone (no matter how far that goes), a prosecutor can permanently destroy reputations and lives.

The United States Supreme Court acknowledged the responsibilities of the prosecutor in *U.S. v. Berger*: "The United States Attorney is the representative not of an ordinary party to a controversy, but of sovereignty whose obligation to govern impartially is as compelling as its obligation to govern at all; and whose interest, therefore, in a criminal prosecution is not that it shall win a case, but that justice shall be done…It is as much his duty to refrain from improper methods calculated to produce a wrongful conviction as it is to use every legitimate means to bring about a just one."[17]

The duties and responsibilities of the defense lawyer, who defends the freedoms of the accused against the awesome power of the government, are similar but not the same. Like prosecutors, defense lawyers are sworn officers of the court. We cannot lie to or mislead a court. We cannot use a witness who tells us he is lying; that would be to suborn perjury. We cannot obstruct justice by concealing or destroying evidence of a crime, such as certain corporate documents or stolen property or perhaps a murder weapon. If we do any of this, we will lose our licenses to practice law and the government will charge us with a crime. We cannot charge the government with anything. The government's responsibility is to all its citizens. Defense lawyers' responsibility is to focus on the citizens we represent, within the boundaries of our roles as officers of the court.

Former Supreme Court Justice White has said that "Law enforcement officers have the obligation to convict the guilty and to make sure they do not convict the innocent…But defense counsel has no comparable obligation to ascertain or present the truth. Our system assigns him a different mission. He must be and is interested in preventing the conviction of the innocent, but, absent a voluntary plea of guilty, we also insist that he defend his client whether he is innocent or guilty. The State has the obligation to present the evidence. Defense counsel need present nothing, even if he knows what the truth is. He need not furnish any witnesses to the police, or reveal any confidences of his client, or furnish any other information to help the prosecution's case. If he can confuse a witness, even a truthful one, or make him appear at a disadvantage, unsure or indecisive, that will be his normal course. Our interest in not convicting the innocent permits counsel to put the State to its proof, to put the State's case in the worst possible light, regardless of what he thinks or knows to be the truth…more often than not, defense counsel will cross-examine a prosecution witness, and impeach him if he can, even if he thinks the witness is telling the truth, just as he will attempt to destroy a witness who he thinks is lying."[18]

Some years ago I received another type of phone call. Jessica Blank and Erik Jensen, two playwrights from New York City, contacted me. Erik and Jessica had attended a conference at Columbia Law School. At that time, eighty-seven innocents had been exonerated. The leader of a workshop on wrongful convictions aired a collect telephone call from an inmate in Illinois. The inmate, who had been convicted on the basis of a false confession, told the listening group that he remained in prison even though his interrogators were later convicted for their coercive actions when interrogating him.

By the end of the call, the members of the group were crying. Both actors and playwrights, Erik and Jessica decided to bring the stories of the wrongfully convicted alive through the theater. They documented their journey to bring the live production of the play, *The Exonerated*, to a worldwide audience and then wrote a book called *Living Justice: Love, Freedom and the Making of The Exonerated*.

With the backing of Culture Project and other activists' organizations, they were able to make their vision a reality. Jessica and Erik brought in extraordinary talent, from producer Allan Buchman to director and renowned actor Bob Balaban. Outstanding actors volunteered their talents to play the parts of the exonerees. Jessica and Erik traveled the country to interview over forty of the eighty-seven exonerees. They videotaped Bo Cochran and Randal Padgett at my office. Bo and Randal were later portrayed as characters in the play. Most memorable was the special performance of *The Exonerated* on December 11, 2010, in the Dag Hammarskjöld Library Auditorium at the United Nations. *The Exonerated* was also turned into a made-for-cable film that starred Susan Sarandon and Danny Glover.

Since the death penalty's reinstatement in 1976, about 1,200 people have been executed.[19] We will never know how many were either innocent or at some stage of redemption. The Supreme Court has ruled that capital punishment does not apply to juveniles or the mentally retarded due to "evolving standards of decency."[20] But I strongly feel it to be indecent to execute even the worst of us.

I always keep in my mind the maxim that history will judge a society by the way it treats its weakest and most vulnerable. Although most would assume that applies to the poor and the elderly, all one has to do is look at those who end up on death row: an overwhelming number are poor, disenfranchised and suffer from some mental defect or even brain damage.

Every once in a while, people with means and advantages commit deadly acts. Such was the case with Nathan Leopold and Richard Loeb, who faced the death penalty for the diabolical and meticulously planned murder of a fourteen-year-old in Chicago in 1924. Attorney Clarence Darrow pleaded to a judge to spare the lives of Loeb, the handsome and privileged eighteen-year-old son of a retired executive, and Leopold, the son of a millionaire box manufacturer. At the end of his twelve-hour summation and hardly able to stand up, Darrow urged the judge: "I am pleading for life, understanding, charity, kindness and the infinite mercy that considers all. I am pleading that we overcome cruelty with kindness and hatred with love. I know the future is on my side...I am pleading for a time when hatred and cruelty will not control the hearts of men. When we can learn by reason and judgment and understanding and faith that all life is worth saving and mercy is the highest attribute of man."[21]

The Chicago papers reported that tears streamed down the judge's cheeks. The entire courtroom sat spellbound. The judge sentenced the boys to life in prison plus 99 years.

It is my fervent belief that Darrow was right—the future *was* on his side. The number of executions is down throughout the country and the death penalty is being eliminated in many states.[22]

The future is uncertain for all of us and promised to none of us, but of one thing I am certain: no matter what lies ahead, my life has not been wasted. As a result of forces seen and unseen, I have contributed to saving many men and women who trusted me with their freedom and their lives.

ACKNOWLEDGEMENTS

I would like to especially thank the editorial team at New Horizon Press: Joan Dunphy, JoAnne Thomas, Joanna Pelizzoni and Charley Nasta, for their superb support, professionalism and skills in making this book a reality. I am very grateful for the efforts of my agent, Verna Dreisbach, who believed in me and this project from the beginning. The following people contributed their time, insights and efforts and to them I am eternally appreciative: David Dees, Patricia Hamilton, Brett Knight, Meredith Gray, Lana Jaffe, Linda Jaffe, David Muhlendorf, Redding Pitt and Henry Frohsin.

Were it not for my mentor Bob Yehling, this book would not exist.

Many years ago, these people supported me in my efforts in many ways when I was less than sure: Judge Jay Blitzman, Sally Boyles, David Dees, Mark Solomon, Maryanne Vollers and Professor Penny White. Thank you!

Finally, I humbly acknowledge the profound influences of Steve Bright, Dean Thomas W. Christopher, Karl Friedman, Robert Gordon, Doug Jones, Mark Mandell, John Mays, Professor Dallas Sands and all the other courageous lawyers upon whose shoulders I stand, and the many clients who trusted me with their lives.

NOTES

Chapter 2
  [1] Diane McWhorter, *Carry Me Home, Birmingham, Alabama: The Climactic Battle Of The Civil Rights Revolution* (New York: Simon & Schuster, 2002).

Chapter 3
  [1] *Whitehurst v. Wright*, 592 F.2d 834 (5th Cir. 1979).
  [2] *Ex parte Day*, 378 So. 2d 1159 (Ala. 1979) (reversed and remanded on the grounds that the testimony of the psychiatrist consulted by the defense in preparation for trial was privileged and could not be offered by state in its case-in-chief.) Mr. Day later entered a guilty plea to a felony assault charge and received probation.

Chapter 7
  [1] Steve Joynt, *Jack's Law: The Rise and Fall of Renegade Judge Jack Montgomery* (Birmingham, AL: Crane Hill Publishers, 1997), 83-86.
  [2] Ibid., 120-21.

Chapter 9
  [1] Henry F. Fradella, "Why Judges Should Admit Expert Testimony on the Unreliability of Eyewitness Testimony," *Fed. Cts. L. Rev.* 2, no.1 (June 2006).
  [2] Constitutional Rights of the Accused 3d § 7:2.
  [3] Fradella, "Why Judges Should Admit Expert Testimony," 14.

⁴ The Innocence Project, "Eyewitness Misidentification," http://www. innocenceproject.org/understand/Eyewitness-Misidentification.php (accessed Sept. 8, 2011).

⁵ Fradella, "Why Judges Should Admit Expert Testimony," 4.

Chapter 11

¹ Roman Polanski is a filmmaker who has directed, produced, written and acted in movies around the world. However, in 1977, Polanski was arrested for the sexual assault of a thirteen-year-old girl. Instead of facing a prison sentence, Polanski fled to France, where he would not be extradited to the United States for these charges.

² An example is the case of *State v. Smith*, 466 So. 2d 1026 (Ala. Crim. App. 1985). Smith was found guilty, but I later appealed the case and had it reversed on the grounds that the medical examiner could not testify to the various positions the victim would have had to be in to receive his wounds.

³ Ala. Code § 13A-5-47 (1975).

⁴ *Ex parte Ward*, 497 So. 2d 575 (Ala. 1986).

⁵ L. Nizer, *My Life in Court*, 1st ed. (New York: Doubleday & Co., 1961).

Chapter 12

¹ *Miranda v. Arizona*, 384 U.S. 436 (1966); *Dickerson v. United States*, 530 U.S. 428 (2000), (upholding the requirement that the Miranda warning be read to criminal suspects).

² Fed. R. Crim. P. 11(c)(1).

³ Ala. R. Crim. P. Rule 14.

Chapter 13

¹ "Ten Leading Causes of Death and Injury," Centers for Disease Control and Prevention, Sept. 3, 2010, http://www.cdc.gov/injury/wisqars/ LeadingCauses.html (accessed Sept. 9, 2011).

² Nancy Lowry, "Jordan Brown's case going to juvenile court," *New Castle News*, Aug. 24, 2011, http://www.ncnewsonline.com/current/x2122765110/ Jordan-Brown-s-case-going-to-juvenile-court (accessed Sept. 9, 2011).

³ Russell Colburn, "15 year old killer gets 20 years," Fox10tv.com, Aug. 1, 2011, 2011. http://www.fox10tv.com/dpp/news/local_news/pensacola/ Warren-Williams,-15,-gets-20.5-years (accessed Sept. 9, 2011).

⁴ Bruce Bower, "Teen Brains on Trial: The science of neural development tangles with the juvenile death penalty," Science News Online, http:// www.phschool.com/science/science_news/articles/teen_brains_trial.html (accessed Sept. 18, 2011).

[5] *Roper v. Simmons*, 543 U.S. 551 (2005) (holding that it is unconstitutional to impose capital punishment on crimes committed when the person was under eighteen).

[6] *Ex parte J.R.*, 582 So. 2d 444 (Ala. 1991).

[7] *Brown v. State*, 353 So.2d 1384 (Ala.1977).

[8] Joseph B. Oakleaf, "Abraham Lincoln: As a Criminal Lawyer," (Rock Island, IL: Augustana Book Concern, 1923), 6-7.

Chapter 14

[1] Jeremy Pelofsky, "Reagan shooter gets more time away from hospital," World News on MSNBC.com, May 5, 2011, http://www.msnbc.msn.com/id/42554508#.TmpWlOz44dU (accessed Sept. 9, 2011).

[2] 18 U.S.C.A. § 17 (West); Ala. Code § 13A-3-1.

[3] "Antidepressants: What You Need to Know About Depression Medication," HelpGuide.org, http://helpguide.org/mental/medications_depression.htm (accessed Sept. 14, 2011).

[4] Ala. Code § 13A-3-1.

Chapter 15

[1] *Ex parte Pruitt*, 673 So. 2d 836 (Ala. Crim. App. 1996).

[2] ABA Death Penalty Guideline 10.7 (2003).

[3] *North Carolina v. Alford*, 400 U.S. 25 (1970).

Chapter 16

[1] "Boaz, Alabama: City of Possibilities," http://www.cityofboaz.org/ (accessed Sept. 9, 2011).

[2] MRPC Rule 1.6.

[3] *Ex parte Monk*, 557 So. 2d 832 (Ala. 1989). Ironically, *Ex Parte Monk* refers to the trial judge in this case whose decision to order open file discovery was appealed by the State, but nevertheless, upheld by the Alabama Supreme Court.

[4] MRPC Rule 1.6.

Chapter 17

[1] MRPC Rule 1.6.

Chapter 18

[1] Joynt, *Jack's Law*, 153-80.

[2] Ibid., 18.

Chapter 20
  [1] *Batson v. Kentucky*, 476 U.S. 79 (1986).
  [2] Ibid.
  [3] A Rule 20 Petition is now referred to in the Federal Rules of Criminal Procedure as Rule 32. Fed. R. Crim. P. 32.
  [4] *Gideon v. Wainwright*, 372 U.S. 335 (1963).

Chapter 21
  [1] *Cochran v. Herring*, 43 F.3d 1404 (11th Cir. 1995).
  [2] *Ake v. Oklahoma*, 470 U.S. 68 (1985).

Chapter 22
  [1] *Gregg v. Georgia*, 428 U.S. 153 (1976).

Chapter 23
  [1] *Monk*, 557 So. 2d at 832.

Chapter 24
  [1] Ala. Code § 13A-5-47.

Chapter 26
  [1] *Ex parte Drinkard*, 777 So. 2d 295 (Ala. 2000).
  [2] "Innocence and the Death Penalty," Death Penalty Information Center, http://www.deathpenaltyinfo.org/innocence-and-death-penalty (accessed Sept. 14, 2011).

Chapter 27
  [1] ABA Death Penalty Guideline 10.7 (2003).
  [2] "Recent Summaries of the Results of Federal Capital Prosecutions," Death Penalty Information Center, http://www.deathpenaltyinfo.org/federal-death-penalty#statutes (accessed Sept. 20, 2011).
  [3] Ibid.

Chapter 29
  [1] 18 U.S.C.A. § 3593(e) (West).
  [2] Ala. Code § 13A-5-46(f) (1975).
  [3] "Judge Override," Equal Justice Initiative, http://www.eji.org/eji/deathpenalty/override (accessed Sept. 18, 2011).
  [4] *Roper v. Simmons*, 543 U.S. 551 (2005).
  [5] 18 U.S.C.A. § 3591 (West).

⁶ *White v. Alabama*, 131 S. Ct. 991 (2011). Leroy White was executed by lethal injection on January 13, 2011.

⁷ See *Thurmond v. Quarterman*, 341 F. App'x. 40 (5th Cir. 2009).

⁸ Charles Montaldo, "Gary Ridgway: The Green River Killer," About. com, Feb. 8, 2011, http://crime.about.com/od/serial/a/Gary-Ridgway.htm (accessed Sept. 13, 2011).

⁹ R. Johnson & S. McGunigall-Smith, "Life without parole, America's other death penalty: Notes on life under sentence of death by incarceration," *The Prison Journal* 88 (2008): 328-346.

¹⁰ *In re Davis*, 130 S. Ct. 1 (2009).

¹¹ "NACDL Resolution Supporting Clemency for Troy Anthony Davis," Death Penalty Reform Resources, http://www.nacdl.org/public.nsf/ defenseupdates/deathpenalty?OpenDocument (accessed Sept. 18, 2011).

Afterword

¹ *Henry VI*, Part 2, Act IV, scene ii.

² Jack Healy, "Surprising View on the Death Penalty," The Huffington Post, http://www.huffingtonpost.com/jack-healey/surprising-views-on-the-d_b_811916.html (accessed Sept. 20, 2011).

³ *U.S. v. Marvin Lee Holley*, No. CR96-B-0208-NE (N. D. Ala. 1998). Holley and his codefendant were charged with the killing of Ronald Avans, an informer who was federalized thus conferring federal jurisdiction to the case.

⁴ Rob Warden, "The Role of False Confessions in Illinois Wrongful Murder Convictions since 1970," Center on Wrongful Convictions Research Report (2003), http://www.law.northwestern.edu/wrongfulconvictions/ issues/causesandremedies/falseconfessions/FalseConfessionsStudy.html (accessed Sept. 14, 2011).

⁵ Rob Warden, "The Snitch System: How Incentivized Witnesses Put 38 Innocent Americans on Death Row," Center on Wrongful Convictions (2004), http://www.innocenceproject.org/docs/SnitchSystemBooklet.pdf (accessed Sept. 14, 2011).

⁶ 18 U.S.C. § 3600 (West 2004).

⁷ ABA, "Evaluating Fairness and Accuracy in State Death Penalty Systems: The Alabama Death Penalty Assessment Report" (June 2006); ABA, "Evaluating Fairness and Accuracy in State Death Penalty Systems: The Georgia Death Penalty Assessment Report" (January 2006).

⁸ "Birmingham News Reverses Its Position on the Death Penalty," Death Penalty Information Center, http://www.deathpenaltyinfo.org/node/1586 (accessed Sept. 14, 2011).

[9] "Facts & Figures," National Coalition to Abolish the Death Penalty, http://ncadp.org/index.cfm?content=5 (accessed Sept. 14, 2011).

[10] David Erickson, "Capital Punishment at What Price: An Analysis of the Cost Issue in a Strategy to Abolish the Death Penalty" (master's thesis, U.C. Berkeley, 1993).

[11] "Scandal-Plagued North Carolina Crime Lab Sued By Exonerated Man," Huffington Post, June 30, 2011, http://www.huffingtonpost.com/2011/06/30/north-carolina-crime-lab_n_887516.html (accessed Sept. 14, 2011).

[12] Marilyn Peterson Armour & Mark S. Umbreit, "The Ultimate Penal Sanction and 'Closure' for Survivors of Homicide Victims," 91 Marq. L. Rev. 381 (2007).

[13] "34 States with Death Penalty," Death Penalty Procon.org, http://deathpenalty.procon.org/view.resource.php?resourceID=1172 (accessed Sept. 14, 2011).

[14] Steve Mill, "What killed Illinois' death penalty," *Chicago Tribune* March 10, 2011; "False testimony by a purported eyewitness landed Anthony Porter on death row," Center on Wrongful Convictions, http://www.law.northwestern.edu/cwc/exonerations/ilPorterSummary.html (accessed Sept. 14, 2011).

[15] Robert Perske, *Deadly Innocence?* (Nashville, TN: Abingdon Press, 1995).

[16] "Innocence and the Death Penalty," Death Penalty Information Center, http://www.deathpenaltyinfo.org/innocence-and-death-penalty (accessed Sept. 14, 2011).

[17] *Berger v. United States*, 295 U.S. 78 (1935).

[18] *United States v. Wade*, 388 U.S. 218, 256-58 (1967) (J. White, concurring).

[19] "U.S. Executions Since 1976," Office of the Clark County Prosecuting Attorney, http://www.clarkprosecutor.org/html/death/usexecute.htm (accessed Sept. 14, 2011).

[20] *Roper v. Simmons*, 543 U.S. 551 (2005); *Atkins v. Virginia*, 536 U.S. 304 (2002).

[21] Clarence Darrow and Arthur Weinberg, *Attorney for the Damned, Clarence Darrow in the Courtroom* (Chicago, IL: University of Chicago Press, 1989).

[22] John Schwartz, "Death Penalty Down in U.S., Figures Show," *New York Times* Dec. 21, 2010, http://www.nytimes.com/2010/12/21/us/21penalty.html (accessed Sept. 18, 2011).